An Emulation of Sanctity

FROM THE AUTHOR

A Priest in Banaras. Bangalore: Asian Trading Corporation, 2020.

Indian Portraits: Eight Christians Encounters with Hinduism. New Delhi: Nirala, 2021.

Pathways of Prayers. Bangalore: Asian Trading Corporation, 2024.

The Trinitarian Philosophy of Jules Monchanin: The French Years (1922–1939). London: Bloomsbury, 2026.

The Trinitarian Mysticism of Jules Monchanin: The Indian Years (1939–1957). London: Bloomsbury, 2026.

An Emulation of Sanctity

Hinduism and Christianity in Dialogue

YANN VAGNEUX

Foreword by

Francis X. Clooney, SJ

Translated by

Roderick Campbell Guion & Caroline Malcolm

PICKWICK *Publications* • Eugene, Oregon

AN EMULATION OF SANCTITY
Hinduism and Christianity in Dialogue

Pickwick Publications
An Imprint of Wipf and Stock Publishers
199 W. 8th Ave., Suite 3
Eugene, OR 97401

www.wipfandstock.com

PAPERBACK ISBN: 979-8-3852-4761-5
HARDCOVER ISBN: 979-8-3852-4762-2
EBOOK ISBN: 979-8-3852-4763-9

Cataloguing-in-Publication data:

Names: Vagneux, Yann [author]. |Campbell Guion, Roderick [translator] | Malcolm, Caroline [translator] | Clooney, Francis X. [foreword writer]

Title: An emulation of sanctity : Hinduism and Christianity in dialogue / by Yann Vagneux, with a foreword by Francis X. Clooney, SJ.

Description: Eugene, OR: Pickwick Publications, 2025 | Includes bibliographical references and index.

Identifiers: ISBN 979-8-3852-4761-5 (paperback) | ISBN 979-8-3852-4762-2 (hardcover) | ISBN 979-8-3852-4763-9 (ebook)

Subjects: LCSH: Christianity and other religions—Hinduism. | Hinduism—Relations—Christianity. | Christianity and culture—India.

Classification: BR128.H5 Y366 2025 (paperback) | BR128.H5 (ebook)

10/20/25

Original French edition:
Une émulation de sainteté. Hindouisme et christianisme en dialogue
© 2024 Groupe Elidia Editions Desclée de Brouwer
10 rue Mercoeur
75011 PARIS

To George Gispert-Sauch, SJ (1930–2020),
in humble pursuit of the path he has showed me

āno bhadrāḥ kratavo yantu viśvataḥ.
Let noble thoughts come to us from all directions.

Ṛg Veda 1.89.1

I have met again with Father de Lubac, alone and at length. . . . He believes that confronted with India I will be able to rethink theology, far better than by digging over the philosophical problems for themselves.

Jules Monchanin

A Christian theology which is not able to enter into a creative dialogue with the theological thought of other religions misses a world-historical occasion and remains provincial!

Paul Tillich

Contents

Foreword by Francis X. Clooney, SJ | ix

1. On the Way | 1
2. Three Millennia of Thought | 12
3. Fire and Spirit | 16
4. The Primordial Sacrifice | 20
5. The Yogin and the Child | 39
6. As a Flash of Lightning | 56
7. The Taste of the Absolute | 83
8. Love in Separation | 109
9. The Tree with Celestial Roots | 133
10. An Emulation of Sanctity | 138

Postscript: A Marriage with Hinduism | 153
Vande Saccidānandaṃ | 167
Bibliography | 169
Name Index | 177

Foreword

When Fr. Yann first showed me this book—I recall that it was the 2024 original French edition that I first saw, in mss form—I welcomed it, as his statement of what his years in India and deep study have meant for him, written down now with the hopes of persuading Hindus and Christians to learn deeply from their own ancient traditions and from one another as well. This is what he has tried to do over the years, and he believes that such learning is urgently needed. He is a witness, calling both Hindu and Christian back to our roots, that on a firm basis we might learn from one another. It is at the same time a useful book. As the Table of Contents shows, the chapters cover a wide range of Hindu wisdom and literatures, and can ably serve an introduction to the spirit of Christian and Hindu traditions told to us by" a person who has prayed, studied, and lived amid the realities of which he writes. For some, indeed, it may be the best of introductions to both Christian and Hindu traditions.

Yann has a wide knowledge of Indian thought, not so much through the extensive reading that he surely does, but through a contemplative reception of ancient texts and their wisdom. He is deeply familiar too with certain currents of Western thought, Christian and secular, citing at every turn an apt quotation from the Bible or the Fathers of the Church, or a later theologian, up to the lifetime of his ideal, Fr. Jules Monchanin (1895–1957). Yann's taste is for the classics of spirituality and their twentieth-century proponents—Henri de Lubac, Hans Urs von Balthasar, and others. Modern academic scholars are rarely quoted, on the Upanisads or bhakti or on the social and political conditions of India today. Since he has lived for years in India, access to most recent scholarship and its trends has been difficult.

As a result, his manner of writing shows a certain timelessness, far removed from the West. He evinces a sense of being unencumbered by the academic struggles of the past decades, postcolonial and orientalist critiques, the modern abhorrence of any hint of essentialism. For Yann, eternal verities still hold. He is very concerned about the West's decay and forgetfulness toward the West's deep wells of spirituality, now seemingly overwhelmed by today's materialism. As he puts it, "the West has forgotten that this reason is not a fixed once and for all faculty, but a disposition called to grow, through the spiritual gift of wisdom, by deepening and simplifying itself so as to be capable of penetrating ever further into the weaving of reality that India designates by the term *tantra*" (156).

While the political realities of modern Indian rarely figure in the book, on occasion, he can be quite direct: "From being the spiritual beacon of the world, Hinduism has become a caricature of itself. In this religion which has become corrupted by politics, there is no longer an ounce of the mystical. After all, is not this worrying spiritual emptiness just the trademark of all extremists, fundamentalists, hardliners and traditionalists? . . . In a religion which is losing its spiritual vitality, only the devotion of the faithful remains, but this has been taken hostage by the *Hindutva*" (160, 161). His view of "export Hinduism" is equally dim: it risks becoming "the religion of the healthy,ġ sanitized to suit the affluent middle classes, by way of "a cheap awakening for those who are only wanting a harmonious and peaceful supplement for their hectic lifestyles. It could be that this decaffeinated version of the religious quest is one of the greatest poisons which Hinduism has to face up to today" (161). All of this too is quite interesting and deserving of discussion and debate. Perhaps Yann will write another book, on Hinduism today as it is actually lived by Hindus inside south Asia, but also in the global diaspora, in dialogue with modern Hindus who are living out their faith in ways he worries about.

One might think that given the evocative timeless tone of the writing in this reflective book, Yann is living in seclusion, in a monastic enclave or hermitage. But I know by experience—my most recent visit to Varanasi in July 2023, when Yann was my host—that he is very well connected with a host of people in that holy city, from shopkeepers and booksellers, to artists, Catholic sisters, Hindu religious leaders and monastics. So many of these people seem to be simply genuine friends of Yann. His Christian ministry and witness is in part by way of friendships, hospitality, generosity with his time and energies. None of this is explicit or central to the book, but it is important to know that in a certain sense, Yann has been a very well-connected priest wherever he has been.

I was intrigued by the word "emulation" in the title. The word is crucial to the book, appearing—the title and page headings—more than a dozen times. I cannot speak to the nuances of "emulation" in French, but it is not a common word in English today, American at least, even if the verb "emulate" will appear now and then. According to the *Oxford English Dictionary*, emulation has often indicated imitation with a competitive edge, the ambition to be at least as good as another. But for Yann it hearkens to a kind of deep mutual learning, captured in the phrase "an emulation of sanctity." Fr. Monchanin himself put it this way, "I would like to see reigning between Hindus and Christians, not an ignorance and mutual contempt and nor, the easy syncretism that smooths away the angles and reduces everything to a rather flat moralism, but a real philosophical emulation and above all an emulation of sanctity" (9–10). Yann adds, "This book would like to call on the best of the Hindu and Christian traditions or rather it would like to allow Hinduism to draw out the best of Christianity and vice versa—all in an 'emulation of sanctity' that will give this departure for the unknown an unexpected fruitfulness" (10). Near the end of the book, he states very clearly how emulation is central to his own life:

> The searing otherness of Hinduism has given me the appetite to rediscover the living springs of the two traditions which are blended together within myself in a unique way. To borrow an appropriate image from Christian de Chergé (1937–1996), the Prior of Tibhirine, I have to tirelessly "dig my well" by living out with Hinduism a genuine "emulation of sanctity" through the face to face experience of the emotive devotion (*bhakti*) of the lowly and the intensity of the search for wisdom (*jñāna*) of so many of those one meets on the road, whether they are still fully engaged in the world or those, such as the *saṁnyāsī*, who are already separated from it. (156)

This is an apt summation of what this book is about.

Though not an autobiography—Yann does not tell us when he first came to India, or where he studied and lived in India, for instance—the book is infused with his personal contemplative yearning whence the "living springs" of Hinduism and Christianity well up within him. It arose out of his teaching, as he states early in the book, but its larger goal is stated movingly near the end: "In fact, I have tried to welcome as generously as possible the alterity of Hinduism into my being and my Christian faith. I have let myself be transformed by it in an ongoing spiritual dialogue, all the more real and burning when the Hindus themselves come to me calling me 'Father Yann' with infinite tenderness, making me their friend, their brother, their father and also their priest. . . . I also know that I will never finish knowing and learning from Hinduism" (163).

His learning from Hindu traditions, as deep as it is, is received within the frame of his staunch Catholic identity. His life and learning are about an "actual expansion through Hinduism of my Catholicism, in order that it can reach its adult maturity," showing "how to be Christian at the heart of Hinduism, and how as a Christian to make myself understood by Hinduism, through speaking its language and in communion with its spiritual quest" (164). We can thank Yann for showing us a very interesting way of being, one might say, Hindu and Catholic at the same time.

Yann is a young man still—so what comes next? Surely his life will entail still further pilgrimages. But for now, *An Emulation of Sanctity* shores up his foundations, on which he can stand however and wherever he thinks, learns, and prays in the years to come.

Francis X. Clooney, SJ, is the Parkman Professor of Divinity at Harvard Divinity School. His own memoir, *Hindu and Catholic, Priest and Scholar: A Love Story* (T&T Clark/Bloomsbury), appeared in 2024.

1

On the Way

"Hail to you who cross to the further shore"[1] sings the *Muṇḍaka Upaniṣad* to the pilgrim desiring the awakening. With an echo that transcends all religious particularism in order to exalt our condition as *homo viator*, the Bible makes the Lord's call to Abram ring out: "Leave your country, your kinship and your father's house, and go to the land that I will show you. I will make of you a great nation, I will bless you, I will make your name great, and you will become a blessing" (Gen 12:1–2) and "Abram went away, as the Lord had told him. . . . He took his wife Sarai, his nephew Loth, all the property they had acquired, and the people they had surrounded themselves with in Harran. . . . Then, from camp to camp, Abram went to the Negev" (Gen 12:4–5, 9).

This book would also like to be a journey somewhat like the one I once made from Rome to Benares in the footsteps of my predecessors who threw a bridge that was as fragile as it was daring between the banks of the Jordan and those of the Ganges. These pages are an invitation to set out, carried by the poet's verses:

> But the true voyagers are only those who leave
> Just to be leaving; hearts light, like balloons,
> They never turn aside from their fatality
> And without knowing why they always say: "Let's go!"[2]

1. *Muṇḍaka Upaniṣad* 2.2.6.
2. Baudelaire, *Les fleurs du mal*, 257.

EXPATRIATION

The first Christians defined themselves as *oi paroikountes*, those who in their exile here below, are still on the way. The term 'parishioners' come from this Greek term, a word that nowadays seems frozen in over much stability, a sclerotic identity even, whereas the early Christians had a light step. For the disciples of Jesus, the only respite granted is the folly of divine love which propels them along all the human pathways: "For God has so much loved the world that he has given his only Begotten Son, that whoever believes in him may not perish, but obtain eternal life" (John 3:16). Thus, the Christian has also to go "from one extreme to the other," as does his Master who "without leaving the bosom of the Trinity, extends himself to the furthest frontiers . . . and He fills the whole space that is between. This extension of Christ, as expressed by the four dimensions of the cross, is the mysterious sign of our dilatation and configures us to itself."[3]

The chapters that follow would hope to go from one extreme to the other, with a sharing of what is *a priori* foreign to us. In fact, there will be a twofold expatriation: the one of the Christian towards the Hindu world and that of the Hindu towards the Christian world. One could then speak of missionary theology not as a disguised proselytism but in terms of a sending forth, of courage and external and interior exodus. Louis Massignon (1883–1962) often summed his thinking up with the term "hospitality." Even if this idea is crucial in his multi-facetted work, perhaps the idea of "expatriation" is for him even more central. Faithful to the Bergsonian intuition which is a process of "sympathy through which one is transported inside an object to coincide with what it has of unique, and consequently of inexpressible," as distinct from analysis which is "the operation which brings the object back to elements already known,"[4] Massignon wrote that "to understand something other is not to *monopolise* the thing, it is to transfer oneself by a decentring to the very centre of the other."[5] There is no better example of this inaugural task than the learning of a new language—missionaries know this so well!—so we would invite readers to make an equivalent exodus by getting to know some Sanskrit words that will certainly be unknown to them. One will doubtless be dismayed by their strangeness but the effort to understand them may then be rewarded by

3. Daniélou, "D'une extrémité à l'autre," 246.

4. Bergson, *Pensée et le mouvant*, 181.

5. Massignon, "L'involution sémantique," 268.

the prodigious philosophical richness they conceal within their remarkable sonic beauty. However, all this is only a preliminary for the "spiritual expatriation"[6] that Massignon urges upon us:

> One only understands the other by mentally substituting oneself for him, by entering into the "made up place" of the other, by reflecting within oneself the mental structure and the thought process of the other. This substitution, which is a going beyond self, is not exempt from suffering because it is also and above all else, an "arising" of God within us: . . . undergoing this pain of not-knowing initially becomes a purification, first of a negative experience, at least in appearance, but very quickly a vision of splendid intellectual discovery, as much for one as for the other, an understanding between one and the other, in God. For the attraction that impelled us to connect ourselves with the other without rejecting any part of him, even the rough edges or shortcomings of his thought, was the very call of God through him, which will make us possess within ourselves the fullness of absolute truth which we will have sought for others, and through them beyond ourselves, renouncing our own spirit, and the solipsism of the system. For the Christian, this is the scope of engagement with our separated brethren, which is neither a denial, nor a low-level complacency, nor a minimisation of the dogmatic absolutes to which our faith adheres, nor a tactic of admiration, agnostic or Gnostic, in respect of the divergences of thought that hold confessions and philosophies apart.[7]

There is no better example of such a spiritual expatriation than Abbé Jules Monchanin (1895–1957), from whom I have received so much. We should read again the image that Henri de Lubac (1896–1991) brought back of his first meeting during the spring of 1930 with the extraordinary chaplain from Lyon who was so passionate about Indian culture: "I have before me, not a learned scholar—even though he reads Asaṅga in Sanskrit—nor one who is curious about strange things, not a humanist seduced by the thinkers he studies without himself participating in their thought, not in the least a dreamer or syncretistic or a spirit who is the least bit exalted: but a man who himself re-lives the spiritual quest of those distant human brothers, as if time and space had vanished. Like them, as a searcher for the Absolute—the Christian has never finished

6. Massignon, *Badaliya*, 50.

7. Massignon, "Nouveau sacral," 349.

searching—but as a peaceful searcher and ever more ardent, as he is already bathed in its dazzling light."[8]

LISTEN

Louis Massignon, Jules Monchanin, Henri de Lubac and Hans Urs von Balthasar (1905–1988) with all their intellectual breadth are amongst the best illustrations of the method of *catholicism*—a unique way of welcoming everything with a perspective whose acuity plunges into the depths of the Trinity in whose image we have been created. Thus catholicism, such as we understand it with our masters, has nothing of the narrow and caricatured identity that some in our own times propagate; on the contrary, we dare to say that such a catholicism is *de jure* the property of every human being, the response to the deepest desire of their heart: for this reason, catholicism is an identity without frontiers. So, whatever their religious affiliation (or lack of it), everyone can make these lines from Benedict XVI (1927–2022) their own, even if the Christian knows that the face of wisdom sought and loved—etymologically the *philosophy*—is the one that the eternal Son has assumed by being born amongst us:

> A Christian professor . . . carries within him a passionate love for this Wisdom! He reads everything in her light; he finds Wisdom's imprints in the elementary particles and in the verses of poets; in juridical codes and in the events of history; in works of art and in mathematic formulas. Without Wisdom not anything was made that was made (cf. John 1:3) and therefore in every created reality one can see Wisdom reflected, clearly visible in different ways and degrees.[9]

With such a vision, the disciple of Jesus, like any *honnête homme*, will never experience fear whilst soaring towards the vast horizons of human thought and spiritual experience in whatever latitude it might be. Never clinging to any fragment of its past but on the contrary, carried away by the powerful flow of the Tradition, true catholicism makes as its own the openness of spirit that was so unique in Origen (185–203), perhaps one of its most iconic representatives:

8. Lubac, *Images de l'Abbé Monchanin*, 14–15. Asaṅga was an Indian Buddhist monk of the fourth century, founder of the Yogācāra school.

9. Benedict XVI, "Celebration of First Vespers."

> He was not trying to lead us astray with his teachings or otherwise, but to save us with a loving, charitable and excellent purpose, and to make us commune with what philosophy has to offer. . . . He wanted us to study the other philosophers, without showing any preference or contempt for any individual philosophical school or doctrine, be it Greek or heathen: we should be listening to all of them.[10]

Listen: the term probably defines the most crucial attitude of catholicism. It is not a question here of listening with a casual ear as if we already knew all about what the other wants to say to us. Worse still, to ventriloquise him by cutting him off in order to speak for him. It is more about keeping quiet—at last!—in order to listen patiently and with kindness. *Ti voglio bene* as an Italian who is so steeped in true Christianity would say: to listen with the very love of the Saviour who wants to lose nothing of what the Father has given him in this world (John 6:39). A desire, that is by definition catholic, to welcome *everything*, to embrace *everything* and as if in an extraordinary mosaic, to find the specific place that the Holy Spirit in its inexhaustible creativity has assigned to everything. It is indeed in order not to be an obstacle to the Spirit that we must first operate an *epokhē* a suspension of our judgment which is neither a resignation nor cowardice but the will to save the other's proposition to the very end as Jesus did, He who loved us "to the end" (John 13:1):

> So that the one who gives the spiritual exercises as well as the one who receives them, may find more help and benefit, it must be presupposed that every good Christian must be more inclined to save the other's proposition than to condemn it; and if he cannot save it, let him think about how he understands it and if he misunderstands it, correct it with love. If this is not sufficient, let him look for all appropriate means for it to be saved.[11]

The learning to which we are called is to form a genuine inner ear for ourselves and "a heart that listens" (1 Kgs 3:9)—the Hindu would here speak of *sādhanā*, literally of spiritual exercise. Like the prophet Elijah, beyond the thunderous manifestations of the hurricane, the earthquake and the fire, we must learn to discern in the other that "sound of sheer silence" by which the Lord comes to meet us (1 Kgs 19:11–12). In a witty manner, Jules Monchanin recalled that "all the cymbals of extremism will not

10. Gregory Thaumaturgus, *Remerciement à Origène* 6.81; 13.151–153.

11. Ignatius of Loyola, *Spiritual Exercises*, 21.

extinguish the whisper of the Spirit"[12] and that "the City of God" cannot "overshadow the temporary tent where the soul and its God were able to dialogue in secret."[13] Certainly, the human tendency is to be contented with trivial melodies but the Spirit has many other ambitions: to bewilder it with an unfamiliar music that John of the Cross (1542–1591) using a splendid oxymoron called the "musica callada," the "silent music," a "harmony of very great music."[14] Already in the early days of the Church, Irenaeus of Lyon (140–202) several times evoked the music that the Triune God plays in his Revelation: "Thus, in many ways, He prepared the human race in view of the symphony of salvation. That is why John says in Revelation, 'And his voice was like the voice of many waters.' For the waters of the Spirit of God are truly multiple, because the Father is rich and abundant."[15] We are not given an easily memorised monodic line here but the harmony of a symphony made up of plurality and a bringing together of opposites—a wonderful sonorous reflection of the unfathomable richness of the Trinitarian life:

> Nonetheless diverse and multiple are so many of the things that have been made: when placed together in the work of creation they appear as if full of proportion and harmony; but with each considered separately they appear as if in opposition to one another and in discord. It is for them like the tones of a sitar which thanks to the very space interval that separates them, can produce a melody that is one and harmonious, even though made up of multiple and opposing sounds.[16]

A catholic ear knows how to listen patiently to the other and discovers, within him, the silent symphony of "the Spirit of the Lord who fills the universe"—"which holds all things together" and "hears all the voices" (Wis 1:7). Also, along with Hans Urs von Balthasar, we are not afraid to affirm that:

> Today, therefore, perhaps the most necessary thing to proclaim and take to heart is that Christian truth is symphonic. Symphony by no means implies a sickly-sweet harmony lacking all tension. Great music is always dramatic: there is a continual process of intensification, followed by a release of tension at a higher level. But

12. Monchanin, unpublished letter to Édouard Duperray.
13. Monchanin, "Religions et civilisations indiennes," 86.
14. John of the Cross, "Spiritual Canticle A," stanza 14, in *Complete Works* (1979), 107.
15. Irenaeus of Lyon, *Adversus Haereses* 4.14.2.
16. Irenaeus of Lyon, *Adversus Haereses* 2.25.2.

> dissonance is not the same as cacophony. Nor it is the only way of maintaining the symphonic tension.[17]

May the reader of this book then listen in that way to the scriptural masterpieces of Hinduism in which he will perceive the imprint of the Spirit of the Risen One, He "in whom are hidden all the treasures of wisdom and knowledge" (Col 2:3).

FRUITFULNESS

Let us make the Lord's call to Abram ring out again: "Go to the land that I will show you. I will make you a great nation, I will bless you, I will make your name great, and you will become a blessing" (Gen 12:1–2) The land that is promised to the one who will be called Abraham and to all his descendants that we are, is the truth. But this is not a plot on which one would be able to plant a sign marked "private property." Truth cannot be inherently possessed; it does not support any enclosure. On the contrary, it is the truth that will increasingly possess us enjoining us to seek it constantly:

> "Seek God and your soul shall live" (Ps 68:33). Let us search for that which needs to be discovered, and into that which has been discovered. He whom we need to discover is concealed, in order to be sought after; and when found, is infinite, in order still to be the object of our search. Hence it is elsewhere said, "Seek His face evermore" (Ps 104:4). For He satisfies the seeker to the utmost of his capacity; and makes the finder still more capable, that he may seek to be filled anew, according to the growth of his ability to receive.[18]

Truth is a pilgrimage, an invitation to a journey that has no end. For our part, there can be no response other than the courage to walk ever further towards it, leaving the familiar shores behind: "It is truth that conquers, not falsehood: by truth is laid out the path to the gods by which the seers, their desires fulfilled, travel to the highest abode of truth."[19] And "ekaṃ sad viprāḥ bahudhā vadanti," a famous śloka of the Hindu tradition exalts the truth as the only light diffracted by the kaleidoscope of the multiple names and forms (*nāmarūpa*) that men give to the gods: "They called him Indra, Mitra, Varuṇa, Agni; and he is heavenly Garuḍa, who has beautiful wings.

17. Balthasar, *Truth Is Symphonic*, 15.
18. Augustine of Hippo, *Homilies on the Gospel of John* 72.1.
19. *Muṇḍaka Upaniṣad* 3.1.6.

The truth is one, but the sages call it by many names; they called him Agni, Yama, Mātariśvan."[20]

Even if the Christian has discovered the face of truth in Jesus who revealed himself as "the Way, the Truth and the Life" (John 14:6), he knows that if he wants to be a "collaborator of the truth," he must always "set out" (3 John 7–8) leaving behind the bastions where routine habit risks turning everything into a sterile statue of salt:

> What we need, however, is respect for the beliefs of others and the readiness to look for the truth in what strikes us as strange or foreign; for such truth concerns us and can correct us and lead us farther along the path. What we need is the willingness to look behind the alien appearances and look for the deeper truth hidden there. Furthermore, I need to be willing to allow my narrow understanding of truth to be broken down. I shall learn my own truth better if I understand the other person and allow myself to be moved along the road to the God who is ever greater, certain that I never hold the whole truth about God in my own hands but am always a learner, on pilgrimage toward it, on a path that has no end.[21]

It is in the courage of risking to venture off the beaten track to the unknown territories that the disciple of Jesus will be faithful to the promises of his baptism because, as Hans Urs von Balthasar said repeating a quote from Charles Péguy (1873–1914), "A Church that is not open to the world in its totality would have ceased to be the Church of Christ. 'We all stand in the frontline.'"[22] Deep down, there is only one virtue necessary for the Christian on the way: the "magnanimity"[23] that "must be in tune with the Spirit of the Risen Jesus, with his freedom to travel the world and reach the peripheries, even those of thought."[24] That is why Pope Francis, tracing the broad outlines of current research within the Church, was able to boldly say: "I dream of Theological Faculties where one lives differences in friendship, where one practices a theology of dialogue and welcoming; . . . where

20. *Ṛg Veda* 1.164.4.

21. Ratzinger, *Many Religions*, 110.

22. Balthasar, "Priestly Existence," 414. Péguy's quote is taken from the 1911 notebook "Un nouveau théologien, M. Fernand Laudet," cited in Péguy, *Mystique et politique*, 872.

23. Cf. Francis, "Interview aux revues culturelles jésuites."

24. Francis, "Theology After *Veritatis Gaudium*."

theological research can promote a challenging but compelling process of inculturation."[25]

It is in response to the Holy Father's desire to see the "theologians . . . encouraging ever anew the encounter of cultures with the sources of Revelation and Tradition"[26] that I have written this new book from India where I now live. It is the outcome of the hospitality I have received from so many Hindu friends—in particular the Brahmin scholars of Benares. It is also the fruit of the hospitality that I wanted to grant to their distinguished tradition in the very name of my Catholic priesthood. And how true is Christ's promise to "he who has left houses, brothers, sisters, a father, a mother, children, or land for his name's sake": he "will receive a hundredfold, and he will inherit eternal life" (Matt 19:29). What true hospitality confers over the years is an ever-increasing family to which we have the privilege of belonging once the latches of our small worlds have been released. "*Vasudhaiva kutumbakaṃ*" sounds out the *Mahā Upaniṣad*, recapturing thus the best of Indian civilisation: "One is a relative, the other stranger, says the small minded. The entire world is a family, lives the magnanimous."[27] But families are composed of unique and irreplaceable members, and this is how a sharing of wealth is possible, an emulation that leads all to give the best of themselves. On the contrary, where the same identity reigns, beyond the comfort of speaking the same language and of having the same points of view, the hour of decadence has already arrived. As for myself, for guidance in the immensity of India which is a veritable shimmering mosaic of multiple cultures and traditions, I have always kept on my lips the *credo* of Jules Monchanin, the prophetic founder of Shāntivanam Ashram which was dedicated to the audacious and challenging encounter between Christianity and Hinduism:

> Does our Shāntivanam deserve its title of "peaceful"? I would like it to. I think it is not necessary to either increase or minimise the differences between Hindus and Christians. But are not these differences properly incentive: a call to fully realise on both sides, what we consider to be the essence of our *dharma*. I would like to see reigning between Hindus and Christians, not an ignorance and mutual contempt and nor, the easy syncretism that smooths away the angles and reduces everything to a rather flat moralism,

25. Francis, "Theology After *Veritatis Gaudium*."

26. Francis, "Theology After *Veritatis Gaudium*."

27. *Mahā Upaniṣad* 6.71–73: "ayaṃ nijaḥ paro veti gaṇanā laghucetasāṃ udāracaritānāṃ tu vasudhaiva kuṭumbakaṃ."

> but a real philosophical emulation and above all an emulation of sanctity.[28]

This book would like to call on the best of the Hindu and Christian traditions or rather it would like to allow Hinduism to draw out the best of Christianity and vice versa—all in an "emulation of sanctity" that will give this departure for the unknown an unexpected fruitfulness. Perhaps here we have the deepest ambition that we nurture in respect of Christian theology, which so often offers the sad spectacle of a rehashing of tired *clichés*, where it would be better to bring forward the startling newness of Christ.[29] As incredulous as Sarah was when she was faced with the unprecedented promise made to her, theology would be able to question itself thus: "Would I really have a child, at my age?" (Gen 18:13). And still with Baudelaire, we would dare to describe the sad shores of its "small and monotonous world" as "an oasis of horror in a desert of boredom!"[30] This is here that generous hospitality brings forward the remedy needed for a rediscovered fruitfulness: "to plunge . . . to the depths of the Unknown to find something new!"[31] At the oaks of Mamre, Abraham experienced this when he invited the three unknown visitors to rest at his table. His hospitality was the pledge of the long-awaited son. Of course, Sarah laughed as the promise contravened the laws of her sterile body. And many will surely laugh at the idea that Christian theology may experience a new spring in the spiritual emulation that the human civilizations will offer to it. Oh, unworthy sons of the Fathers of the Church of a time when "Christendom that still carried its thought into the limitless space of the nations and still trusted in the world's salvation"![32] Oh, representatives of such a provincial theology that condemns the risen Christ to become bogged down in the "black cool pool" of the "water in Europe"[33] as Arthur Rimbaud (1854–1891) feared. Let them hear the warning of this ancient homily: "We should not hold our Saviour in low esteem for if we esteem him but little, we may hope to obtain but little from him"![34] On the contrary, the Christ that we proclaim has already mysteriously come, in the power of the Spirit, to meet Hinduism, Buddhism, Jainism,

28. Monchanin, Letter to M. Divien. "*Dharma*" can be translated here as "religion."

29. Cf. Scholtus, *Petit christianisme d'insolence.*

30. Baudelaire, *Les fleurs du mal*, 262.

31. Baudelaire, *Les fleurs du mal*, 263.

32. Balthasar, *My Work*, 49.

33. Rimbaud, *Poésies completes*, 22.

34. Clement of Rome, *Second Letter to the Corinthians* 1.

Islam and all the quests for the Absolute in this world. And we ourselves, we are only following in the wake of his light by running behind the One who is truly the "man with the soles of wind."

"Perhaps," said Emmanuel Mounier (1905–1950), "it is only Christianity that has the broad enough gesture, so may it haul the mainsail up the mast and having set out from the ports where it is stagnating, may it soar up towards the furthest stars without heed of the night that envelops it."[35] And Monchanin, from the depths of his Indian roots, became clairvoyant:

> Spiritualities that have yet to come into being, contemplative modes, new formulations of the Mystery, types of worship and consecrated life doubtless await, will wait for centuries perhaps, the advent of civilisations such as those of India and China into the heart of a one and multiform Church. The Christianity that was yesterday, that is today, that will always be "the one who comes."[36]

35. Mounier, *L'affrontement chrétien*, 120.

36. Monchanin, "Religions et civilisations indiennes," 86.

2

Three Millennia of Thought

"IN THE BEGINNING WAS the word" Hinduism might say. In its first maṇḍala, the *Ṛg Veda* stated that "the word (*vāc*) is measured in four quarters. The wise who possess insight knows these four divisions. Three quarters, concealed in secret, cause no movement. The fourth is the quarter that is spoken by men."[1] Many centuries later, Abhinavagupta, the genius of Kashmir, took up this Vedic vision to distinguish four states of the one and transcendent Absolute: the 'Supreme Word' (*parāvāc*) which is pure consciousness and pure light, "seminal reality [which] contains all that will constitute the universe—both things and words";[2] the 'seeing one' (*paśyantī*), a subtle vibration which "initiates . . . a movement towards manifestation, thus to differentiations and limitations";[3] the "middle one' (*madhyamā*), "the inner language of one who speaks to oneself or reflects clearly, though without vocal expression";[4] and finally, the 'spread-out one' (*vaikharī*) which "assumes a well-differentiated form by manifesting itself in clearly separated letters, words and sentences"[5] Surprisingly, India has described an annihilation of the Word or rather a "descent" of the Absolute which, by expressing itself in fragile words calls us back to the incomparable purity of the unstruck primordial sound: the *anāhata śabda*. If India has spoken so much through her sages and thinkers, it is to make us sense, beyond words,

1. *Ṛg Veda* I.164.45.
2. Scheuer, *Parole et silence*, 168–69.
3. Scheuer, *Parole et silence*, 169.
4. Scheuer, *Parole et silence*, 170.
5. Abhinavagupta, *Parātrīśikāvivaraṇa*.

the density of a silence. Almost two thousand years after the first verses of the *Ṛg Veda* were uttered, and following thousands of pages of scholarly treatises, Indian thought wanted to catch its breath in an aphorism cleaved like a diamond, which summed up in two words what had led her along so many paths of thought: "athāto brahmajijñāsā,"[6] "And now the quest for the Absolute." A splendid *sūtra* in which the adverb "athāto" indicates that the quest has already begun before one becomes conscious of it; "jijñāsā": a desiderative form with a doubling of the syllable to suggest all that is still lacking in knowledge (*jñāna*) and thereby excite desire; and finally, *Brahman*, the Absolute, whose etymology refers back to the Sanskrit root [*bṛh*], to grow, to increase, like the things of the Spirit which expand the hearts of those who love them. "Athāto brahmajijñāsā": the secret of India is beautifully revealed in these words.

Slightly longer than the first *Brahmasūtra* is the first description which the Catholic Church gave of a religion which in 1965 was still quite unknown to her: "Thus in Hinduism, men contemplate the divine mystery and express it through an inexhaustible abundance of myths and through searching philosophical inquiry. They seek freedom from the anguish of our human condition either through ascetical practices or profound meditation or a flight to God with love and trust."[7] Succinct as it may be, this sentence aptly describes the journey that the studies in this book hope to accomplish.

Before going any further, a brief chronology of Indian writings is in order. Traditionally, the beginning of Hinduism, thirty-five centuries ago, is marked by the *Veda*, an imposing set of liturgical hymns born of the visions of sages which were then transmitted orally to their disciples before being recorded in writing later. The *Veda* are the first corpus of the *Śruti*—literally "that which has been heard." They were followed by the *Brāhmaṇa*, ritual treatises developing an abundance of religious myths. Then, in a gradual internalization, appeared the *Araṇyaka* or "forest treatises" and the *Upaniṣad*, veritable spiritual gems, the oldest of which are contemporary with the awakening of Siddhārtha Gautama (563–483) known from then on as the Buddha. This first era of Vedic revelation was followed by the time of the *Smṛti*, which etymologically recalled the crucial breakthroughs achieved and encouraged new developments. The most emblematic of these is the *Bhagavadgītā*, a short treatise from the oceanic epic of the *Mahābhārata* which seems anterior to the other epic of the *Rāmāyaṇa* known by every

6. *Brahmasūtra* I.1.1.

7. Paul VI, *Nostra Aetate* 2.

Indian child. The *Bhagavadgītā* was a confluence of fifteen centuries of thought and enabled the unfolding of the three spiritual paths (*mārga*) of Hinduism: the *karmamārga* or "path of selfless action," the *jñānamārga* or "path of spiritual knowledge" and the *bhaktimārga* or "path of devotion."

Even more brief than the *Bhagavadgītā* are the *sūtra* which, in various fields, wanted to extract the quintessence of the achievements of Indian thought. Many treatises should be mentioned here, but we shall retain only the *Brahmasūtra* of Bādarāyaṇa whose fortune was remarkable in medieval Hinduism. Indeed, like the *Sentences* of Peter Lombard (1100–1160), the *Brahmasūtra* were commented on by various masters of the *vedānta*, such as Śaṅkara (788–820) and Rāmānuja (1017–1137) who, in their singular reading of these obscure aphorisms, laid the foundations for their own interpretation of the scriptures. The *vedānta* was the last of the *darśana*, the six philosophical schools[8] that emerged from Vedic orthodoxy. From the fifth–seventh centuries, another set of texts called *āgama* appeared. They are at the origin of the tantric currents which transfigured Hinduism and Buddhism which was still prevailing at that time in many parts of India. The ambition of the *Tantra* was to lead human beings to final liberation more rapidly. In the land of Kashmir, these new schools produced masterpieces of mystical speculation with Utpaladeva (900–950) and Abhinavagupta (950–1020), considered by many to be the pinnacle of Indian thought.

Still in the first millennium CE, the mythical narratives of the *Purāṇa*, such as the Krishnaite *Bhāgavata Purāṇa*, contributed to the emergence of different religious traditions (*saṃpradāya*) attached to one or the other form of the gods or goddesses, reflections of the one Absolute in the world of manifestation. This notable change was the fertile ground for the *bhakti*, which drew India into a veritable fire of love fuelled by remarkable men and women, both mystics and poets. Two of them will accompany our journey: the young Āṇḍāl (eighth century) in Tamil Nadu and the blind bard Sūrdās (fifteenth century) in the Braj.

We will not give a similar chronology for the Christian thinkers who will be summoned throughout these pages to echo the spiritual and philosophical breakthroughs of Hinduism. Many Church Fathers, witnesses of an unalterable springtime of thought, will intervene: Irenaeus of Lyon (140–202), Origen of Alexandria (185–253), Gregory of Nyssa (335–395), Augustine of Hippo (354–430) and Bernard of Clairvaux (1090–1153), the

8. The six *darśana* are the *vyāya*, the *vaiśeṣika*, the *sāṃkhya*, the *yoga*, the *mīmāṃsā* and the *vedānta*.

final representative of this noble tradition. Following them will come the great mystics whom India can recognise as distant brothers and sisters in the Spirit: Hadewijch of Antwerp (1200–1260), John of the Cross (1542–1591), Thérèse of Lisieux (1873–1897) and Mother Teresa (1910–1997) who, in Calcutta, made the newness of Christ shine in the darkness. By personal attraction, the thinkers of the twentieth century will have a place of choice as creative heirs of the ecclesial tradition: Romano Guardini (1885–1968), Henri de Lubac (1896–1991), Hans Urs von Balthasar (1905–1988), François-Xavier Durrwell (1912–2005) and Joseph Ratzinger-Benedict XVI (1927–2022). Finally, in this conversation between Hinduism and Christianity, it was imperative to invite those who were the artisans of this necessary dialogue: Brahmabāndhav Upādhyāya (1861–1907), Jules Monchanin (1895–1957), Henri Le Saux-Swāmī Abhishiktānanda (1910–1973), Raimon Panikkar (1918–2010), without forgetting Bettina Sharada Bäumer (born in 1940), to whom these pages owe so much.

We still have to say a word about the origin of this book. It was born almost involuntarily with the writing of a study on the *viraha*, love in separation, in September 2016. At the same time, the course on the sacred scriptures of Hinduism, which I was beginning to give for future Indian Catholic priests, led me year on year to study a significant aspect of Indian thought. Slowly, a book was being composed, with an architecture reminiscent of the Hindu temples or Christian cathedrals. Indeed, after an entrance porch on the mystery of fire and the Spirit, the reader will enter two inner courtyards—which may also be the nave and transept—to be led into the inner *garbhagṛha* where shines the figure of the *jīvan-mukti*, the "one who is liberated in this life," to whom from the choir of the cathedral will respond the splendor of the Risen One, whom I was trying to contemplate with an invincible hope during the spring of 2021 when along with my people of India and Nepal we were swept away by the tragic wave of the COVID-19 pandemic. From this most sacred of places, we will have to go back to the various courtyards and cross the porch again with the promise of new and fruitful horizons.

3

Fire and Spirit

"BERESHIT," "IN THE BEGINNING" (Gen 1:1). As many commentators have pointed out, the Bible opens with a *beth*, the second letter of the Hebrew alphabet, and not with an *aleph*. In this inaugural *beth* is masterfully demonstrated the otherness of creation in relation to the Creator, to whom alone the primacy of the *aleph* belongs: "Bereshit bara Elohim et hashamayim ve'et ha'aretz," "In the beginning, God created the heaven and the earth" (Gen 1:1). On the contrary, in the "Agnimīle purohitaṃ," the *Ṛg Veda*, the threshold to the imposing scriptural temple that is Hinduism, opens with an *a*, the first letter of the Devanagari alphabet, which according to later tantric traditions is the vowel *bīja*, the seed at the origin of all earthly manifestation of the primordial Word: "The first phoneme, the first sound that arises within the Word at its highest level, is *a*. It is the highest and purest form of Śiva's energy: *cit-śakti*, the energy of pure consciousness. It is the unexcelled, the peerless one: *anuttara*, or the Absolute. *A* is the original phoneme, which comes before all others, whence they all proceed and where all of them will return." This is the "supreme matrix of sound," says Abhinavagupta.

> Thus, it is fullness (*pūrṇatā*). The fullness of the pure and absolute supreme consciousness, fullness also in that this consciousness is inclusive of all the worlds and that like it, the phoneme *a* is inclusive of the countless number of phonemes which will bring the worlds into existence, sustain them, and eventually dissolve them.[1]

1. Padoux, *Vāc*, 235–36.

"Agnimīle purohitaṃ yajñasya devaṃ ṛtvijaṃ hotāraṃ ratnadhātamaṃ," "I pray to Agni, the household priest who is the god of the sacrifice, the one who chants and invokes and brings most treasure."[2] Such is the first of the verses by which, in infinite number, Hinduism has exalted the mystery beyond everything. It is a contemplation of the sacrificial fire, which tradition calls the "mouth of the gods," because by its ardor it consumes all human offerings so that they reach their ultimate destination. It is in this sense that fire is the priest *par excellence*, the mediator who re-establishes the constantly threatened balance between the worlds of men and gods: "To you, Agni, who shines upon darkness, we come day after day, bringing our thoughts and homage to you, the king over sacrifices."[3] Besides its eminently sacerdotal role in the Brahmanic sacrifice (*yajña*), fire has since the dawn of time been the liturgical witness of human life. It is the "faithful friend" presiding over each rite of passage—the *saṃskāra* that unfold from birth to death to lead the human being to greater religious perfection. In a moving way during the final *saṃskāra*, fire becomes the *tāraka*, the ferryman leading to the further shore the one who has nothing left to offer but his own body delivered to the flames. The image of cremation finally introduces us to the greatest significance that Hinduism has given to fire: that of bringing about union with the Absolute and thus for the first time answering the eternal question that has inhabited Indian thought for three and a half thousand years. Indeed, for those who watch its graceful glow in the hearth, fire is a vivid metaphor for the philosophical question of the one and the many: diverse in its countless flames and yet always the same. It is in its metaphysical sense that fire is similar to the vowel *a*, for from its ardor everything comes and everything returns—similar thus to the Absolute that India has never ceased to seek in an incandescent quest: "Here is the truth: as from the flaming fire issue forth, by thousands, sparks of the same form, so from the Immortal proceed the various beings and they find their way back into It."[4]

Fire, on the other hand, is scarcely present in the Catholic liturgy, which over time has become increasingly anaemic by losing its cosmic dimension. Fire does however open the most beautiful of celebrations, that of the Easter Vigil, often in the form of a rather paltry brazier, whereas it should be the glorious herald of the "new creation" (2 Cor 5:17) in which the old world has been definitively consumed. During the holy night "which

2. *Ṛg Veda* I.1.

3. *Ṛg Veda* I.7–8.

4. *Muṇḍaka Upaniṣad* 2.1.

shines like the day" (Ps 138:12), it is from its flames that the Easter candle is lit, the very symbol of the presence of the Risen One in the midst of his Church. Step by step this unique fire is then propagated in multiple lights carried by the faithful:

> On this, your night of grace, O holy Father, accept this candle, a solemn offering, the work of bees and of your servants' hands, an evening sacrifice of praise, this gift from your most holy Church. But now we know the praises of this pillar, which glowing fire ignites for God's honour, a fire into many flames divided, yet never dimmed by sharing of its light.[5]

At the heart of the Solemn Vigil, the fire illustrates the *agraphon* related by Origen: "Whoever comes near me comes near the fire." It reminds us that the body of the Risen One has become entirely possessed by the Holy Spirit. The "new heaven" and the "new earth" (Rev 21:1), for which the glorified flesh of the Saviour represents the anticipation, are the universe where nothing escapes hold of the Spirit's—a Pentecost that has already begun, where the same fire that Jesus came to "cast on the earth" (Luke 12:49) burns in a unique way on the Virgin and the Apostles:

> When the day of Pentecost came, at the end of the fifty days, they were all together. Suddenly a sound came from heaven like a violent gust of wind, and the house where they were sitting was filled with it. And there appeared to them tongues as of fire, and they were divided, and one tongue fell on each of them. And they were all filled with the Holy Spirit and began to speak in other tongues, each one speaking according to the gift of the Spirit. (Acts 2:1–4)

Fire is the Risen Christ, fire is his Spirit of love "whose secret joy will always be to establish communion and restore the likeness, playing with the differences,"[6] fire is the Church which is truly Catholic which "knows that the various customs hallowed by her confirm the unanimity of her faith."[7]

It is by meditating on the burning fire and listening to the whispering of the Spirit, of whom a papal adage says that "He himself is the harmony,"[8] that we want to cross the threshold to penetrate into the Hindu temple as

5. From the *Exsultet*, the Proclamation of Easter.

6. Chergé, "Spiritual Testament."

7. Lubac, *Catholicism: A Study*, 153.

8. "Ipse harmonia est." Pope Francis regularly uses this adage which he attributes to Basil of Caesarea. It is in fact an extrapolation of the Cappadocian in his *On the Holy Spirit* 16.38.

into the Catholic cathedral. May we be nourished by both religious traditions, recalling the last verses of the *Ṛg Veda*: "United your resolve, united your hearts, may your spirits be at one, that you may long together dwell in unity and concord!"[9] and with the invocation that begins all Eastern Christian prayer: "O Heavenly King, the Comforter, the Spirit of Truth, who are everywhere and fills all things, Treasury of Blessings, and Giver of Life—come and abide in us, and cleanse us from every impurity, and save our souls, O Good One."

9. *Ṛg Veda* 10.191.4: "samānī va ākūtiḥ samānā hṛdayāni vaḥ samānaṃ astu vomano yathā vaḥ susahāsati."

4

The Primordial Sacrifice

THE *VEDA* ARE THE foundation of Hinduism: the *sanātana dharma*. Etymologically, *Veda* signifies "vision" and thus "true knowledge." In India, one would simply say "awakening." In this sense, the four collections of hymns and liturgical formulas of the *Ṛk*, *Yajuḥ*, *Sāma* and *Atharva Veda* refer to what the *ṛṣi*, the first sages, saw when, facing the mystery of the universe, they sensed, as much in the infinity of the heavens as in the depths of their own hearts, an Absolute that surpassed them. Contemplating the creation in its fundamental bounty, they perceived a generosity at the origin of everything: "We have crossed towards the further shore beyond darkness. The radiant dawn extends her rays, smiling like a lover seeking conquests, she brings light to all and with the charm of her countenance awakens us to bliss."[1] Above all, the light was the guide for their awakening, the light of the dawn and the dusk, the blinding light of the sun at its full height when all darkness has been dispelled: "Let us meditate on that excellent glory of the divine vivifying Sun, May he enlighten our understanding."[2] The light itself became the final goal of their quest—not just the external light, but the interior light which shines at the depth of the heart: "Gazing beyond the dark we reach the supreme Light and attain the Sun, the God of Gods, the Light."[3]

In the dazzling horizon of the sun, Man is the primordial priest when, stretching his hands towards the glowing orb, he unites the world here below with the world of the gods. Such is the original connection—the

1. *Ṛg Veda* 1.92.6.
2. *Ṛg Veda* 3.62.10. This is the *Gāyatrī* mantra that is recited each day by the Brahmins.
3. *Ṛg Veda* 1.50.10.

re-establishment of the balance of the universe, to which all future sacrifices will be committed—the *yajña* that the *Veda* detailed meticulously from the humble offering of the water, right up to the impressive sacrifice of the horse (*aśvamedha*). One can then easily understand why Raimon Pannikar (1918–2010) in his master work *The Vedic Experience*, was able to write: "If one had to choose a single word to express the quintessence of the Vedic Revelation, the word *yajña*, sacrifice, would perhaps be the most adequate."[4]

Among the sacrifices documented in the *Veda*, one of them over the millennia has generated an unfailing interest. It is described in the tenth mandala of the *Ṛg Veda* in the *Puruṣa-sūkta*,[5] a hymn of more recent composition in a corpus that is some 3,500 years old. It is not about a sacrifice that man can do because it is a sacrifice brought about before man ever was. However, up to the present day there is scarcely a liturgy that is not accompanied by the recitation of at least several of the sixteen Sanskrit verses that make up the *Puruṣa-sūkta*. Furthermore, the importance of the myth of the Puruṣa within Indian thought has been such that whoever would want to understand only just a tiny part of its tangled developments will always have to come back to one of the most penetrating visions that were given to the first *ṛṣi*.

THE PURUṢA-SŪKTA

Puruṣa signifies man in general but in the case of the *Puruṣa-sūkta*, one has to say: the primordial Man. Two etymologies can be put forward for the Sanskrit term. The first comes from the verbal root (*pṛ*), to fill, from which comes the idea of totality and plenitude and the transcendent dimension. The second would be associated with *pura*—the fortress, the city—to which the verbal root (*sad*) is joined, to sit or (*sī*) to dwell, from which comes the idea of the spirit residing within the interior of the human body and the immanent dimension. In a sense, one can say that the whole evolution of the archetype of the Puruṣa has played on this double etymology. However, before following its thread across the centuries, it is worth coming back to its place of origin in the *Ṛg Veda*.

In the introduction to his translation of several hymns from the *Veda*, Louis Renou (1896–1966) wrote concerning the *Puruṣa-sūkta*: "Immolated

4. Panikkar, *Vedic Experience*, 347.

5. Cf. *Ṛg Veda* 10.90.1–16.

during the course of a vast sacrifice (the first of the sacrifices) the limbs of the Giant, in being scattered across the expanse, gave birth to the world. This hymn . . . is the one that had the greatest impact: did it not embrace the creation of the world within the same impulse as that of the sacrifice, the two primordial events?"[6] To understand how this vision has pervaded Indian thought, there is no better way than to listen to the recitation of it by the Brahmins, as they clearly emphasise the alliteration of the initial S—"sahasraśīrṣā puruṣaḥ sahasrākṣaḥ sahasrapāt"—which immediately describes the cosmic immensity of the Puruṣa:

The Puruṣa has a thousand heads,
a thousand eyes, a thousand feet.
He pervaded the earth on all sides
and extended beyond it as far as ten fingers.

It is the Puruṣa who is all this,
whatever has been and whatever is to be.
He is the ruler of immortality,
when he grows beyond everything through food.[7]

The Primordial Man is the quintessence of the cosmos in its original unity. He fills everything, he is the fullness of everything, according to the first possible etymology of the Puruṣa. However, that unity has been disseminated and it is from the dismemberment of the body of the primordial Man that the whole creation is born by means of a sacrifice that the *Puruṣa-sūkta* describes further on:

When the gods spread the sacrifice
with the Puruṣa as the offering,
spring was the clarified butter,
summer the fuel, autumn the oblation.

They anointed the Puruṣa, the sacrifice born at the beginning,
upon the sacred grass.
With him the gods, Sādhyas, sages sacrificed.[8]

With a paradox typical of the Vedic spirit, the Puruṣa is at the same time both the victim that the gods have sacrificed at the very beginning and the one for whom the sacrifice (*yajña*) is offered. The Sanskrit here displays

6. Renou, *Hymnes spéculatifs*, 12.
7. *Ṛg Veda* 10.90.1–2.
8. *Ṛg Veda* 10.90.6–7. The Sādhyas are a category of the Vedic gods.

a real genius by using only three words: "yajñena yajñamajayanta devāḥ," which begin the last verse of the hymn:

With the sacrifice the gods sacrificed to the sacrifice.
There were the first ritual laws.
These very powers reached the dome of the sky
where dwell the Sādhyas, the ancient gods.[9]

Previously, the *Puruṣa-sūkta* had presented the fruits of the primordial sacrifice. These were first the start of the liturgical cult which was of prime importance for the Vedic man. Afterwards, following on from the dismemberment of the *Puruṣa*, the whole animal and human creation arose, in particular, the division of society into four castes (*varṇa*):

From that sacrifice in which everything was offered,
the verses and chants were born,
the metres were born from it,
and from it the formulas were born.

Horses were born from it,
and those other animals that have two rows of teeth.
Cows were born from it,
and from it, goats and sheep were born.

When they divided the Puruṣa,
into how many parts did they apportion him?
What do they call his mouth,
his two arms and thighs and feet?

His mouth became the Brahmin (*brāhmaṇaḥ*);
his arms were made into the Warrior (*rājanyaḥ*),
his thighs the merchant (*vaiśyaḥ*),
and from his feet the servant (*śūdraḥ*) was born.[10]

The breaking up of the unity represented by the Puruṣa, in as far as it was the totality of the universe of space and time is not however a pure loss in an overwhelming multiplicity. The worlds of men and the gods remain mysteriously connected to the body of the Puruṣa and the Vedic liturgy is specifically the place where this original unity allows itself to be intuited again. Furthermore, the mysterious connections between the cosmos and

9. *Ṛg Veda* 10.90.16.
10. *Ṛg Veda* 10.90.9–12.

the Puruṣa, such as they are set out at the end of the hymn, had a considerable future in the *Upaniṣad* whose only objective, etymologically speaking, was to rediscover the connections re-establishing the scattered unity:

> The moon was born from his mind;
> from his eye the sun was born.
> Indra and Agni came from his mouth,
> and from his vital breath the wind was born.
>
> From his navel the middle realm of space arose;
> from his head the sky evolved.
> From his two feet came the earth, and the quarters of the sky
> from his ear.
> Thus they set the world in order.[11]

Such, in this over brief exposition, is the central message of the *Puruṣa-sūkta*: the sacrifice is at the beginning of everything—an offering up of the unity itself so that the multiplicity can appear. One final detail concerning the primordial sacrifice is here worthy of mention. It concerns the vertical axis represented by the wood to which the Puruṣa was bound, a veritable cosmic ladder erected between the three worlds of the earth, the intermediate space and the heavens:

> They were seven enclosing-sticks for him,
> and thrice seven fuel-sticks,
> when the gods, spreading the sacrifice,
> bound the Puruṣa as the sacrificial beast.[12]

It is interesting to note here that when the temples appeared on Indian soil in the post-Vedic era, according to the architectural treatises (*vāstu śāstra*) the archetype of the Puruṣa was again found in the two horizontal and vertical dimensions of the new venue for the sacrifice:

> The Puruṣa is not only related to site and ground plan. The elevation of a temple (śikhara: abode of the *garbhagṛha* or sanctum) is also likened to the body of Puruṣa, and the different parts of the temple are named after the limbs of the body, the soul being the consecrated image in the sanctum. The temple is thus a symbol of the Cosmic Man which is all in one body and soul, parts and the whole.[13]

11. *Ṛg Veda* 10.90.13–14.

12. *Ṛg Veda* 10.90.15.

13. Bäumer, "Purusa," 46. Here is what A. K. Ramanujan wrote about the analogy between the Hindu temple and the human body: "Indian temples are traditionally built

This important observation brings our focus now to the center of the temple—the place of the sacrifice itself, in what some authors have called "Brahminism"—a new development of Hinduism which follows on from the first insights in the *Veda* concerning the mystery of the origins.

THE SACRIFICE OF PRAJĀPATI

The epoch of the *Brāhmaṇa* opened up a new phase in Indian thought. After the grand inaugural visions of the *Ṛg Veda* and the liturgical formulas of the *Yajur Veda*, this new corpus wanted to exponentially develop the sophistication of the ritual by describing it in ever greater detail. For a non-Brahmin—and *a fortiori* a foreigner—the thousands of pages of the *Brāhmaṇa* can be somewhat forbidding. However, to the careful reader, they promise a wealth of riches, as was the case at the end of the nineteenth century for Sylvain Lévi (1863–1935) in his magisterial work *La doctrine du sacrifice dans les Brâhmanas.*[14]

What caught the attention of Levi in the *Brāhmaṇa* was the recovery of the myth of the sacrifice of the Puruṣa in the figure of Prajāpati, the lord of creatures,[15] who was scarcely mentioned in the *Veda*. On several occasions, the *Śatapatha Brāhmaṇa* describes the creation of the world through the sacrifice of Prajāpati in order to show that "at the origin of every being there is a sacrifice that has produced it. The texture of the universe is sacrifice, which is the act *par excellence* which produces all that is."[16] For example, it is written that: "Prajāpati produced living beings, and having produced living beings he went upwards—he went to that world where that sun now shines. Indeed, there was then no other victim except Prajāpati, whom the gods could offer in sacrifice. Wherefore it is with reference to

in the image of the human body. The ritual for building a temple begins with digging in the earth, and planting a pot of seed. The temple is said to rise from the implanted seed, like a human. The different parts of a temple are named after body parts. The two sides are called the hands or wings, the *hasta*; a pillar is called a foot, *pāda*. The top of the temple is the head, the *śikhara*. The shrine, the innermost and the darkest sanctum of the temple, is a *garbhagṛha*, the womb-house. The temple thus carries out in brick and stone the primordial blueprint of the human body" (*Speaking of Śiva*, 19–20).

14. Lévi, *Doctrine du sacrifice*. More recently the Italian philosopher Roberto Calasso has published a very penetrating study of the *Śatapatha Brāhmaṇa*: Calasso, *Ardor*.

15. Cf. *Śatapatha Brāhmaṇa* 6.1.1.5: "That same *Puruṣa* became Prajāpati, the Lord of all creatures."

16. Panikkar, *Vedic Experience*, 348.

this that the *ṛṣi* has said (*Ṛg Veda* X, 90, 16), 'With the sacrifice the gods sacrificed to the sacrifice,'—for by sacrifice they did offer up Prajāpati, the sacrifice."[17]

Other mythological accounts from the *Śatapatha Brāhmaṇa* describe the same reality, namely that Prajapati is the very personification of the sacrifice. In a striking way, it is said that Prajapati, no longer wanting to be alone, yet having nothing at his disposition to create the world, dismembers himself to produce a descent, up to the point where he becomes drained of all life. Thus, "creation is pictured here as the self-immolation of the Creator. It is only because Prajāpati sacrifices himself fully that he can give to creation his whole self."[18] One finds here, in the way that Prajāpati became the father of all creatures, the vein of the *Puruṣa-sūkta*. The text does not hesitate to say besides that "Puruṣa is indeed the sacrifice."[19] However, the *Śatapatha Brāhmaṇa* took a new step. Then, with Prajāpati on the verge of death, the creatures to whom he gave life became frightened. Thus, with the help of Agni, the sacrificial fire, they decide to seek a way to bring their father back to life by piecing together his dismembered body through a new ritual sacrifice. So, "it is only by the same sacrifice in the opposite direction, by the same sacrifice in which he has himself been offered as oblation, that Prajāpati is snatched back from death. He has been sacrificed and he lives; he has been dismembered but stays the same because the sacrifice has recomposed him."[20] Then a double sacrifice appears: the primordial sacrifice by which Prajapati created the world by himself dying and the ritual sacrifice by which Prajapati was brought back to life. However, the reconstitution of the dismembered unity was not carried out on one occasion at the beginning, but it happens each time that a ritual sacrifice is carried out. This is the crucial innovation introduced by the *Brāhmaṇa*.

The purpose of a very particular sacrifice is to symbolically reconstruct the dismembered body of Prajāpati. It is known as *agnicayana* and its complex ritual is set out at length in books 6 to 10 of the *Śatapatha Brāhmaṇa*. Etymologically it concerns the construction of the altarpiece of the fire that is so essential in the Vedic cult: "When one builds up the fire-altar one reconstructs space and time, the body of Prajāpati."[21] To perform

17. *Śatapatha Brāhmaṇa* 10.2.2.1–2.
18. Panikkar, *Vedic Experience*, 78.
19. *Śatapatha Brāhmaṇa* 1.3.2.1.
20. Panikkar, *Vedic Experience*, 78.
21. *Śatapatha Brāhmaṇa* 6.1.2.17.

the *agnicayana*, the four classes of the Vedic priests are required: the *hotṛ* of the *Ṛg Veda*, the *adhvaryu* of the *Yajur Veda*, the *udgātṛ* of the *Sāma Veda* and the *brāhmaṇa* of the *Atharva Veda*. The meticulous study of the ritual is of fundamental concern here. The dismembered corpse of Prajapati is represented by the large number of scattered bricks (*istaka*) required for the construction of the altar. As in former times, the sons of Prajapati gave life back to their father by constructing a sacrificial altar, which would be a new body for him, likewise the priests of the *agnicayana* carry out gesture by gesture the different stages of the lifesaving sacrifice. After a preliminary initiation (*dīkṣā*) lasting one year, they mark out on the ground a sacred space upon which they are going to construct an altar with 10 800 bricks set out in five rows built on top of each other. Previously they will have buried in the foundation of the future altar a mysterious golden effigy of a man along with a living tortoise as well as the heads of five animals. When the human effigy is lodged, the *Puruṣa-sūkta* is sung, making thus a concrete link with the ancient sacrifice of the Puruṣa.[22] Then, each day and each night a brick is put in place, accompanied by an appropriate mantra, faithful to the injunction of the *Śatapatha Brāhmaṇa* to recover the unity and the continuity of time: "The officiant recites the verses continually, without interruption: and so he makes the days and nights of the year continuous, and so the days and nights of the year alternate continually and without interruption."[23] Once the ritual which has lasted for years[24] is over, the altar is ready to receive the *āhavanīya*, the sacred fire, which finally gives life back to Prajāpati, for whom from that time the altar acts as an immortal body, over which time no longer has control.

In an exemplary way, the *agnicayana* reveals the objective of the whole sacrificial system of the *Brāhmaṇa*: to re-establish the universe in its equilibrium between the world of men and of the gods by recovering the broken unity. Therefore, it is no longer only a primordial sacrifice by which the world is created, as was the case in the *Puruṣa-sūkta*. There is thereafter a continuity, with the sacrifice, being repeated indefinitely so that the body

22. The image of the Puruṣa lying at the foundation itself of the altar is very powerful. One can recall here that the relics of the Buddha and of his disciples were place placed in the foundation of the ancient stupas—as is the case at Sarnath and at many other Buddhist holy places. On this matter, we can consult the penetrating study of Mus: "Où finit Puruṣa?"

23. *Śatapatha Brāhmaṇa* 1.3.5.16.

24. The last time that the *agnicayana* was carried out in India, at Pannal in Kerala, the ritual took less time and only lasted from April 12–24 in 1975.

of Prajāpati can be forever recreated. In a way that is even more radical than the *Veda*, the *Śatapatha Brāhmaṇa* places the sacrifice (*yajña*) at the centre of all reality since all sacrifice recreate, at a given time and place, the archetypal primordial sacrifice. The *yajña* of the Brahmin priest is thus the continual creation and re-creation of the world—the most secure preservation of the cosmic equilibrium:

> Sacrifice is the centre of the world, its force, that which gives it the strength to be, to be what it is and what it shall be, that which supports the cosmos and maintains it in existence. Sacrifice is not primarily a human affair, but a cosmic venture, and God and the Gods are the prime actors in it. Sacrifice is not only the creative act; it is also both the conservational and the actively transforming act of the whole universe.[25]

The never ending repetition of the sacrifice which sustains the cosmos has a name; the *ṛta*, which can be translated as 'cosmic order' because the reality of the world carries on in as far as the Brahmanical sacrifice is carried out. In the idea of the order of the cosmos, there is nothing static, but by contrast everything is in motion as the image of the fire of Agni who presides over all the Vedic liturgies. Thus "*ṛta* is the ultimate foundation of everything; it is the 'supreme'"[26]

In exactly the same way, the *Veda* and the *Brāhmaṇa* address the question of the return to unity which is, *par excellence*, the driving thread of Indian thought. As much in the myth of the sacrifice of Puruṣa as in that of the self-immolation of Prajāpati, one can contemplate the destruction of the primordial unity in order that the cosmic multiplicity can be made possible. This then, without being an original sin, cannot satisfy man. He needs to rediscover what has been lost. The goal of the Vedic liturgy is none other than to re-establish the harmony of the world of man and of the gods, which is continually threatened by the non-virtuous acts (*pāpa*) that punctuate life. To allow everything to rediscover its proper order within the primordial unity, there is no other way than the different ritual sacrifices (*yajña*) duly carried out in the prescribed way. Such is the grandeur of man at the centre of creation: "He can experience that bliss and sense of fullness [of the identification with the Absolute] only when he is busily engaged in building up again the body of Prajāpati after it has been dismembered

25. Panikkar, *Vedic Experience*, 98.

26. Panikkar, *Vedic Experience*, 350.

and before his new creative act."[27] However—and this is the obstacle that emerges rapidly in the Vedic and Brahmanical world—man is caught up in a "process . . . of having to re-construct again and again the unity long-wished" because "he loses his unity and identification with the Absolute at the end of every sacrifice."[28] Such an instability cannot permanently satisfy an India driven by the desire for unity.

THE PURUṢA, SUN-COLORED, BEYOND DARKNESS

We have to come back to the *Puruṣa-sūkta*. As we have seen, the *Brāhmaṇa* exploited the full potential of the idea of sacrifice (*yajña*) which is central to the Vedic hymn. However, in essence this contains another thread leading to further developments. In fact, two strophes of the hymn evoke a mystery hidden at the heart of the cosmic manifestation of the Puruṣa filling the entire universe:

Such is his greatness,
and the Puruṣa is yet more than this.
All creatures are a quarter of him;
three quarters are what is immortal in heaven.

With three quarters the Puruṣa rose upwards,
and one quarter of him still remains here.
From this he spread out in all directions,
into that which eats and that which does not eat.[29]

As a matter of fact, only a quarter of the mystery of Puruṣa has been made manifest, three quarters remain "concealed in secret,"[30] as it is also the case with the primordial word (*vāc*). At a new stage of Indian thought, the *Upaniṣad* had no other objective than to pierce the mystery in its sealed virginity: "So far goes his greatness, and the Puruṣa is greater than that. A foot of him is all beings: three-footed, he has immortality in the sky."[31] The *Upaniṣad* know that everyday man cannot know everything as the Mystery remains, for the most part, untouched. However, it is men of will who have had the courage to set out to discover the Mystery in its totality and to be

27. Vesci, *Heat and Sacrifice in the Vedas*, 285.
28. Vesci, *Heat and Sacrifice in the Vedas*, 286.
29. *Ṛg Veda* 10.90.3–4.
30. Cf. *Ṛg Veda* 1.164.45.
31. *Chāndogya Upaniṣad* 3.12.6.

permanently blinded by its light. These men were no longer satisfied by the repetition of the sacrifice which in their eyes had become sterile. The multiplicity of the creation was no longer to them a source of bounty, but instead of ignorance and of being led astray. For them, there was only one final goal: The One in his static perfection. It is then that these men—who for the most part had left human company for the solitude of the forests—proceeded to abandon Agni, the fire of the sacrifice, the priest and mediator between the world of men and that of the gods, to devote themselves to the heat of the more interior fire of *tapas*—literally the ascesis, "the primordial fervour, the original fire, the supreme concentration, the ultimate energy, the creative force that initiates the whole cosmic movement."[32] Thanks to the fire of *tapas*, they undertook an interior pilgrimage, turning back the cosmic manifestation in order to rediscover the hidden source. This was an interior pilgrimage into the mysterious cave of the heart—the *guhā*—because the masters had said to them that: "The *Ātman* [the Absolute] pierced holes outward. Therefore, one looks outward and not inside oneself. Desiring immortality, a certain sage turned his eyes inward and saw the *Ātman* within."[33]

What happened here was an actual transfiguration of the sacrifice. It was no longer about an unsatisfactory external sacrifice, that was not able to lead to the desired liberation (*mokṣa*) through an unbreakable union with the Mystery. On the contrary, all that mattered was the inner sacrifice within which man sacrifices everything, by sacrificing himself. Here, it is no longer a plant or animal-based sacrifice to be delivered to the flames of Agni. Only the ego (*ahaṃkāra*) and the mind (*manas*) are the burnt offering of the mystical sacrifice in the heat of *tapas:* "The ascetic has to burn, to consume, all his thoughts and overcome all his desires, . . . because such an ascesis corresponds to the very structure of reality: the sacrifice of the intellect re-enacts the primordial sacrifice."[34] Thus the inner sacrifice as proposed by the *Upaniṣad* is the most perfect participation in the primordial sacrifice of the Puruṣa. Even more, by the sacrifice of his ego and the mind that makes him a prisoner in the restricted sphere where only a quarter of the Puruṣa is manifest, man becomes able to understand the entirety of the hidden mystery, being himself, in an entirely interior way, the glorious Puruṣa. Such is the deliverance (*mokṣa*) in the way of wisdom (*jñāna*) opened up by the seers of the *Upaniṣad*:

32. Panikkar, *Vedic Experience*, 52.

33. *Kaṭha Upaniṣad* 4.1.

34. Panikkar, *Vedic Experience*, 420.

> But by his own divinisation, the [seer] identifies himself with that Absolute which revealed Itself to him beyond the cosmic activity, in the Silence and Non-Activity of the by now Immobile Perfection. . . . Thus the [seer] gradually arrives at a stage where he stops offering sacrifice, at first simply to avoid any external activity and to interiorize its effects by meditation, but then to deliver himself totally to the pure awareness of the Perfect Unity. In this perception he can then contemplate, in an unmoved and detached manner, the flow of the world and of the universe which unfolds itself in front of him without touching him, and in his experience of the Absolute remains forever identified with It.[35]

Since the seer of the *Upaniṣad* has himself become the Puruṣa, simultaneously sacrificed at the interior level and also led back to his primordial unity in the mystical integration, which is brought about by the inner awakening, it is not surprising that the archetype of the Puruṣa found a new relevance in this very focused corpus of writing. The *Upaniṣad* furthermore exploited the two dimensions contained within the possible etymologies of the Sanskrit term. First of all, in the dimension of wholeness and transcendence the Puruṣa is an equivalent of the *Brahman*—the Absolute as the cosmic Mystery. The *Chāndogya Upaniṣad* here contemplates "the Puruṣa made of gold who is seen within the sun, with golden beard, golden hair, all golden to the tips of the nails."[36] The more recent *Muṇḍaka Upaniṣad* affirms that "just as flowing rivers go down into the sea leaving name and form behind, the one who knows, freed from name and form, reaches the Puruṣa, higher than the highest."[37] The awakening here is the recognition that one is really Brahman or the Puruṣa, the light that covers everything with its glory: "The Puruṣa who is seen in the sun am I. I am he."[38] However, it is above all the dimension of interiority of the Puruṣa that has been the most crucial in the *Upaniṣad* and one can justifiably say that "the transformation of the Cosmic Archetypal Person into the innermost divine presence in the human being was the Copernican revolution of the *Upaniṣad*."[39] Here the Puruṣa is associated with the *Ātman*, the Absolute that is our deepest inner mystery. Thus, the *Bṛhadāraṇyaka Upaniṣad* did not hesitate to re-write the myth of creation of the *Śatapatha Brāhmaṇa* upon which

35. Vesci, *Heat and Sacrifice in the Vedas*, 287.
36. *Chāndogya Upaniṣad* 1.6.6.
37. *Muṇḍaka Upaniṣad* 3.2.8.
38. *Chāndogya Upaniṣad* 4.11.1.
39. Bäumer, "From Puruṣa to Śakti," 33.

this *Upaniṣad* depends: "In the beginning was the *Ātman*, in the likeness of a Puruṣa. Looking around he saw nothing but himself."[40] Some other *Upaniṣhad* preferred to evoke the profound mystery of the "Puruṣa who is seen within the eye,"[41] such "a light without smoke":[42] "A Puruṣa, a thumb in length, rests in the midst of the *Ātman*, Lord of past and future."[43] Finally, when the *Upaniṣad* settled the equation of the *Brahman* and the *Ātman* into the formula of the awakening, they reconciled the two dimensions of transcendence and immanence of the Purusa: "I see the light that is your most beautiful form. That Puruṣa—I am he";[44] "'The Puruṣa who is seen in the eye is the *Ātman*,' he said. 'It is the immortal, the fearless. It is *Brahman*.'"[45] It is not surprising then that in a later *Upaniṣad*, the Puruṣa ended up being the personification of the ardently longed deliverance (*mokṣa*): "I know this great Puruṣa, sun-colored, beyond darkness. Knowing him, one goes beyond death. There is no other path by which to go. All this is filled by the Puruṣa, the one, who stands in the sky, forms as a tree. There is nothing higher or lower than he, no one smaller or larger."[46] Such is the ultimate knowledge of the sealed three-quarter part of the mystery of the Puruṣa—a knowledge about which another *Upaniṣad* said that "it can be won by the one whom the *Ātman* chooses. To him the *Ātman* reveals its own form."[47]

THE LAMB SLAIN BEFORE THE CREATION OF THE WORLD

Having thus traversed almost a thousand years of Indian thought has allowed us to gauge the boundless fecundity of the myth of Puruṣa in its many developments: the sacrifice at the beginning of all creation in the *Ṛg Veda*, a true sacrificial system (*yajña*) that allows the preservation of the world in the *Brāhmaṇa* and finally the inner sacrifice in the *Upaniṣad*, where man himself becomes the glorious Puruṣa. It is hardly surprising that such an archetype had a permanent effect on the first Christians who

40. *Bṛhadāraṇyaka Upaniṣad* 1.4.1.
41. *Chāndogya Upaniṣad* 1.7.5.
42. *Kaṭha Upaniṣad* 4.13.
43. *Kaṭha Upaniṣad* 4.12.
44. *Īśa Upaniṣad* 16; *Bṛhadāraṇyaka Upaniṣad* 5.15.2.
45. *Chāndogya Upaniṣad* 4.15.1.
46. *Śvetāśvatara Upaniṣad* 3.8–9.
47. *Kaṭha Upaniṣad* 2.23.

became interested in "the dismembering of the primordial Puruṣa' from which 'springs the life that fills the universe."[48] Among these must be counted Henri Le Saux-Swāmī Abhishiktānanda (1910–1973)[49] who wrote in his personal diary: "No doubt the Puruṣa will help me rediscover, as if afresh, the universal dimension—the eternal dimension—of the mystery of Jesus."[50] However he added, to demarcate the distance separating the myth from the reality of the salvific Incarnation: "Good Friday. The Cross: at this point, the Puruṣa is no longer enough to explain the mystery of Jesus, nor the mystery of the human being at its greatest depth. . . . The Puruṣa is not sacrificed for the world's salvation. He does not suffer—Jesus suffers."[51] Having said that, it is undeniable that for an Indian Christian the myth of the Puruṣa is remarkable when it is illuminated *a posteriori* by the fullness of the Mystery of Christ. In fact, does the First Letter of Peter not write that we have been "ransomed by the precious blood of Christ, like that of a lamb without defect or blemish . . . destined before the foundation of the world but revealed at the end of the ages for our sake" (1 Pet 1:18–20)? In an even more striking way, the Apocalypse talks of "the Lamb slaughtered since the foundation of the world"[52] (Rev 13:8). There was a need for a reader as attentive to the final book of the Bible as Hans Urs von Balthasar (1905–1988) to extract the full theological richness of such a statement. This had already caught the attention of S. Bulgakov (1871–1944) and P. T. Forsyth (1848–1921):

> Christ's sacrifice began before he came into the world, and his Cross was that of a lamb slain before the world's foundation. There was a Calvary above which was the mother of it all. His obedience, however impressive, does not take divine magnitude if it first rose upon earth, nor has it the due compelling power upon ours. His

48. Swāmī Abhishiktānanda, *Ascent to the Depth*, 255 (April 13, 1963).

49. To Henri Le Saux's name must be added those of his friends Raimon Panikkar, Bettina Bäumer, Uma Marina Vesci who have studied the Puruṣa in the works cited previously. The Indian priest George Praseed should also be mentioned, who devoted his doctoral thesis to this theme: cf. Praseed, *Sacrifice and Cosmos*. Finally, we must not forget other important works in French such as Biardeau and Malamoud, *Le sacrifice dans l'Inde ancienne*.

50. Abhishiktānanda, *Ascent to the Depth*, 346 (April 24, 1972).

51. Abhishiktānanda, *Ascent to the Depth*, 341 (March 31, 1972).

52. Certain new translations have separated the "apo katabolēs kosmou" from the "tou arniou tou esphagmenou" but that goes against the more prevalent tradition.

> obedience as a man was but the detail of the supreme obedience which made him man.[53]

For sure, the doctrine of the *Ur-Kenosis*—the "fundamental Kenosis"[54] as briefly sketched out by von Balthasar—has been much discussed within the Church; nevertheless, one easily understands that a Hindu, bathed in the light of Puruṣa, can readily grasp that there is a sacrifice at the heart of all reality, as its most intimate foundation.

For want of being able to enter too far into a recent theological debate, which deserves deeper consideration, we can allow the Indian myth of the sacrificed Puruṣa to resonate in order to gather new light upon the mystery of the Eucharist that is celebrated every day in innumerable parts of the world. For that, it is beneficial to listen further to Henri Le Saux in his Indian hermitage at Gyansu in the midst of a Hindu world:

> The morning mass in my mezzanine, in the external form of the Indian rite, integrating the Vedic praise and the hymns of the Puruṣa, the real Hindu title for Christ (certainly not in the sectarian modern Hinduism, but in the great tradition of the *Śruti* [Scriptures]).[55] In the name of all those around about me. Giving a voice to their silence, revealing Christ in their call to God. . . . To plunge into the depth of India in the name of the Church, to discover Christ there, the pre-existing Puruṣa—more so actually than in the Greek *logos*—and waiting there for his unveiling. I still believe what I wrote: the Indian Church awaits to give birth to the idea that deep down in a Hindu heart, the Puruṣa awakens himself as Christ![56]

Conventionally, the holy sacrifice of the mass has been theologically understood as the sacramental commemoration of the bloody sacrifice of the Cross, accomplished once and for all on Golgotha: "The Sacrifice which is offered every day in the Church is not distinct from that which Christ Himself offered, but is a commemoration thereof."[57] Three altars

53. Forsyth, *Person and Place of Christ*. This citation is taken up in Balthasar, *Mysterium Paschale*, 39.

54. Balthasar, *Mysterium Paschale*, 39.

55. The *Śruti* are the collected sacred Scriptures of Hinduism: *Veda*, *Brāhmaṇa*, *āraṇyaka*, and *Upaniṣad*. The *Bhagavadgītā* can also be included in this list.

56. Henri Le Saux, Letter to Sister Thérèse Lemoine, Oct. 24, 1966, in Le Saux and Thérèse de Jésus, *Le Swami et la Carmélite*, 205.

57. Thomas Aquinas, *Summa Theologiae* IIIa, q. 22, a.3, 2um. For further details we would draw attention to Andia, "Le sacrifice Parfait."

can be discerned here. First of all, the altar of the Cross where the one who makes the sacrifice is himself offered as the sacrifice: "by commending himself to you for our salvation, showed himself the Priest, the Altar, and the Lamb of sacrifice."[58] Then reference is made in the Canon of the Mass to a mysterious celestial altar—the *sublime altare tuum*—the archetype where the liturgy of the Son, the eternal High priest is celebrated: "In humble prayer we ask you, almighty God: command that these gifts be borne by the hands of your holy Angel to your altar on high in the sight of your divine majesty, so that all of us, who through this participation at the altar receive the most holy Body and Blood of your Son, may be filled with every grace and heavenly blessing."[59] Without doubt here is one of the liturgical keys to understanding along with von Balthasar "the everlasting aspect of the sacrifice of Golgotha."[60] Finally, it is the stone altar where the mass is celebrated and within which are incorporated the relics of the martyrs whose sacrifice bore witness to the greatest Love. To understand the theological richness associated with the stone altar, it is necessary to re-read the preface that was used at the time of its consecration:

> Having become both the true Priest and the true oblation, he [Christ] has taught us to celebrate for ever the memorial of the Sacrifice that he himself offered to you on the altar of the Cross. Therefore, Lord, your people have raised this altar, which we dedicate to you with joyful praise. Truly this is an exalted place, where the Sacrifice of Christ is ever offered in mystery, where perfect praise is rendered to you and redemption flows forth for us. Here is prepared the table of the Lord, where your children, fed by the body of Christ, are gathered into the one, the holy Church. Here the faithful drink of your Spirit from the streams that flow from Christ, the spiritual rock, through whom they, too, become a holy oblation, a living altar.[61]

58. "Fifth Preface of Easter," in *Daily Roman Missal*, 743.

59. "The Roman Canon," in *Daily Roman Missal*, 779. Cf. Irenaeus of Lyon, *Adversus Haereses* 4.18.6: "The altar, then, is in heaven (for towards that place are our prayers and oblations directed)."

60. Balthasar, *Mysterium Paschale*, 40: "And what does the 'sublime altare tuum' of the Roman Canon mean if not the everlasting aspect of the sacrifice of Golgotha, which is likewise represented in the Lamb slain before time began, seated eternally with the Father on that throne from which issue 'the flashes of lighting, and voice, and peals of thunder' (Apocalypse 4,5) of God's glory?"

61. "Preface during the Mass for the Consecration of an Altar," in *Daily Roman Missal*, 2111.

The symbolic and theological richness of the stone altar is remarkable. One single aspect concerns us here. The altar is the place where, by the sacrifice of the mass, the Church is made manifest when the many become one, without losing any of their singularity: "The cup of blessing that we bless, is it not a communion of the blood of Christ? The bread that we break, is it not the communion of the body of Christ? Because there is one bread, we who are many are one body, for we all partake of the one bread" (1 Cor 10:16–17). The Apostle states it clearly: in his sacramental communion with the sacrificial body of Christ, the multiplicity of the creation returns to unity but a unity of communion (*co-esse*);[62] thus the Church is built, of which the Host is the most transparent sign. An ancient eucharistic prayer from the first Christians spoke in terms that were almost the same of the eucharistic unification of the world: "As this broken bread was scattered upon the mountains, but was brought together and became one, so let thy Church be gathered together from the ends of the earth into thy kingdom."[63] On the altar at the Mass, day after day the Pleroma of Christ is manifested when all the singular realities of the world, signified by the bread and the wine, "fruits of the earth and the work of human hands," are gathered up and united in the strength and the light of the Risen One. Thus, each mass that is celebrated at a particular time and place has no purpose other than to sacramentally extend the power of the Resurrection to that time and place, assumed, purified and transfigured in Christ. Doing this, each "white stone" (Rev 2:17) of the singular human circumstances where the mass is celebrated is embedded in the mystery of the Church which "will not be complete, will not be the whole body of Christ, until it has incorporated all the civilisations and all the cultural and spiritual riches of the entire world."[64] Jules Monchanin (1895–1957), who was called Purush by his friends, said that "Christ, by the Resurrection *totus Deus*, deifies everything, man and the whole world,"[65] and he added:

> In the Church and through it Christ prolongs his Redeeming Incarnation until the end of time, incorporating within himself all those who are redeemed, animating them with the Holy Spirit and leading them to the Father. With him and in him, they share in his mystery and are incorporated within the Holy Trinity. This

62. Cf. Vagneux, *Co-esse*, 530–34.

63. *Didachē* 9:4.

64. Monchanin, "L'hindouisme," 66.

65. Monchanin, "Spiritualité de l'Inde," 237.

> mystical body of Christ, which is the continuation through the Resurrection of his physical body, is no longer constrained by space and time. It can only possess its full "ecumenicity" by integrating itself with the whole of humanity, with all cultures and in all eras. Time is only granted to the world for the preparation of the catholicity of the Church.[66]

We have here a broader meaning for the mystery of the Mass, which too often suffers from ideological reductions. The echoes brought by the *Puruṣa-sūkta* and also by the sacrificial doctrine in the *Brāhmaṇa* allow us to understand with greater acuity the mystery which takes place in the Eucharist celebrated daily in each part of the world: the unification of the whole of the creation in the dismembered body of the crucified Christ and in his glorious Risen Body. Such is the gracious wish of the Father: "to recapitulate all things in Christ, things in heaven and things on earth" (Eph 1:10). The Eucharist is thus the sacrament which allows the fullness of Christ to invade and recover everything. It is necessary here to recapture the vastness of the vision of Teilhard de Chardin (1881–1955) in order to prevent any harmful reduction of the Eucharist:

> There is only one Mass in the world, throughout all time: the true Host, the full Host, it is the universe that the Christ penetrates ever more intimately and brings to life. From the distant origin of things up until their unpredictable consummation, through innumerable turmoils in limitless space, the entire Nature undergoes, slowly and irresistibly the Great Consecration. Only one thing occurs in the Creation, deep down, from all time and for ever: the body of Christ.[67]

The *Letter to the Ephesians* has the merit of finding an appropriate balance, in our understanding of the Eucharist, between the remembrance of the Passion and the proclamation of the Resurrection that both occur within the sacrament. Without doubt, it is with this landmark of the emerging ecclesial theology that the myth of Puruṣa would have the most to engage, because the *Letter to the Ephesians* in the same way contemplates the cosmic plenitude of Christ: "He that descended is the same also that ascended far above all the heavens, that He might fill all things" (Eph 4:10). If the Christ is able thus to extend his transcendent power to the whole creation, it is because he dwells within the intimacy of each being: "In order

66. Monchanin, "Essai de spiritualité missionnaire," 164.

67. Teilhard de Chardin, "Panthéisme et christianisme," 90.

that the Father may give you according to the riches of his glory, to be strengthened with power by his Spirit in the inner man and that Christ may dwell by faith in your hearts, that you will be rooted and founded in love" (Eph 3:16–17). Being thus within them, Christ can lead believers on the road of spiritual sacrifice which is the real adoration: "Therefore I urge you, brothers, by the mercy of God, to present your bodies as a living sacrifice, holy and pleasing unto God, which is your spiritual service" (Rom 12:1). In this same movement towards a greater truth, which was the same as that of the *Upaniṣad*, Pope Gregory the Great (550–604) asked himself: "What else do we understand the altar of God to be but the soul of the just man, which lays on itself, before His eyes, as a sacrifice all the good deeds he has performed?"[68] The only duty of the disciple of Christ is then to become a living altar, in the image of his Master who made himself "the altar, the priest and the victim"! And to the Christian in India, the call to give flesh to Puruṣa—mysterious 'premonition' of the fullness of Christ to come: "This evening celebrated Mass with the hymn to the Puruṣa. . . . The celebration of the birth of the Puruṣa, before time and beyond all times. The celebration of each one's birth, of the birth of the Man in each one who is born."[69]

68. Gregory the Great, *Homilies on Ezekiel* 2.10.19.

69. Swāmī Abhishiktānanda, *Ascent to the Depth*, 363 (Dec. 25, 1972).

5

The Yogin and the Child

IN THE SACRED GEOGRAPHY of India, the *saṃgama*—the confluence—has a particular importance. In this place, the rivers come together and flow further from their respective sources, moving towards the ultimate *saṃgama* with the vast ocean wherein they will lose both name and form (*nāmarūpa*)—the mystical symbol of the awakened being who completely immerses himself in the infinite splendor of the Absolute.[1] Speaking about the *Bhagavadgītā*, Jules Monchanin (1895–1957) accurately used the appropriate image of the *saṃgama*, saying that

> The *Bhagavadgītā* is a confluence and a mirror. It is a confluence which invites us to go up along several rivers (*sāṃkhya*, *yoga*, *bhakti*, *post-upanishadic* and *prevedantic jñāna*[2]) to their sources, known or lost. . . . It is also a mirror of the Indian mind: a thousand facets in which the ineffable unity is glittering.[3]

Written at the turn of the Christian era and included in the sixth book of the *Mahābhārata*, the *Bhagavadgītā* is a culmination of a number of undercurrents that moulded the *sanātana dharma*—better known as Hinduism, at the risk of losing its inherent diversity within this specific appellation. However, as a *saṃgama* of so many spiritual influences, the *Bhagavadgītā* is also the starting point for a new way pledged to transform

1. Cf. *Praśna Upaniṣad* 6.5.

2. Jules Monchanin here makes reference to two Indian philosophical systems (*darśana*): the *sāṃkhya* and *yoga* as well as the way of devotion (*bhakti*) and that of spiritual knowledge (*jñāna*).

3. Monchanin, "*Bhagavadgītā*."

the face of Hinduism: the *bhaktimārga* or the way of devotion. This, whilst undergoing a remarkable development, has not in the meantime caused the disappearance of the other ways; these are the *jñānamārga* or the way of mystical knowledge so admirably sketched out in the blaze of the *Upaniṣad* and also in the *karmamārga* or the way of selfless action that has its original inspiration in the *Bhagavadgītā* itself. There, once again the image of *saṃgama* is a precious aid for orientating ourselves in the labyrinths of Hinduism because it obliges us take the high ground in order to contemplate the many meanders and confluences in the journey of the Spirit making its way towards the final liberation (*mokṣa*).

Another way of orienting ourselves in the eighteen complex chapters of the *Bhagavadgītā* would be to put in place some overall figures which will provide a synthesis of the various parts of this text which has nowadays become one of the most popular in Hinduism. Next to the *bhakta*, the devotee or servant of the Lord, the figure of the *yogin* is central and when these two figures are fused into one single person, he is then promised to the ultimate accomplishment: "Be a *yogin*, Arjuna! Because the *yogin* goes beyond those who only follow the path of the austere (*tapasvin*), or of wisdom (*jñānin*), or of work (*karmin*). And the greatest of all *yogī* is he who with all his soul has faith, and he who with all his soul loves me."[4] Amongst the various *yogī* who appear throughout the *Bhagavadgītā*, one of them was committed to a remarkable destiny, taking upon himself the entire message of this book: the *karmayogin*. In fact, in the dialogue between Arjuna and his divine charioteer Kṛṣṇa, a crucial question torments the conscience of the Prince on the battlefield at Kurukṣetra where he has been called, along with his other Pāṇḍava brothers, to fight their Kaurava cousins and some of their uncles as well as the teachers who had educated them since childhood: "How to accept such a bloodbath that will generate an accumulation of bad *karman*?" For Arjuna there would be a considerable temptation to retreat if Kṛṣṇa were not there to remind him of his princely status: his *dharma* of *kṣatriya*. And it is precisely the fulfilment of *dharma* according to the own way of *karmamārga*—the way of selfless action (*niṣphala*)—that guarantees Arjuna his liberation: "Set thy heart upon thy work (*karman*), but never on its reward (*phala*). Work not for a reward; but never cease to do thy work."[5] A bit later, using the keyword "detached" (*asakta*), Kṛṣṇa describes the heart of *karmayoga* which has been crucial in the life for so many

4. *Bhagavadgītā* 6.46–47.

5. *Bhagavadgītā* 2.47.

Indians: "In liberty from the bounds of attachment (*asakta*), do thou therefore the work to be done: for the man whose work is pure attains indeed the Supreme."[6] Summarizing the new message given during the approach to the decisive combat, Raimon Panikkar (1918–2010) wrote:

> The true *yogin* is not the man who does not act but the man who acts with detachment, that is, without hankering for the results of his actions, not only on a moral but also on an ontological plane. The true ascetic not only has perfect control over himself and total equanimity, but he is also liberated from all desires, sees the Lord everywhere and everything in the Lord, and is ready for action when it is required and seen as his duty.[7]

It is obvious that the *karmayoga* had a crucial impact upon the Indian mind. However, it must not be forgotten that the *Bhagavadgītā* suggests other yogas: the *jñānayoga* or the yoga of mystical knowledge, the *bhaktiyoga* or the yoga of devotion and one even finds in these writings some echoes of the yogic exercises of the *śramana* who in the fifth century BC were the first to explore the mysterious connections between the body and the spirit. Perhaps so many distinctions between the different yogas poses a risk of leading us astray amongst what the *Bhagavadgītā* wanted to draw together in such a luminous way. Also, we would like to simply re-read this iconic writing using the archetype of the *yogin* in the way it appears throughout the book, setting out a figure in which the Indian soul reads its own spiritual quest within itself as if in a mirror.

THE BEING WHO IS UNIFIED

"Yukta ityucyate yogī," "the *yogin* is the one who is brought together":[8] this is how the *Bhagavadgītā* defines the *yogin*, going back to the Sanskrit root [*yuj*]: to join, to attach and then unify. The *yogin* is etymologically the being who is unified and who remains thus at the centre of every passion: "He whose mind is untroubled by sorrow, and for pleasure he has no longings, beyond passion, and fear and anger, he is the sage of silence (*munin*) of unwavering mind."[9] Beyond the alternation of good and bad fortune, a

6. *Bhagavadgītā* 3.19.
7. Panikkar, *Vedic Experience*, 444.
8. *Bhagavadgītā* 6.8.
9. *Bhagavadgītā* 2.56.

deep peace settles upon him and such is his spiritual accomplishment: "The man who forsakes all desires and abandons all pride of possession and of self reaches the goal of peace supreme."[10]

In order to achieve such a state of equanimity, a *sādhanā* (that is a spiritual exercise rather than a technique) is necessary in order that the *yogin* can conquer his senses (*yatendriya*) which continue to drive him towards the outside whilst scattering him. Also he has to walk on the path that is the opposite of the innate tendencies of his nature, activating the drawing together of his senses and his spirit into the silence of the depths in the extreme concentration implied by the root [*yam*] used in the adjective *yata*, "bound, unified," present in the beautiful description "yogī yuñjīta satatam ātmānaṃ" that Lord Kṛṣṇa makes of the *yogin*:

> Day after day, let the *yogin* practice the inner unification: in a secret place, in deep solitude, master of his mind (*yatacittātman*), hoping for nothing, desiring nothing. Let him find a place that is pure and a seat that is restful, neither too high nor too low, with sacred grass and a skin and a cloth thereon. On that seat let him rest and practice yoga for the purification of his spirit: with the life of his body and mind in peace; his spirit in silence before the one. With upright body, head, and neck, which rest still and move not; with an inner gaze which is not restless, but rests still between the eyebrows. With the soul in peace, and all fear gone, and strong in the vow of holiness, let him rest with mind unified, his spirit on me, his god supreme.[11]

Such a *sādhanā*, if practised till the end, should lead the *yogin* naturally to the *mokṣa*, the liberation to which India aspires:

> When the sage of silence closes the doors of his spirit and, resting his inner gaze between the eyebrows, keeps peaceful and even the ebbing and flowing of breath; and with life and mind and reason unified (*yatendriya*), and with desire and fear and wrath gone, keep silent his spirit before final liberation (*mokṣa*), he in truth has attained final liberation.[12]

Thus is the *yogin*, also called *yogayuktātman*:[13] the being who is joined together and who is then unified. We can easily understand then

10. *Bhagavadgītā* 2.71.
11. *Bhagavadgītā* 6.10–14.
12. *Bhagavadgītā* 5.27–28.
13. *Bhagavadgītā* 6.29.

how the spiritual ideal that the *Bhagavadgītā* has just sketched out through incorporating several traditions of the *śramana*, was promised a tremendous future within Indian thought and its spiritual practice. As proof of this we have the *Yogasūtra* of Patañjali with their commentary by Vyāsa but also the subsequent developments as much in Hinduism (in particular of the *haṭhayoga* of the mythical guru Gorakhnāth), as in the Buddhism of the *yogācāra* and the *vajrayāna* tradition, and also in Jainism, making yoga to be thus "an age-old pan-Indian dimension of the spirituality of India . . . one—or the most characteristic—of its essential manifestations."[14] However the seed of all of these subsequent developments can already be seen in wonderful descriptions that the *Bhagavadgītā* has given of the figure of the *yogin*. This is why it is worth relating some of them here.

In the twelfth chapter, the *yogin* meets again the figure of the devotee (*bhakta*) on the way of perfection:

> The man who has a good will for all, who is friendly and has compassion; who has no thoughts of "I" or "mine," whose peace is the same in pleasures and sorrows, and who is forgiving; this *yogin* of unification, ever full of my joy, whose spirit is unified (*yatātman*) and whose determination is strong; whose mind and inner vision are set on me—this man loves me (*bhakta*), and he is dear to me. He whose peace is not shaken by others, and before whom other people find peace, beyond excitement and anger and fear—he is dear to me. He who is free from vain expectations, who is pure, who is wise and knows what to do, who in inner peace watches both sides, who shakes not, who works for God and not for himself—this man loves me, and he is dear to me. He who feels neither excitement nor repulsion, who complains not and lusts not for things; who is beyond good and evil, and who has love—he is dear to me. The man whose love is the same for his enemies or his friends, whose soul is the same in honour or in disgrace, who is beyond heat or cold or pleasure or pain, who is free from the chains of attachments; he who is balanced in blame and in praise, whose soul is silent, who is happy with whatever he has, whose home is not in this world, and who has life—this man is dear to me.[15]

Another description of the *yogin*'s cloak of virtues is given in the sixteenth chapter:

14. Monchanin, "Problèmes du yoga chrétien," 258.

15. *Bhagavadgītā* 2.13–19.

> Freedom from fear, purity of heart, constancy in sacred learning and contemplation, generosity, self-harmony, adoration, study of the scriptures, austerity, righteousness; non-violence, truth, freedom from anger, renunciation, serenity, aversion to fault-finding, sympathy for all beings, peace from greedy cravings, gentleness, modesty, steadiness; energy, forgiveness, fortitude, purity, a good will, freedom from pride—these are the treasures of the man who is born from heaven.[16]

Lastly, the final eighteenth chapter concludes by depicting the *yogin* at the height of his *sādhanā*, when he has become *brahmabhūta*, the being who is completely united with the Absolute (*Brahman*), his Lord:

> Hear now how he reaches *Brahman*, the highest vision of light. When the vision of mind is clear, and in steadiness the inner unification is completed; when the world of sound and other sense is gone, and the spirit has risen above passion and hate; when a man dwells in the solitude of silence, and meditation and contemplation are ever with him; when too much food does not disturb his health, and his thoughts and words and body are in peace; when freedom from passion is his constant will; and his selfishness and violence and pride are gone; when lust and anger and greediness are no more, and he is free from the thought "this is mine"; then this man has risen on the mountain of the Highest: he is worthy to be one with *Brahman*. He is one with *Brahman* (*brahmabhūta*), and beyond grief and desire his soul is in peace. His love is one for all creation, and he has supreme love for me.[17]

Such a perfectly recollected *yogin* is essentially a hidden being in the secret of the night of all beings.[18] Therein this place of interior unification with the Absolute (*Brahman*), he awakens and takes wing, like the great Golden Swan (*paramahaṃsa*): "He is not bound by things outside (*asaktātman*), and within he finds inner gladness. His soul is one in *Brahman* (*brahmayogayuktātman*) and he attains everlasting joy";[19] "He has inner joy, he has inner gladness, and he has found inner Light. This *yogin* attains the *nirvāṇa* of Brahman (*brahmanirvāṇa*[20]): he is one with

16. *Bhagavadgītā* 16.1–3.

17. *Bhagavadgītā* 18.50–54.

18. Cf. *Bhagavadgītā* 2.69: "In the dark night of all beings awakes to Light the tranquil man (*saṃyamin*). But what is day to other beings is night for the sage who sees."

19. *Bhagavadgītā* 5.21.

20. On various occasions the *Bhagavadgītā* uses the expression *nirvāṇa* which had

God and goes unto God (*brahmabhūta*)."[21] This man who is totally free can from now on say: "I am not bound (*asakta*) by this vast work of creation (*karman*). I am and I watch the drama of works."[22] However—and such is both the paradox and great newness of the *Bhagavadgītā* in its teaching on the way of selfless action (*karmamārga*)—the *yogin*, whilst being detached from everything (*asakta*) does not flee to the desert far away from people and this comes from the fact that in the midst of the waves of the *saṃsāra*, he is attached to the one and only Absolute:

> The integrated man is both *yukta*, yoked to the whole of reality, involved in the net of relationships, and *vimukta*, free, liberated. He is committed but not concerned, he is detached but not unattached, he is involved but not entangled. Hence derives his "holy indifference," his serenity, his peace, which is not one of having taken refuge in an ivory tower or an inaccessible eyrie but is the result of being situated in the very heart of reality.[23]

To this fully liberated *yogin*, we can finally apply the same words that the *Bhagavadgītā* uses to describe the supreme Spirit with which the *yogin* has now become one: "It is never born, and it never dies. It is in Eternity: it is for evermore. Never born and eternal, beyond times gone or to come, it does not die when the body dies."[24]

THE CHILD WHO COMES FORTH FROM THE ETERNAL NEWNESS

Faced with the sublime figure of the *yogin* who for all time has been for India the unblemished mirror of her spiritual quest, the Christian is entitled to ask himself which figure represents the outcome of his spiritual way. On several occasions,[25] the Swiss theologian Hans Urs von Balthasar

---

an immense fortune within Buddhism. Cf. *Bhagavadgītā* 2.72: "This is the Eternal (*Brahman*) in man, O Arjuna. Reaching him all delusion is gone. Even in the last hour of his life upon earth, man can reach the *nirvāṇa* of Brahman—man can find peace in the peace of his God"; *Bhagavadgītā* 6.15: "The *yogin* who, lord of his mind, ever prays in this inner unification, attains the peace of *nirvāṇa*, the peace supreme that is in me."

21. *Bhagavadgītā* 5.24.

22. *Bhagavadgītā* 9.9.

23. Panikkar, *Vedic Experience*, 444.

24. *Bhagavadgītā* 2.20.

25. The principal texts of Hans Urs von Balthasar on childhood are: *Unless You*

(1905–1988) liked to make a contrast between the pagan sage who "with his power declining, achieves the distance required for serenity and religious wisdom"[26] and the immutable youth of the Christian sage: "In the figures of the great saints the truth is crystal clear: Christian childlikeness and Christian maturity are not in tension with one another. Even at advanced age, the saints enjoy a marvellous youthfulness."[27] Von Balthasar had elsewhere found confirmation for his suggestion in a quote from Saint Augustine who liked to say: "Let not our progress through life turn us from new men into old; rather, let our growth be a growth in newness itself."[28]

Of course, von Balthasar's contrast between the pagan world and the Christian world might need to be nuanced. However, it has the merit of bringing us to the heart of the unique figure of spiritual accomplishment that Christ himself described for us in his teaching: that of the child. Teaching his disciples, one day Jesus "took a little child and put it amongst them, and taking it in his arms, he said to them: 'Whoever welcomes a child such as this in my name, welcomes me'" (Mark 9:36–37). Another time, he said to them: "Let the little children come to me; do not stop them; for it is to such as these that the kingdom of God belongs. Truly I tell you, whoever does not receive the kingdom of God as a little child will never enter it" (Mark 10:14–15). It is worth noting that the words of Christ are found to be identical in the three synoptic Gospels[29] and this confirms how the image of the child is the fulcrum of all types of Christian holiness each in its own way diffusing the unique holiness of Christ which strictly speaking is his spirit of childhood. In fact, if Jesus has thus proposed the child as the royal path for those who follow him, it is, as the Gospels show it, because the Son is the child *par excellence*. It is moving here to underline how Hans Urs von Balthasar, at the end of his immense theological career, wished to "show the essential traits of the man who lives this childhood in God as an adult"[30] for "inasmuch as childhood uniquely interweaves loving trust (in those who care for the child's needs) and unquestioning obedience, it possesses an affinity with the Father's eternal child."[31]

Become Like This Child; "Eternal Child"; and "Young Until Death."

26. Balthasar, "Young Until Death," 218.

27. Balthasar, *Unless You Become Like This Child*, 41.

28. Augustine of Hippo, *Ennarationes in Psalmos* 131.1.

29. Mark 9:33–37 // Matt 18:1–5 // Luke 9:46–48; Mark 10:13–16 // Matt 19:13–15 // Luke 18:15–17.

30. Balthasar, *Unless You Become Like This Child*, 44.

31. Balthasar, "Eternal Child," 214.

To understand how the way of childhood in Christianity is the perfect expression of the *sequela Christi*, we have to hold a psychological view that is orientated more towards the qualities of childhood itself together with a theological perspective that contemplates the mystery of Christ. To illustrate the psychological viewpoint, few pages can rival the magnificent description of spiritual childhood given by Romano Guardini (1885–1968) in his masterwork *The Lord*. Meditating on the words of Christ to his disciples the German theologian made a contrast with the adult spirit by emphasizing the openness of the child to the reality through a pure welcome and availability:

> The adult is self-centred; he is constantly examining, testing, judging himself. Herein lies the earnestness of life, which consists of a feeling of responsibility, conscious living. The immediacy of things and people is broken in the grown-up world, for the adult is constantly projecting himself between them and him. The child does not reflect. His life moves outside himself. He is open to the world and everything in it. Unconsciously he stands straight and looks straight at things as they really are.[32]

Such an openness creates a radical humility within the child, which allows him to disappear when faced with the reality greater than himself: "In the child's attitude towards life lies his humility. . . . He does not drag his small ego into the foreground; his consciousness brims with objects, people, event—not himself. Thus is the world is dominated by reality: that which is and really counts."[33] Such an interior openness then allows the child be led into the newness of the Kingdom and to dance with his Lord who 'playing the flute' requires this of him in the same way as "children, sitting in the marketplace and calling one to another" (Matt 11:17):

> Because the child is natural, open, without intentions or fear of failing to assert himself, he is receptive to the great, revolutionary ideas in Christ's teaching of the kingdom. The same teaching is met with reserve by the more mature listener. His cleverness condemns it as impossible; his caution warns him of the consequences; his self-esteem is soon up in arms; his hard grasp cannot let go. He has encysted himself in artificialities, and fearful of his brittle little world, he prefers not to understand. Fear has made

32. Guardini, *Lord*, 289.

33. Guardini, *Lord*, 289.

> his eyes blind, his ears deaf, his heart dull; as Jesus would say, he is over-mature.[34]

Thus, according to Guardini, an abyss opens up between the ever-new universe of the child and the prematurely aged world of adults:

> The child is young. It has the simplicity of eye and heart which welcomes all that is new and great and salutary; it sees it for what it is, goes straight to it and enters in. This simplicity, *naturalis christianitas*, is the childlikeness . . . Jesus means nothing sentimental or touching; neither sweet defencelessness nor gentle malleability. What he values is the child's clarity of vision; the ability to look up and out, to feel and accept reality without ulterior motives.[35]

All of this allows Guardini to conclude by affirming:

> The spiritual childhood Jesus means emanates from God's Fatherhood. Everything comes to the child from its father and mother, is related somehow to them. They are everywhere, the origin, measure and order of all things. The adult soon distances himself from his parents; in their place stands the world, irreverent, disinterested or hostile. Once the parents have gone, everything becomes homeless. For the child of God a fatherly Someone is again omnipresent; to be sure, he must not be distorted to a superprojection of an earthly father, but must remain who he is, as he has revealed himself: God our Father and Lord Jesus Christ who helps us to accomplish his will. The childlike mind is the one that see the heavenly Father in everything that comes into his life. . . . To become a child in Christ's sense is to reach Christian maturity.[36]

The discovery of the benevolent presence of the celestial Father as the source of our existence brings the psychological view of the child back to theology because our destiny to "become children of God" (John 1:12) is completely rooted in the figure of the eternal Son, who, according to the incomparable prologue to the Gospel of Saint John was "with God" and "was God" (John 1:1). That is why von Balthasar could write that: "the youthfulness of Jesus and of his genuine followers is a mystery that far transcends psychology. For it springs from the most hidden depths of theology, from the very mystery of the triune God."[37] In fact, this is the spiritual childhood

34. Guardini, *Lord*, 290.
35. Guardini, *Lord*, 290–91.
36. Guardini, *Lord*, 291.
37. Balthasar, "Young Until Death," 224.

promised to the disciples of Christ through their ontological roots in the mystery of the Trinity, in the place where Jesus eternally dwells: "The divine Child—even when he is sent out into the world—is ever springing forth as the fruit of the Father's generative act. There is no routine habit here, only constantly fresh amazement, eternal gratitude, and eternally ready obedience."[38] And it is in the depths of the Trinitarian exchange that all newness and all renewal in this world find their unique source:

> Jesus's eternal youthfulness is no obstacle to his adult manhood. The mystery of his origin is also the mystery of the ever-renewed act of his release. God the Father lets God the Son be God—not a subordinate divinity, but God equal in dignity to the Father. And both let the Holy Spirit be the co-equal expression of their love. The Father's begetting and the Son's letting himself be begotten; the Father's and Son's inspiration of the *Pneuma* and the Spirit's letting himself be spirated [*sic*]—all of this is both eternal act and eternally complete result. . . . This is why God's eternity is eternally youthful and surprising, why it is an abyss of newness.[39]

Having thus re-read, in the light of the words of Christ, the penetrating reflections of Guardini on the psychology of childhood and the equally penetrating theological research of von Balthasar on the trinitarian newness, we more easily understand how much childhood is the mirror of the Christian journey towards the mystery of the eternal birth within God as it is sung on the eve of Christmas: "in splendoribus sanctorum, ex utero, ante luciferum, genui te."[40] It is this mystery of generation which in Christianity is the framework of the whole of reality: the mystery of the endless game of the divine Logos[41] in his creative enthusiasm, the mystery that inextricably

38. Balthasar, "Young Until Death," 221.

39. Balthasar, "Young Until Death," 222.

40. "In the splendour of the sanctuary, from the womb of the dawn, I have begotten you." This comes from a verse of Psalm 110 that the Gregorian liturgy uses as a communion antiphon on the Christmas eve Mass so as to evoke, as does the gradual "Tecum Principium," the eternal generation of the Word. In these immortal pieces, the music rises to summits of theological expression, which the feeble words of our intelligence cannot rival.

41. This divine game is also a drama, as von Balthasar clearly showed concerning the entry of the coming of the eternal Son onto the world scene: "And even death itself turns out to be an essential part of the game. Jesus, now grown and with a full measure of responsibility, returns all his earthly achievements to the hands of the Father. It is as if he were trustfully asking the Father to repair a broken toy or a spoiled game, like an earthly child who knows that fathers can do anything. His child's gesture—'into your hands'—is

unites time and eternity, as the old Heraclitus (535–475) foresaw in such an impressive way: "Time is a child playing draughts, the kingly power is a child's."[42]

MERGED IN THE MYSTERY

It is obvious that the figure of the *yogin* and that of the child may seem at first sight to be at opposite sides of an unbridgeable abyss, especially as the Christian will always be tempted to take up the old theological quarrels about grace and apply them to other spiritual paths. However, by too hastily setting the advanced age of the wise man against the immutable freshness of the "God who died so young,"[43] he may prevent his interlocutor from setting out the entire depth of his argument. The Indian tradition is undeniably much more spiritually subtle, and it is cautious about too radically opposing what is gleaned through the efforts of extreme ascesis against what is received as a fruit of the divine grace. To convince oneself of this one has only to read the magnificent dialogue in the *Bṛhadāraṇyaka Upaniṣad* between the sage Yājñavalkya and Kahola, where it is written:

> Therefore a brahmana should turn away from learning (*pāṇḍityaṃ*), and desire to live like a child (*bālyena*). When he has turned away from both childhood and learning, he is a "silent one" (*munin*). When he has turned away from both non-silence and silence, he is a brahmana (*brāhmaṇaḥ*)—a true knower of *Brahman*.[44]

It is worthy of note here that in order to describe the spiritual way of mankind, the *upaniṣad* blends together the figure of the child (*bāla*) with that of the *yogin* in its different aspects of scholar (*pāṇḍita*), silent one

thus the perfect act of trust in the Father, who will straighten every crooked line and retrieve every lost moment. There is a close connexion between childhood and death: the essential secret of both consists, quite simply, in the act of handing over the gift. It is in physical nakedness that the child enters the world, and it is in spiritual nakedness that he must entrust himself, stripped of all power, to the mystery of the Father. Everything between birth and death is a parenthesis. The seriousness of this parenthesis is part of God's game, but at either end it is the aspect of play that stands out most prominently. The Father's Child who proceeds from him eternally also returns to him eternally and in every moment of time. And this is the game that we, God's other children, are invited to play as well" (*Eternal Child*, 216–17).

42. Heraclitus, fragment 52.

43. Cf. Boyer, *Le dieu qui était mort*.

44. *Bṛhadāraṇyaka Upaniṣad* 3.5.1. Cf. Le Saux, "Dans le pays tamoul," 124.

(*munin*) and one who is united with the Absolute (*brāhmaṇa*)—aspects that the *Bhagavadgītā* has itself adopted whilst it has ignored the child. Also remarkable is the fact that in his *Commentary on the Brahmasūtra*,[45] Śaṅkara (788–820) returned to the same verse of the *Bṛhadāraṇyaka Upaniṣad* in order to explain the term *anāviṣkurvan*, "without any display," that is present in the *sūtra* "anāviṣkurvannanvayāt" of Bādarāyaṇa. In doing this, Śaṅkara stands against the interpretation of those who in the *Upaniṣad* under discussion, read the term *balya* with a short *a* signifying "force" instead of *bālya* with a long *a* signifying "childhood." With the short *a* rejected by Sankara, it would mean "the sage must try to live by that strength which comes from knowledge" whereas for him the text should read as "that the sage renounces knowing and becomes like a child (*bālya*)." This then allows him to affirm that:

> Hence by the term *bālya* is to be understood here some inward state of a child such as having immature functional ability. That fact is referred to by the *sūtra* in, "without display" (*anāviṣkurvan*). That is to say, without showing himself off by parading his wisdom, learning, virtuousness. . . . He should be free from pride, conceit . . . like a child who, owing to the immaturity of his senses, does not try to make a display of himself before others.[46]

The interpretation that Śaṅkara has here made of childhood could not avoid challenging a Christian immersed in Hinduism as was Henri le Saux-Swāmī Abhishiktānanda (1910–1973). In a short and almost ignored text written in 1972 to the Carmel of Lisieux, he declared that:

> In the commentary on the *Brahmasūtra* (III, 4, 50), Śaṅkara asks himself what is to be understood by this state of childhood . . . what characterises the (spiritual) childhood is the absence of malice and vanity. Childhood has no idea of putting forward its persona and its own value—the exact opposite of what the *upaniṣad* calls *pāṇḍityaṃ*, the satisfaction of knowledge and the display of that knowledge. The child, himself, is itself quite simply, without a viewpoint or reflection on what he is or on the way that he is.[47]

Śaṅkara, the master of Vedanta, has thus used the image of the child to comment on the term *anāviṣkurvan*, 'without any ostentation.' Pushing his reflection further, he declared, returning to an ancient tradition, that:

45. Cf. Śaṅkara, *Brahmasūtra Bhāṣya* 3.4.50 (pp. 806–7).
46. Śaṅkara, *Brahmasūtra Bhāṣya* 3.4.50 (pp. 807).
47. Le Saux, "Dans le pays tamoul," 124–25.

> He is a *brāhmaṇa* whom nobody recognizes either as an aristocrat or a commoner, either as well-read or not well-read, either as well-behaved or not well-behaved. A man of enlightenment should resort to unostentatious behaviour while following his spiritual practices in secret. He should roam over the earth like a blind man (not attracted by sense-objects), like one benumbed (i.e. without the sense of taste . . .), like one who is dumb (i.e. without active organs), and 'without any out sign and with unostentatious behaviour (*anāviṣkurvan*).[48]

Even more subtly, for Henri le Saux, the 'without any ostentation' (*anāviṣkurvan*) was above all a spiritual attitude that was completely interior. It is the naked experience of the child (*bāla*), fully open within a pure openness to reality, without any turning back upon itself. Thus, the child is fully hidden within the mystery, as distinct from the adult who knows (*pāṇḍita*) and above all wants it to be known that he knows:

> The vedantic ascesis can be defined as a return to the origins, to that inherent state within ourselves which has not reached the process of becoming and that is not able to experience the modifications that the subsequent conditions of our existence bring about in our body and our thought. Back to the origins? More precisely, the discovery of that within us that is beyond all beyond all origin lived, thought or felt. Even when the adult has recognised this most interior mystery of his being, is he not constantly seeking to make of formulation of it, seize it, whereas *that* is actually as present to him as the light in his eyes and the air in his lungs?[49]

And Henri le Saux adds:

> Without a doubt it is this transparency to oneself of the child over and above all reflective thought, which is more commonly found in Indian thought when it contemplates the state (more than the way) of spiritual childhood—at least at the level of the way of wisdom or *jñāna*; because the *bhakti* tradition (loving devotion) will certainly be responsive to the attitude of trust and surrender to the paternal love that was so strongly emphasised by the saint of Lisieux.[50]

As the most secure remedy for the temptation towards complexity that is woven into the hearts of adults, the child is worthy of "the blessed

48. Śaṅkara, *Brahmasūtra Bhāṣya*, 807.
49. Le Saux, "Dans le pays tamoul," 125.
50. Le Saux, "Dans le pays tamoul," 125.

simplicity"[51] by which Raimon Panikkar described the monk as universal archetype. For the Catalan theologian, the child is truly the future of mankind who, on the threshold of maturity, "has, at this stage, two ways open to him: either to begin all over again and increase and broaden the flow of information, or to begin to simplify, to condense, to concentrate, so that all once again becomes simple, more transparent, as if he were recovering his lost innocence, though in a higher degree and a deeper sense."[52] However, through the eyes of Indian wisdom, the child does not represent the final outcome of mankind's spiritual pilgrimage. In fact, after having exhorted "the sage to renounce learning (*pāṇḍityaṃ*) in order to become like a child (*bālya*)," the *upaniṣad* previously mentioned goes even further, proposing a higher and more reconciliatory ideal in the image of the *munin* and above all that of *brāhmaṇa* of which the *Bhagavadgītā* says that he has become one with the Absolute (*brahmayogayuktātman*[53]/*brahmabhūta*[54]): "When he has turned away from both childhood and learning, he is a 'silent one' (*munin*). When he has turned away from both non-silence and silence, he is a brahmana (*brāhmaṇaḥ*)."[55] Commenting on this new spiritual stage, Henri le Saux wrote:

> One might think that everything has been said, once the ideal of the child has been proposed; but no, it is necessary just as much to renounce being a child as being a scholar and to become a *munin* (or better a silent one: one who is led by the inspiration from within), then it is necessary to abandon all interest in being or not being silent or inspired. Only then does one become a true sage, one who knows from intimate experience the very mystery of *Brahman*.[56]

And with an extreme finesse that issues from the original outpouring of the *upaniṣad* that he was wanting to recover above and beyond all the commentaries from the subsequent tradition, the monk from Brittany clarified all the new contradictions that emerge along the path of awakening:

> The child, himself, is unaware of his carefree indifference and of his freedom, he does not think that he is acting as a child. But the adult who has become a child again finds it difficult to forget that

51. Panikkar, *Blessed Simplicity*.
52. Panikkar, *Vedic Experience*, 767.
53. *Bhagavadgītā* 5.21.
54. *Bhagavadgītā* 5.24.
55. *Bṛhadāraṇyaka Upaniṣad* 3.5.1.
56. Le Saux, "Dans le pays tamoul," 125.

> he has become a child again; and, in the very development of his state of infancy, he becomes again an adult: in so doing he is the same as the one who is in silence. When he becomes aware that he has attained this silence from outside, he has already broken the silence and he is no longer a *munin*. At the level of ultimate experience, of the perfect childhood and of total silence, it is as if everything that could be said of wisdom, of childhood and of silence has evaporated, only the *Brahman* remains, alone and without another. The crystal that reflects the light is so much at one with that light that it no longer knows anything of itself or the light. There is not a word to describe that mystery; there is no action to attain it. *That is*, quite simply as the child is, and is itself, without thinking about it.[57]

Indian wisdom here reaches the virginal silence covering the human being, who from henceforth being nothing but pure astonishment in the face of the infinite newness of the Mystery, completely embedded in the Mystery and above all, without a possibility of turning back to himself, lets the Mystery simply *be*. In an impressive way India has here come so close to the mysterious one who gathers within himself the figure of the perfect "*gnostic*" (*pāṇḍita*) using the term of Clement of Alexandria (150–215), the figure of the child (*bāla*) or *ho pais*[58] as Clement of Rome (35–99) called him and the figure of the silent one (*munin*) of whom Ignatius of Antioch (35–108) said he was "the Word that came from silence"[59]—in short, the one who is perfectly united with the Absolute (*brāhmaṇa*) because "at the beginning he was with God, he was God" (John 1:1), in other words Jesus himself, the eternal Son hidden for eternity in the bosom of his Father, upon whom he gazes

> with eternal childlike amazement: "The Father is greater than I" (John 14:28). Indeed, he is irretrievably greater in so far as he is the origin of all things, even of the Son, and the Son never thinks of trying to 'catch up' to this his Source: by so doing he would only destroy himself. He knows himself to be sheer Gift that is given to itself and which would not exist without the Giver who is distinct from the Gift and who nonetheless gives himself within it.[60]

57. Le Saux, "Dans le pays tamoul," 126.

58. Clement of Rome, *First Letter to the Corinthians* 16.1–3: "The Christ belongs to humble souls, to those who do not raise themselves above the flock. . . . We have announced him like a small child."

59. Ignatius of Antioch, *Letter to the Magnesians* 8.2.

60. Balthasar, *Unless You Become Like This Child*, 44.

Dwelling in "God's eternity that is eternally youthful and surprising," immersed in the trinitarian exchanges which are "an abyss of newness,"[61] "in the Absolute Spirit of Love," the Son "marvels at Love itself as it permeates and transcends all that is."[62] But such a newness, source of the inexhaustible wonder of the Son, is also what is promised to all those who are called to be sons in Him, participants in Him in the trinitarian exchanges where they will be completely united with God: "Unceasingly, the divinised soul, in tune with the trinitarian rhythm, comes to the Father in the Spirit and by the Word, and goes from the Father to the Spirit through the Word, it is gathered into the One, it expands itself into the Three, having itself become mutual indwelling (*circumincessio*)."[63] For those who travel this path of unification in the present day by again becoming the little children to whom the Kingdom of the Father, of the Son and of the Holy Spirit is promised, there is a vow to accompany them all along their journey:

May God give us a renewed mind
For nobler and freer love:
To make us so new in our life;
That Love may bless us
And renew, with new taste,
Those to whom she can give new fulness;
Love is the new and powerful recompense
Of those whose life renews itself for love alone.
Those who newly wish to know
In the new springtime, the new love.[64]

61. Balthasar, "Young Until Death," 222.
62. Balthasar, *Unless You Become Like This Child*, 46.
63. Monchanin, Unpublished note: "Contemplation."
64. Hadewijch of Antwerp, *Vale Millies* 9 in *Complete Works*, 130.

6

As a Flash of Lightning

"As when lightning has flashed—Aah!—and made us blink—Aah!"[1] The unique beauty of the *Upaniṣad* is to communicate spiritual experience to us in its purest form. Long before the scholarly treatises expounded on the Awakening and its modalities, the words of the ancient sages led back to the original outpouring of light: the glare of a flash of lightning that in a second tears open the interior heavens, the cry of a human being who from now on sees everything in an unimagined clarity. We could speak here of a primordial poetic magma, remembering that the very etymology of poetry is *poiein* in the Greek: to create, to bring out a newness that is absolute. Even more powerful is the Sanskrit term *kavi* which designates the poet, that is to say literally the seer, the one who "knows the mystery of the past, the present and the future"[2]—qualities that ultimately are those of the Absolute: "kaviṃ purāṇaṃ anuśāsitāraṃ," "the Poet, the most Ancient One, the Controller."[3]

The *Upaniṣad* brought a climax to the fascination with the light that inhabited the *ṛṣi*, the seers of the Vedic era. But whereas their elders fixed the splendor of the sun in its glorious rising, the later masters set out in a search for the interior sun, the supreme witness that shines motionless at the depths of the heart. They allowed themselves to be filled with a longing for the light whose sovereign freedom is the very symbol of the infinite consciousness which in the Awakening no longer knows any obstacle to

1. *Kena Upaniṣad* 4.4.
2. *Bhagavadgītā* 7.26.
3. *Bhagavadgītā* 8.9. See also *Bhagavadgītā* 10.37: "kavīnāṃ uśanā kaviḥ."

its flight into the immaculate azure. Moreover, the sages of the *Upaniṣad* ascended once again the pathway of the cosmic manifestation to rediscover the luminous dark source, the place where they disappeared forever, engulfed in the mystery.

THE INNER DAZZLING

It took courage and ardor for the ascetics to undertake the pilgrimage towards the *guhā*, the "secret cave of the heart," "the utmost height."[4] Above all, they had to be chosen by the Absolute because the *Ātman*, the Self, the inner principle that is sought, "cannot be won by speaking, not by intelligence or much learning. It can be won by the one whom It chooses. To him the *Ātman* reveals its own form."[5]

Faced with the enigma of the world, the sages chose the most unexpected way to identify the source of the light, by first immersing themselves in the darkened fabric of the world by going back against all the evidence. But once they were able to tear aside its dense texture of ignorance (*avidyā*), they reached a greater darkness—that of the infinite mystery that fills the cave of the heart: "Those who worship ignorance enter into blind darkness: those who delight in knowledge (*vidyā*) enter into greater darkness."[6] Surrounded on all sides by vertiginous paradoxes through which they later expressed their *upaniṣad*, they understood that "the gods seems to love the mysterious, and hate the obvious."[7] This, so to speak, was the inner ritual of their mystical initiation up to the moment where the Awakening burst forth in all is brilliance, to "lead them from the unreal to the real, from darkness to light, from death to immortality"[8] allowing them to discover in an instant of eternity that "ahaṃ brahmāsmi,"[9] "I am *Brahman*," the very mystery of the cosmos manifested as the innermost mystery of the human being.

"Seeing above darkness the highest light, seeing, each for himself, the highest, we have reached the sun, the god among gods, the highest light—the highest light"[10] sings the *Chāndogya Upaniṣad*, taking up on a deeper

4. *Kaṭha Upaniṣad* 3.1: "guhāṃ praviṣṭau parame parārdhe."
5. *Kaṭha Upaniṣad* 2.23.
6. *Īśa Upaniṣad* 9.
7. *Bṛhadāraṇyaka Upaniṣad* 4.2.2.
8. *Bṛhadāraṇyaka Upaniṣad* 1.3.28.
9. *Bṛhadāraṇyaka Upaniṣad* 1.4.10.
10. *Chāndogya Upaniṣad* 3.17.8.

level the jubilation of the seers of the *Ṛg Veda.*[11] Every night can then fade in front of the sun that will shine forever in the depths of the heart: "When it has risen above, it will not rise and will not set, but will rest, solitary, in the middle. . . . It does not rise and set for him: it is always daytime for the one who knows the mystery of *Brahman*."[12] It is in these terms so simple yet of an inexhaustible richness that the ancient *Upaniṣad*, still very close to the overwhelming spiritual experience of the sages, describe the experience of the Awakening to the divine light which, obtained in a flash as brief as lightning, frees the human being from all binding and conditioning. This is the supreme gift that no spiritual technique can obtain and that gives the world in its original glory back to the seer when he comprehends from the depths of his being that "all this, everything that moves on the earth should be covered by the Lord."[13] As Henri Le Saux-Swāmī Abhishiktānanda (1910–1973) who devoted his life to examining the jewels of Hindu mysticism wrote:

> The Upanishadic seer is much less the man who "knows this or that," than the man who "knows *thus* (*evaṃ*)," as the *Upaniṣad* constantly reiterate, calling him *evaṃvid*. It is like a new knowing, a new way of looking at things, at the world, a new illumination which makes one perceive everything quite differently. It is essentially a matter of passing on an experience of oneself, which does not convey any new information, so to speak, but which is much more an awakening to an unsuspected depth in oneself, an awakening to oneself, to things, to the mystery which, when projected, is called God.[14]

Awakening, the term that governed the wonder of the *Veda* before the splendour of the cosmos is launched at a new depth to designate a mystical knowledge, a definitive enlightenment. A blinding vision of the Absolute identified with a light which, in its glory, is the very fabric of the world, the secret engraved at the foundation of everything: "tameva bhāntamanubhāti sarvaṃ tasya bhāsā sarvamidaṃ vibhāti," "The sun does not shine there, nor the moon and stars. Lightning does not shine there, let alone fire. When It shines, everything shines with its light and everything is a reflection of its splendour."[15]

11. *Ṛg Veda* 1.50.10.
12. *Chāndogya Upaniṣad* 3.11.1–3.
13. *Īśa Upaniṣad* 1.
14. Abhishiktānanda, "Upanishads," 62.
15. *Kaṭha Upaniṣad* 5.15.

Already, the *Īśa Upaniṣad* affirmed that the dearest wish of the man preparing himself to leave his body was to enter into the light which at the moment of death he discovers to be his own mystery: "The face of truth is concealed by a golden vessel. Reveal it, Pūṣan, to my sight, which has truth as its *dharma*. Pūṣan, Ekarṣi, Yama, Sūrya, son of Prajāpati, draw apart your rays and draw them together. I see the light that is your most beautiful form. That very person (*puruṣa*)—I am he."[16] But for those who in the Awakening have reached "the further shore beyond darkness,"[17] death is definitively dead in this present life and the final liberation (*mokṣa*) is already obtained in this carnal condition of which all limitations are finally transcended: "That serene being which, after having risen from out of this earthly body, and having reached the highest light, appears in its true form. 'That is the Self,' thus he spoke. This is the immortal, the fearless, this is *Brahman*. The name of *Brahman* is 'truth.'"[18] The seer understands clearly then that "sarvaṃ khalvidaṃ brahma," "everything is indeed *Brahman*":[19] everything is plenitude, spaciousness, light, an ocean of glory. Free from all ignorance, his being no longer presents any obstacle to the experience of fullness that the recognition of the *Ātman* or *Brahman* at the heart of everything obtains for him: "Seeing this, thinking this, knowing this—taking pleasure in the *Ātman*, playing in the *Ātman*, making love with the *Ātman*, delighting in the *Ātman*—one becomes one's own ruler, and wins freedom to move in all worlds."[20] Such is the fullness of light and freedom that India has sought with an unparalleled degree of fervour: "Om! That is full (*pūrnaṃ*), this is full. Fullness comes forth from fullness. When fullness is taken from fullness, only fullness remains."[21]

A good many centuries after the first ecstatic cries of the seers of the *Upaniṣad*, the *Bhagavadgītā* again took up, by drawing them together in an almost similar manner, the themes of light, of the journey beyond death and of the inner liberation already in this present life:

> When a man knows this, he goes beyond death. It is *Brahman*, without beginning, supreme: beyond what is and beyond what is not. It is invisible: It cannot be seen. It is far away, and It is close,

16. *Īśa Upaniṣad* 15–16.
17. *Chāndogya Upaniṣad* 7.26.2.
18. *Chāndogya Upaniṣad* 8.3.4.
19. *Chāndogya Upaniṣad* 3.14.1.
20. *Chāndogya Upaniṣad* 7.25.2.
21. *Īśa Upaniṣad* 1.

> It moves, and It does not move, It is inside everything, and It is outside of everything. It is One in all things; and It seems as if it were multiple. It carries all beings: destruction comes from It, and creation also comes from It. It is the Light of all lights that shines beyond the darkness. It is the vision and the end of the vision that is achieved by the vision—which remains at the heart of all things.[22]

Testimony of the unique spiritual quest of an entire people continually launched towards the supreme place where "the sun shines not, nor the moon gives light, nor fire burns, for the Light of my glory is there. Those who reach that abode return no more."[23]

LIBERATION IN THIS LIFE

Contemporary with the sages of the *Upaniṣad*, Siddhārtha Gautama (563–483) is the most emblematic figure of the Awakening, the *bodhi*, to the extent of only being referred to as the Buddha: the Awakened One. With him, the only state that the human being is authorised to desire appeared in full light in the darkness of the world, like the blooming of an immaculate lotus from the depths of a muddy pool. However, the Buddha never defined the reality of *nirvāṇa*. He only stated four noble truths: the reality of the painful impermanence of all things (*duḥkha*), its cause, the possibility of its cessation, and the eightfold path that leads to it. A major event in the history of humanity, the Awakening of Siddhārtha Gautama has however notably shifted Indian thought towards a negative connotation of the world from which it is now necessary to escape in order to obtain liberation from the endless cycle of births (*saṃsāra*). Here the primordial optimism of the *Veda*, for which the human being could receive no greater blessing than to "live a hundred autumns"[24] before leaving to join his fathers, seemed to be lost. Parallel to the rise of Buddhist thought which drew Hinduism in new directions, the key term *mokṣa*, deliverance, underwent a significant evolution. From one of the four *puruṣārtha*—the values that fulfil a human life in a completely happy way—*mokṣa* has gradually supplanted *dharma*, *artha* and *kāma*[25] to become the sole reality that is pursued. The final liberation

22. *Bhagavadgītā* 13.13–17.

23. *Bhagavadgītā* 15.6.

24. *Ṛg Veda* 10.18.

25. *Dharma* is the religious aspect of life and also conformity to the demands of the

from the *saṃsāra* and the attainment of the ultimate plenitude became then the horizon for all the paths that the many Hindu schools subsequently undertook. From the Sanskrit root [muc] meaning "to untie, to release, to liberate," three derivatives were granted a considerable future: *mokṣa*, the desire for liberation, the quest for deliverance; *mukti*, the achievement of this objective and *mukta* which designates the one who is established in such a state. Fruit as much of the enlightenments of the *Upaniṣad* as of the destiny of the Buddha, the ideal of *jīvan-mukti*—the deliverance (*mokṣa*) obtained in this very life, unlike the *videha-mukti* which is granted only after bodily death—has set itself as the peak of all spiritual realisation, the vanishing point towards which the *mumukṣu* tends—literally the one who aspires to the final liberation.

Śaṅkara (788–820) is the thinker within Hinduism who deployed the theme of *jīvan-mukti* with a rare intensity, an immense figure whose influence extends right up to the present day. Admittedly, many of his detractors denounced him for showing over much influence from Buddhism that he nevertheless fought against. It is obvious, for example, that like the disciples of the Awakened One, his teaching was aimed at liberation of self from the illusory world to enter the definitive light. Whilst Buddhists in a radical manner weaned the human being away from any permanent support with their central doctrine of *anātman*, the non-self, Śaṅkara nevertheless assigned the final word to the plenitude of *Brahman*: "Anyone who knows *Brahman* becomes *Brahman*."[26] Beyond all the mythological accretions with which tradition adorned his life and all the later treatises that were generously attributed to him, Śaṅkara's principal contribution was to reestablish Vedic Orthodoxy, commenting not on the four ancient *Veda* but on the three sets (*prasthānatrayī*) of the more recent texts: the *Upaniṣad*, the *Bhagavadgītā* and the *Brahmasūtra*.[27] In general, he stuck to it word for word to elucidate the difficulties of comprehension but for some passages, he proposed new interpretations upon which the school of *advaita vedānta* was

caste; its importance is central to the *Mahābhārata* of Vyāsa or in the *Manusmṛiti* (*Laws of Manu*). *Artha* is the economic and political aspect of life, masterfully exposed in the *Arthaśāstra* of Kauṭilya. Finally, *Kāma* is the dimension of sensual pleasure as shown in the famous treatise of the *Kāmasūtra* of Vātsyāyana.

26. *Muṇḍaka Upaniṣad* 3.2.19.

27. The *Brahmasūtra* are a set of brief proposals shedding light on the difficulties contained in the *Upaniṣad*. This major text of Hindu thought was commented on, among others, by Śaṅkara, Rāmānuja (1017–1137), Madhva (1238–1317) giving birth to the different schools of the *vedānta*.

founded, based on a radical reading of the statement "ahaṃ brahmāsmi,"[28] "I am *Brahman*." For Śaṅkara, the spiritual fulfilment which the Scriptures witness was the *jīvan-mukta*, the one who in this current life has realized his strict non-duality (*advaita*) with the Absolute and who is therefore delivered from all fear—this being the most undeniable outer sign of his inner liberation: "O Janaka, you have certainly attained *Brahman* that is fearlessness."[29] The *Ekaślokī*, attributed to Śaṅkara, summarised in a single Sanskrit verse the doctrine of the *advaita vedānta* and its mystical journey:

> *Teacher*: What is the light for you?
> *Student*: For me, sun is the light in the day, and lamps in the night.
> *Teacher*: All right, tell me what is the light that makes you see the sun and the lamps?
> *Student*: Eyes.
> *Teacher*: What is the light when you close your eyes?
> *Student*: Intellect.
> *Teacher*: What is the light for you to perceive the intellect?
> *Student*: It is me.
> *Teacher*: Thus, you are the Ultimate Light.
> *Student*: Yes, Lord, I am That.[30]

Śaṅkara's masterpiece is the *Bhāṣya*, his commentary on the *Brahmasūtra* offering new clarifications for the interpretation of the *Upaniṣad*. In the fourth and final section of the book, the fulfilment of *jīvan-mukti* is widely present. It is based mainly on an elucidation of the famous passage "eṣa saṃprasādo" from the *Chāndogya Upaniṣad*: "That serene being which, after having risen from out of this earthly body, and having reached the highest light, appears in its true form. 'That is the Self,' thus he spoke. This is the immortal, the fearless, this is *Brahman*."[31] Śaṅkara writes: "The soul than attains liberation (*mukta*) . . . becomes free from its erstwhile bondage and continues as the pure Self."[32] It is above all the final lines of the *Bhāṣya* that make the ideal of *jīvan-mukti* ring out most powerfully in the light of the ultimate *brahmasūtra*,[33] taking up the final

28. *Bṛhadāraṇyaka Upaniṣad* 1.4.10.

29. *Bṛhadāraṇyaka Upaniṣad* 4.2.4.

30. Śaṅkara, *Ekaślokī*.

31. *Chāndogya Upaniṣad* 8.3.4.

32. Śaṅkara, *Brahmasūtra Bhāṣya* 4.4.2 (p. 896).

33. "Anāvṛittiḥ śabdādanāvṛittiḥ śabdāt," "There is no return on the strength of the Upanishadic declaration, there is no return."

declaration of the *Chāndogya Upaniṣad*, "na ca punar āvartate na ca punar āvartate," "there is no return, yes, there is no return!":[34]

> For such Upanishadic passages as, "Going up through that nerve one gets immortality,"[35] "They no more return to this world,"[36] "Those who proceed along this path of the gods do not return to this human cycle of birth and death,"[37] "He reaches the world of Brahman and does not return under here."[38] . . . Non-return stands as an accomplished fact for those from whom the darkness of ignorance has been completely removed as a result of their full illumination and who therefore cling to that liberation as their highest goal which exists ever as an already established fact. The non-return of those who take refuge in the qualified *Brahman* becomes a fact only because they too have that unconditioned *Brahman*[39] as their ultimate resort. The repetition of the *sūtra*, "There is no return on the strength of the Upanishadic declaration," shows that the Scripture ends here.[40]

Śaṅkara's followers brought scholastic refinements to the *advaita vedānta* by resounding the *mahāvākyāni*, the four great statements from the *Upaniṣad*: "ahaṃ brahmāsmi," "I am *Brahman*";[41] "tat tvaṃ asi," "you are that";[42] "ayaṃ ātmā Brahma," "this *ātman* is *Brahman*"[43] and "prajñānaṃ Brahma," "consciousness is *Brahman*."[44] Among the later treatises attributed to the Master, the *Vivekacūḍāmaṇi* took up the figure of *jīvan-mukta* but it reserved this ideal for the lone renunciant, the *saṃnyāsin*—as in the original Buddhism, only the monk (*bhikṣu*) was able to claim the state of awakening (*arhat*). As one late *Upaniṣad* puts it: "The mystery of Glory and immortality, raised to the highest heavens, hidden in the secret of the heart,

34. *Chāndogya Upaniṣad* 8.15.

35. *Kaṭha Upaniṣad* 3.16; *Chāndogya Upaniṣad* 6.5.

36. *Bṛhadāraṇyaka Upaniṣad* 6.2.15.

37. *Chāndogya Upaniṣad* 4.15.5.

38. *Chāndogya Upaniṣad* 8.15.1.

39. To harmonize the seemingly contradictory statements of the *Upaniṣad*, Śaṅkara made a distinction between the *saguṇa Brahman*, the Absolute manifested in the multiplicity of the world and qualified by it, and the *nirguṇa Brahman*, the Absolute detached from any relationship with the illusory world.

40. Śaṅkara, *Brahmasūtra Bhāṣya* 4.4.22 (p. 912).

41. *Bṛhadāraṇyaka Upaniṣad* 1.4.10.

42. *Chāndogya Upaniṣad* 6.8–16.

43. *Māṇḍūkya Upaniṣad* 1.2.

44. *Aitareya Upaniṣad* 3.1.3.

where only those who have renounced everything can penetrate."[45] A truly spiritual guide, the *Vivekacūḍāmaṇi* assigns to the renunciant journeying towards the Awakening the necessary quality of being a *mumukṣu*, that is to say a being totally desiring the *mokṣa*. A splendid paradox of the only permitted desire because "the stopping of desire is what is called freedom even in this life itself—*jīvan-mukti*."[46] This is followed by the description of the *brahmavidyā*, the knowledge of *Brahman* possessed by the living liberated being, who having removed the veil of the *māyā*, the cosmic illusion that covers everything, contemplates only the light of the Eternal: "He who knows no difference between the world and *Brahman* in his real consciousness—he is a *jīvan-mukta*, free even in this life."[47] The whole treatise then sings over and over of the greatness of the being who has realized in mystical knowing (*jñāna*) his non-dual unity with the Absolute: "In the consciousness of *Brahman*, staying there forever, free from external desires, enjoying the blessedness unknown by others, seeing this world as in his dream, and yet full in established understanding—surely he is the enjoyer of endless merits. He is blessed indeed. He is to be followed in this world."[48] Peace and the absence of fear attest to his Awakening: "Those ascetics and great souls whose desires have been fully fulfilled, who have become full of peace, who have made themselves fully controlled, knowing the Supreme Truth and uniting themselves with That, attain this blissful state of freedom."[49] The *Vivekacūḍāmaṇi* dared to push the paradox to the point of asserting that the *jīvan-mukta*, living by the absolute freedom of *Brahman*, can choose to remain invisible to the eyes of the world that is incapable of recognizing his grandeur: "Sometimes he appears like a fool, sometimes like a wise man, sometimes as a king—full of possessions—sometimes as an ignorant man, sometimes quiet, sometimes in that great snake that attracts with its mesmeric power, sometimes like a worthy man very much respected, sometimes in servitude, sometimes unknown—the wise one wanders thus, always delighted in the Bliss Supreme."[50] Whatever the external conditions in which his bodily life now unfolds, the living liberated one is permanently established in *samādhi*, the state of equanimity of his

45. *Mahānārāyaṇa Upaniṣad* 12.14.
46. Śaṅkara, *Vivekacūḍāmaṇi* 317.
47. Śaṅkara, *Vivekacūḍāmaṇi* 439.
48. Śaṅkara, *Vivekacūḍāmaṇi* 425.
49. Śaṅkara, *Vivekacūḍāmaṇi* 471.
50. Śaṅkara, *Vivekacūḍāmaṇi* 542.

spirit that is immersed in the beatitude of *Brahman*. His consciousness has expanded to become the very consciousness of the *Brahman* which fills the universe and contemplates its glory in all things: "*Samādhi* comes to him alone who is full of the spirit of renunciation. Those who practice *samādhi* become established in the understanding of *Brahman*, and from that established understanding comes the freedom from all bondages. One who becomes free from all bondages feels eternal Bliss."[51] These quotations from the *Vivekacūḍāmaṇi* have the merit of reminding us that in the eyes of Śaṅkara and of his first and recent commentators, the *advaita vedānta*, beyond its speculative austerity, is the testimony to the spiritual experience of *jīvan-mukti*, the final horizon that illuminates all of the Scriptures and the realisation of what in truth we have always been. Indeed, it is because he is plunged into ignorance (*avidyā*) that the human being lives like a sleepwalker, always passing his deepest identity by. To awaken him, he will require the compassion of the *jīvan-mukta*, some later evolutions of which will affirm that like the *bodhisattva* of Buddhist wisdom, his bountiful help will never fail humanity until all attain the *nitya-mukti*, the final and total deliverance where no one will be left in the shadows of the illusory world.

Vidyāraṇya (1297–1386), twelfth pontiff of Śṛngēri (one of the four monasteries that Śaṅkara had founded to perpetuate his teaching), is the author of the *Jīvan-mukti-viveka*.[52] In this classic work of the *vedānta* offering an overview of the spiritual ideal of *jīvan-mukti*, the author has been particularly interested in how the living being who is liberated continues to exist in his body in the midst of worldly activities, without producing any karmic acts that will lead to a new birth. In what is above all a work of anthology, Vidyāraṇya has made some sparkling quotations from the tradition available to his readers, such as this one from the *Laghu Yogavāsiṣṭha*: "The *jīvan-mukta* is he who does not frighten the world, nor is he afraid of the world; he is free from joy, anger and fear as well."[53] More recently, Swāmī Nikhilānanda (1895–1973), monk from the Ramakrishna Mission, described in a very beautiful synthesis, the form of spiritual fulfilment in Vedantic wisdom:

> A *jīvan-mukta* demonstrates by his life and action, the reality of *Brahman* and the illusoriness of the names and forms (*nāmarūpa*) of the relative world. Having himself crossed the ocean of birth

51. Śaṅkara, *Vivekacūḍāmaṇi* 375.
52. Swāmī Vidyāraṇya, *Jīvan-mukti-viveka*.
53. *Laghu Yogavāsiṣṭha* 5.95.

> and death, he helps others to the shore of Immortality. . . . Completely free from the illusory notion of the physical individuality he is aware of his identity with all beings. He is conscious that he feels through all hearts, walks with all feet, eats through all mouths, and thinks with all minds. He regards the pain and pleasure of others as his own pain and pleasure. Physical death and birth have no meaning for him, a change of body being to him like a change of garments or like going from one room to another. . . . He does not have to come back to the world of darkness again; for he has entered into the world of Light. If compassion for mankind moves him to assume again a body, he is born as a free soul always conscious of his divine nature.[54]

THE LIGHT OF THE TANTRA

Whilst the *vedānta*, also known as *uttara mīmāṃsā*, was being elaborated with Bādarāyaṇa to whom the *Brahmasūtra* are attributed, and then by Gauḍapāda in the sixth century and Śaṅkara in the eighth century, another movement was appearing in an India that was experiencing the same spiritual simmering as during the time of the *Upaniṣad* and the Buddha. Re-assuming the ascetic heritage of the *śramana*, the ancient ascetics who were the first to be attentive to the importance of breath in human existence, new thinkers craving for spiritual experience were paying greater attention to the states of consciousness—especially to the inner equanimity of the *samādhi*. This led them to develop techniques of recollection and of a state of inner aloneness (*kaivalya*), better known under the generic name of *yoga*. To their eyes, here was to be found the royal path of union with the Absolute, surpassing in its spiritual effectiveness the Vedic ritual (*yajña*) or the purely speculative knowledge (*jñāna*): "High as a mountain a thousand leagues long, sinfulness accumulated throughout life! Only the practice of meditation can destroy it: there is no other way."[55] The corpus of the *Upaniṣad* was then enriched by a new series of texts called "Yoga Upaniṣad" in which the ideal of the *jīvan-mukta* shines out in all its glory as the culmination of the *sādhanā*, the spiritual exercise of the *yogin*:

> When he manages to practice the meditation described as "non-qualified," the adept will in twelve days achieve this supreme goal

54. Swāmī Nikhilānanda, "Introduction."

55. *Dhyānabindu Upaniṣad* 6. Cf. Varenne, *Upanishads du Yoga*, 50.

> of yoga, the final enstasis. He is, therefore, one who is liberated in this life thanks to his ability to hold his breath as long as he wishes and the fact that his individual soul has been able to unite with the universal Soul. He can thus, if he so desires, abandon his body and rest forever in the womb of the supreme *Brahman*, or, on the other hand, preserve his bodily integrity; he can, if he so desires, travel the worlds thanks to his powers such as the ability to move around at will; he can become God, if he wants to and enjoy the pleasures of Heaven, or transform himself at will into man, animal or genie, become a lion, a tiger, an elephant, a horse, or even attain the status of Supreme Lord! These different metamorphoses are only a matter of differing practices, the ultimate goal remains the same which is to reach the state of absolute aloneness (*kaivalya*).[56]

Apart from the increasingly refined description of the techniques for breath retention (*kuṃbhaka*) and bodily postures (*āsana*), as well as the wondrous powers (*siddhi*) acquired by the *yogin*, these new trends developed an astonishing symbolic vision of the body—a true microcosm of the universe and a vessel for the Absolute—centred around seven centres (*cakra*) which from the base of the spine up to the top of the skull which with the help of three nerve channels (*nāḍī*), offer a path of light for the ascent of the *kuṇḍalinī*, the primordial energy, the ancient serpent that is coiled within the depths of the human being. When the *kuṇḍalinī* is "awakened through appropriate practises," it "brings the *yogin* to the state of liberation by uniting the individualised energy and consciousness with the universal consciousness."[57] Then, as the *Yogakuṇḍalinī Upaniṣad* affirms, "cleansed of all defilement, delivered from the state of bewilderment where it is retained by its captive condition, the subtle body shines out: it is made of pure consciousness, it is the very essence of the person, since it is none other than the universal Soul that is present in all beings!"[58]

As a result of new intuitions on the path of spiritual liberation, the Tantric currents transfigured Hinduism and Buddhism from the fifth to the seventh centuries. The etymology of the term "*tantra*" brings together two Sanskrit roots: [*tan*] designating the fabric, the expansion and [*tra*] the liberation. By addressing not only the *saṃnyāsin* but also "the whole of mankind without restriction of race, caste, sex or creed,"[59] this sophis-

56. *Yogatattva Upaniṣad* 106–11. Cf. Varenne, *Upanishads du Yoga*, 65–66.

57. Padoux, *Vāc*, 125.

58. *Yogakuṇḍalinī Upaniṣad* 77–78. Cf. Varenne, *Upanishads du Yoga*, 103.

59. *Vijñāna Bhairava*, 8.

ticated esoteric pathway wanted to discover the fabric of reality through an expansion of the human consciousness into the spaces of the Divine Consciousness which alone can provide the definitive liberation. Presenting themselves as teachings generally revealed by Śiva to the Goddess, the *Śakti* or divine energy, the *Tantra* were considered by their followers as "superior to the *Veda* (and as its continuation), for they are more effective in leading humans towards liberation, leading them more rapidly and up to higher spiritual plane than the *Veda*-based teachings. They also claim to be better adapted to the needs of beings living in the present dark cosmic age (*kaliyuga*), where desire or passion (*kāma*) prevails."[60]

If the tantric currents spread throughout India, it is probably in Kashmir between the ninth and tenth centuries that they found their mystical and speculative climax, particularly with Abhinavagupta (950–1020), by re-orchestrating, into a powerful synthesis, the traditional themes of light, consciousness and freedom of which Śiva-Bhairava—the ultimate reality—is the absolute plenitude: "The innermost light of illumination, the manifestation of the unique Lord, pure Consciousness, is worshipped in the limited form of a wave of Consciousness, the wheel of beneficial energies."[61] This light, which is the Infinite Consciousness of Śiva, continually gives itself freely in its divine shining (*prakāśa*) which the whole worldly reality reflects (*vimarśa*):

> Bhairava, the Light, is self-evident; without beginning, He is the first and last of all things, the Eternal Present. And so what else can be said of Him? The unfolding of the categories of existence (*tattva*) and creation, which are the expansion of His own Self, He illumines, luminous with his own Light, in identity with Himself, and because He illumines Himself, so too He reflects on his own nature, without his wonder (*camatkāra*) being in any way diminished.[62]

Since the supreme reality is the Consciousness of Śiva-Bhairava, the whole path of inner liberation will consist for the human being to return to the splendor of the One, plunging his limited consciousness (*cittapralaya*) into the infinite Consciousness. The *Vijñāna Bhairava* states here that "if one contemplates simultaneously that one's entire body and the universe consists of nothing but Consciousness, then the mind becomes free from thoughts and the supreme Awakening occurs."[63] As Lilian Silburn (1908–1993) wrote

60. Padoux, *Hindu Tantric World*, 8.
61. Abhinavagupta, *Tantrāloka* 1.116.
62. Abhinavagupta, *Parātriṃśikāvivaraṇa*.
63. *Vijñāna Bhairava* 63; cf. 106.

commenting on this famous tantric treatise, in "the illuminating splendour" of this state of liberation where "the Self perpetually blazes," "the illumined thought fades away completely in the face of the indestructible Light (*citprakāśa*) whilst the internalised cosmos identifies itself with the absolute, Paramaśiva."[64] This is a return to our deepest nature that we have never in fact left, even if it had been covered by different impurities (*mala*) due to spiritual ignorance: "Liberation is in fact nothing other than the revelation of our own nature, which, in turn is simply the full awareness of our own self and nothing else."[65] "The *yogin*, resting even for an instant is this ocean of consciousness, intent on devouring time, becomes instantly a 'Wanderer in the Sky' (*khecara*) and is liberated";[66] Abhinavagupta says that such a being has "devoured time" because "in this very moment, . . . in the present, actual moment, when the mystical experience is realised," the "past and future are found to be excluded. But then in turn, the present moment in its turn is also rejected since it depends upon the other two. As a consequence, we overcome the present moment and enter into the eternal which is liberated from temporal duration."[67] Lilian Silburn notes here that the surest sign for recognizing an awakened being who is totally established in the Supreme Consciousness is "the wonder that he experiences":

> The most ordinary things appear extraordinary to the *yogin* who is contemplating them in their essence. A simple touch of Consciousness is enough for a sound or a colour to appear to him as divine. The entire body, the things perceived, being impregnated with pure consciousness, are transfigured. So, the spontaneous bliss engendered in this way is new at every moment.[68]

Having acquired the absolute freedom of the divine Consciousness, the yogin "dives into [an] ocean of immortality" and, "flooded by the waves of nectar,"[69] he becomes even in his flesh fully permeable to the divine energy: "He walks at will in the Self, for everywhere he finds only the Self or Bhairava. He absorbs himself so deeply into the free Bhairava that he identifies

64. *Vijñāna Bhairava*, 65.

65. Abhinavagupta, *Tantrāloka* 1.156.

66. Abhinavagupta, *Mālinīvijayavartikā*.

67. *Vijñāna Bhairava*, 61–62.

68. *Śivasūtra et Vimarśinī de Kṣemarāja*, 132–33.

69. *Netra Tantra* 7.48: "He should pour out the energy, thereby becoming all pervasive, flooded by the waves of nectar. Being established in the flood of nectar he dives into that ocean of immortality"; cf. Bäumer, *Yoga of Netra Tantra*, 178–79.

with Him."[70] But all of this is the work of the sudden and extremely intense descent of the divine energy (*śaktipāta*)—a grace that is not the result of any technique, but which generally relies on the mediation of the *guru*, who is so important in the Tantric traditions. At this moment where the Self is revealed in a blazing manner, the ecstasy of the fifth *śivasūtra* is fully experienced: "udyamo bhairavaḥ,"[71] "the upsurge of Bhairava."

It is indeed the journey of the human being towards *jīvan-mukti* that the tantric traditions of Kashmir from Vasugupta (800–850) to Kṣemarāja (975–1025) have described with an unequalled detail and refinement, making their works one of the pinnacles of Indian thought. The *jīvan-mukta* ideal which emerged in the first *Upaniṣad* and was later thematised by Śaṅkara and his successors, found a remarkable centrality within Tantrism: "jīvann api vimukto 'sau kurvann api ca ceṣṭitaṃ," "he is liberated although he still remains in this life and although he indulges in ordinary activities,"[72] declares the one hundred and forty-second verse of the *Vijñāna Bhairava* that Lilian Silburn commented upon thus: "The human being freed from his bonds while he still lives (*jīvan-mukta*) retains his vital principle whilst having permanently recognised his own identity with the Ultimate Consciousness. His body remains perceptible; he experiences pleasant or painful feelings, and he performs his daily tasks."[73] Of this being that "strictly speaking one cannot . . . designate by the term 'liberated' (*mukta*) since it contents itself with regaining consciousness of its inalienable freedom that can neither be lost nor found,"[74] it will be said that he is the *mṛtyuñjit*, the "conqueror of death."[75] It is also the one who has definitively overcome all fear, like Bhairava of whom the *maṅgalasūtra* of the commentary that Kṣemarāja made of the *Vijñāna Bhairava* praises: "Glorious is the Supreme whose nature is Consciousness who bestows fearlessness to the fearful and hence is the cause of the overcoming of fear of those afflicted by worldly existence, who is revealed in the innermost abode of the heart, the Lord of the fearful, the Ender of Death, who removes fear, along with his own

70. *Śivasūtra et Vimarśinī de Kṣemarāja*, 133.

71. *Śivasūtra et Vimarśinī de Kṣemarāja*, 18.

72. *Vijñāna Bhairava*, 162.

73. *Vijñāna Bhairava*, 163.

74. *Vijñāna Bhairava*, 64.

75. *Netra Tantra* 7.51: "Having attained the state of *amṛteśa*, the subtle one, he becomes immortal. Thus having become immortal, he is *mṛtyuñjit* (conqueror of death), there is no doubt"; cf. Bäumer, *Yoga of Netra Tantra*, 179.

Energy, Lord Bhairava, who fills the whole Universe." Finally, when he reopens his eyes,[76] the *jīvan-mukta* contemplates the universe emerging from the absolute Consciousness—that is to say, from his own consciousness in total non-duality:

> everything that he perceives, the world and his body, forms his own person that has become universal because he is no longer restricted by dependence on his individual body. . . . In the absence of the division between subject and object, the *yogin* cannot distinguish what belongs to him in his own right from what belongs to the universe: the whole world is the Self; and the Self is the whole world. Indeed, for him a single undifferentiated energy fills them both. Such is the expansion of the inner glory.[77]

We can only bow before the grandeur of such an experience that India bears witness to through so many mystical treatises and even more through those whom over the ages she has considered as *jīvan-mukta*. The splendid horizon of her spiritual quest where "words break down, the mind swirls made frantic by the great light that everywhere surrounds and absorbs it in a flash."[78] If this mystical fulfilment may seem inaccessible to us, it nevertheless radiates a light that we can already recognise (*pratyabhijñā*) as being that which shines at the very depths of our hearts.

THE FIRSTBORN FROM THE DEAD

For a disciple of Christ, how could the Indian visions of the *jīvan-mukta* not find a powerful echo in the Risen One, totally freed from the bonds of death and living forevermore since his awakening on Easter morning? For certain, the Christian faith confesses that Christ died and then rose again, he is the "firstborn from the dead" (Col 1:18), the one who by his death destroyed death forever. Here, a Hindu could easily consider the resurrection of Christ as a case of *videha-mukti*, a liberation after death, a lower stage compared with the *jīvan-mukti*. However, instead of making hasty comparisons that lead to erroneous judgments about one tradition or the other, could we not take time to allow them to mutually enlighten each other, so that new and hitherto unsuspected perspectives might appear for

76. Cf. *Śivasūtra et Vimarśinī de Kṣemarāja*, 45: "bhūyaḥ syāt pratimīlanaṃ," "Again there is reopening of the eyes."

77. *Śivasūtra et Vimarśinī de Kṣemarāja*, 134–35.

78. Ajātānanda, *Années de grâce*.

each of them? It is remarkable to see the Greek verbs *egerein*, "to awaken" and *apoluein* "to untie" that are used in the New Testament to evoke the resurrection, appear in a dramatic light on the horizon of the *jīvan-mukta*. The resurrection, whose "time and hour" were known only to the "blessed night" that saw "the victorious Christ rising from the underworld"[79] is an event hidden within the secret of God that the Scriptures evoke with the brilliance of "the lightning that flashes and lights up the sky from one side to the other" (Luke 17:24). The liturgy in the great office of the Easter Vigil, represents it as an explosion of imperishable light that expands throughout the world to the very depths of the human heart: "For it is God who said: 'let light shine out of darkness' who has shone in our hearts to give the light of the knowledge of the glory of God in the face of Jesus Christ" (2 Cor 4:6). The evangelists describe the Risen One manifesting himself (*ōphtē*[80]) to his disciples in the sovereign freedom of his glorious body freed from the laws of space and time: "Constituted in the fullest dignity of his sonship, Christ has done with servitude. The flesh, that mark of slavery imprinted upon Christ on earth which made it possible for his divine liberty to be fettered, has been destroyed."[81] The Paschal greeting "Peace be with you" (John 20:19) reveals a being who has gone beyond all fear and penetrated into the "new creation" (2 Cor 5:17), a transfigured world that has regained its original beauty in the glorious body of Jesus: "The Risen One is the irruption and the first representative of the future world; it is an eschatological reality that 'touches' this world and is verifiable in its effects; it is a *reality* and a *story*, but not in the manner of a worldly story linked to time and mortality."[82] Moreover, faced with the penetrating developments about the consciousness of *jīvan-mukta*, we can venture to ask ourselves how the Risen One apprehended the world, what new perceptions inhabited him—he who now contemplated everything from the "further shore" (John 6:25) to which he had acceded, plunging time into eternity. The Christian

79. Cf. "Exultet of the Easter Vigil" in *Daily Roman Missal*, 473: "O vere beata nox, quæ sola meruit scire tempus et horam in qua Christus ab inferis resurrexit."

80. Cf. 1 Cor 15:5–7. The divine passive *ōphtē*, which we can translate as "he made himself seen," "he was manifested," means that the Resurrection is the gift par excellence that the Father gave to the Son. If as Christians we hold the Resurrection to be the greatest divine gift, the Hindu quest should not be caricatured as the work of a single human being left to his own strength. The Tantric tradition clearly states that the state of *jīvan-mukta* is obtained by *śaktipāta*, a descent of grace that finds its ultimate *raison d'être* in the Absolute.

81. Durrwell, *Resurrection*, 134.

82. González de Cardedal, *Cristologia*, 146.

Scriptures here have a confusing sobriety that easily gives rise to the disturbing fable[83] from the poet Jean Grosjean (1912–2006) of a Messiah disconcerted before his apostles who were so mired in the old world that they had not the slightest idea of the kingdom of light in which their Master was now moving. Moreover, the terror grips us facing the fact that in a certain sense, the Resurrection remains the great unthought of Christian theology, or at the very least it has been "relegated to the second rank,"[84] being the subject of only three of the five hundred and twelve questions in the *Summae Theologiae*[85] of Saint Thomas Aquinas (1225–1274). There is however a promising vein that we can follow from Saint Paul to Teilhard de Chardin (1881–1955), the one who was granted his wish to die on Easter Day. Amongst those who over the ages have meditated on the Resurrection, we find furthermore the Redemptorist François-Xavier Durrwell (1912–2005) who re-captured the whole centrality of the great mystery of the Christian faith by receiving remarkable spiritual intuitions that allowed him to take up anew the legacy of the Fathers, in particular Irenaeus of Lyon (140–202). In August 1939, Durrwell understood that the Resurrection is the complete outpouring of the Holy Spirit into the man Jesus offered to his Father on the Cross. He then realized that death and resurrection for Christ meant the end of life according to the flesh and entry into the life of the Spirit. Moreover, through his Paschal Mystery, Christ has become a source of salvation for those who come to drink of the Spirit that flows from his pierced side and enter into communion with him, even beyond the institutional boundaries of the Church.[86] To hear now these too rare theologians of the Resurrection, after having been taught by the thinkers of the *jīvan-mukti*, will certainly be of great benefit in the rich change of spiritual scenery that the meeting between the Hindu and Christian traditions will bring about.

The Resurrection of Christ is nowadays the subject of a serious misunderstanding in the Christian consciousness. Most of the time, mortal biological life—*bios* in Greek—is confused with the eternal life of the Spirit, the Trinitarian communion: *zoē*. Nevertheless the Scriptures never use *bios*

83. Grosjean, *Le Messie*.

84. González de Cardenal, *Cristologia*, 147.

85. Cf. Thomas Aquinas, *Summa theologiae*, IIIa, q. 53–55.

86. Cf. Paul VI, *Gaudium et Spes* 22: "And this applies not only to those who believe in Christ, but to all people of good will, in whose hearts grace invisibly acts. In fact, since Christ died for all and man's final vocation is truly unique, namely divine, we must hold that the Holy Spirit offers to all, in a way that God knows, the possibility of being associated with the Paschal Mystery."

for the Resurrection because it is not a palingenesis but an access to a new existential dimension operated by the Spirit, the definitive entry into the divine life:

> The resurrection appears as the anticipated form of the new existence that God will grant to all creation at the time of the final consummation. It therefore has nothing to do with a simple return to the biological life that existed before (as was the case for Lazarus, to whom his previous life was returned . . . but to die again). On the contrary, Jesus entered into the new life, the life that will never end, being the eternal life of God himself: "Christ, raised from the dead, will no longer die again; death no longer has dominion over him" (Rom 6:9).[87]

In the Resurrection, human nature, eternally assumed by the Son, undergoes a qualitative transmutation: it is fully glorified by the Spirit and participates without any obstacle in the divine life (*zoē*) of the intra-Trinitarian relationships. This is the new existence of the Risen Christ, true God and true man:

> The resurrection of Jesus is the supreme form of God's closeness to the world, being the supreme form of the integration of a part of the world into the divine life. The risen Jesus is humanity assumed by God, redeemed from the power of death, immersed in the very life of God and become thus the salvation of the creation.[88]

To speak here of God's ultimate proximity to the world leads us to consider the newness that the Resurrection brought to human nature in relation to the Incarnation—a subtlety that few theologians have highlighted as acutely as Hilary of Poitiers (315–367) did. In his *De Trinitate*, the holy bishop spoke of "offensio unitatis," "offence to unity," to characterise the consequences in Jesus of the assumption of the "forma servi."[89] The incarnate Son certainly still lives in the intra-Trinitarian relationships but under a kenotic mode that Hilary calls "vacuitatis dispensatio," "the economy of being brought to annihilation."[90] At the Resurrection, there was an unsurpassed newness in the full reintegration of the Son, with his glorified flesh,

87. González de Cardedal, *Cristologia*, 149.

88. González de Cardedal, *Cristologia*, 154.

89. Hilary uses here the Pauline vocabulary of "forma servi" or "slave condition" (Phil 2:7) and "forma Dei" or "divine condition" (Phil 2:6). Later, the Council of Chalcedon (451) spoke of the two natures of Christ, divine and human.

90. Hilary of Poitiers, *De Trinitate* 41.

in the "forma Dei." Human nature is now fully assumed into the Trinitarian relationships without the screen imposed by the "offensio unitatis": "The newness brought by the economy had inflicted an offence on the unity and there could be no perfect unity, as it previously was, if the flesh assumed were not glorified by the Father."[91] In the same vein, in his great work[92] François-Xavier Durrwell recalled a penetrating interpretation that Origen (185–253) made of the promise of Jesus: "Let anyone who is thirsty, come to me and let the one who believes in me drink!" to which the Evangelist adds: "According to the word of Scripture: 'Out of his heart shall flow rivers of living water'" (John 7:37–38). By punctuating the text differently from the most commonly admitted version, Origen[93] asserted that it was not from the believer that the living water flowed but rather from the glorified bodily humanity of Christ that became the source of the Spirit—that "Spirit which believers were to receive; for as yet there was no Spirit, because Jesus had not yet been glorified" (John 7:39). Making the Risen Christ thus the source of the Spirit was consistent with Saint Paul's statement, "The first man, Adam, became a living being the last Adam—Christ—became the spiritual being who gives life" (1 Cor 15:45):

> Christ was not always this life-giving spirit, but "became" so. He was the son of our common ancestor and moulded into his image, before becoming the principle of spiritual humanity. To him also applied the law that "that was not first which is spiritual, but that which is psychic" (1 Cor 15:47). The life-giving spirit, the "heavenly man," as the Apostle also calls him, can be identified with the God-man only in as much as the divinity of Christ is consummated in the Resurrection. *Ambrosiaster* comments, "The second Adam became a living spirit through the Resurrection."[94]

Through the gift of the Father at the Resurrection, Christ's glorified human nature has been totally spiritualized:

> Christ is spirit, reality, truth, it is he who gives history its meaning and its fulfilment, because he himself is wholly saturated by the Holy Spirit. He is so filled by him that he is transformed into his

91. Hilary of Poitiers, *De Trinitate* 38: "dispensationis novitas offensionem unitatis intulerat, ut perfecta antea fuerat, nulla esse nunc poterat, nisi glorificata apud se fuisset carnis adsumptio."

92. Durrwell, *Resurrection*, 81.

93. Origen, *Homilies on Exodus* 11.2.

94. Durrwell, *Resurrection*, 100.

> shining glory and his power of life and becomes in his turn a principle of life and of glory. . . . Christ is so completely transformed by the Holy Spirit that everything in him is changed into spiritual reality.[95]

From now on, nothing of the glorified flesh of the Risen One will resist the grip of the Spirit, as revealed by Saint Paul's impressive oxymoron "sōma pneumatikon," "the spiritual body" (1 Cor 15:44). Thus,

> seen from this angle, the Resurrection is the definitive outpouring of the Spirit in Jesus, which carries the Incarnation to that fullness in which the Word makes real the possibilities of the divine nature, reaching the extreme limit of what it can fulfil and be in the human being. At the same time, it is the fullness of human existence brought to the maximum possible participation in God. Thus, the fullness of God's incarnation in humanity and the fullness of mankind's participation in the life of God in the Spirit match each other in the Resurrection.[96]

To evoke the glorified humanity of Jesus that reaches the summit of the glory possessed by the Son from all eternity, Scripture resorted to the moving psalm: "You are my Son, today I have begotten you" (Ps 2:7; cf. Acts 13:33), making the Resurrection a new and definitive birth following the eternal generation of the Son in the womb of the Father and of his temporal birth from the womb of Mary. The Letter to the Colossians, in a declaration with the promise of a considerable theological destiny, affirmed that "in him the whole fullness of deity dwells bodily" (Col 2:9). But the "firstborn from the dead" (Col 1:18) is also the "firstborn of a multitude of brethren" (Rom 8:29) and what was accomplished once and for all in the glorified human nature of the Risen One has become a promise for the whole of the living:

> The resurrection becomes the pivot of salvation: in it is realised the greatest possible conjugation between God and human being, and at the same time the definitive rooting of human being in God, through the integration of all human beings into the humanity of Jesus. Jesus is therefore salvation personified: he is the saved humanity, that is to say fulfilled, perfected, irreversibly present to God; and he is also salvific humanity, which is inclusive for all, shared by all.[97]

95. Durrwell, *Resurrection*, 103.
96. González de Cardedal, *Cristologia*, 172.
97. González de Cardedal, *Cristologia*, 172.

Few theologians have meditated with the vigor of Saint Irenaeus on the glorification of the flesh "capable of receiving and containing the power of God"[98] and on the promise that this flesh, which having received in fullness the anointing of the Spirit, has become for all mankind: "The light of the Father has burst forth in the flesh of our Lord, then shining from his flesh, it came into us, and so man attained incorruptibility, enveloped as he was by this light of the Father."[99] In a fully Christian way that can contrast with other spiritual horizons, Irenaeus combined the two inseparable dimensions of the flesh and the Spirit. "Caro salutis est cardo,"[100] "the flesh is the pivot of salvation," wrote Tertullian (160–220); "caro et Spiritus," more precisely according to Irenaeus because "it is the Spirit of God who descended on [Jesus]—the Spirit of that very God who, through the prophets, had promised to confer on him the Anointing, so that, we ourselves receiving from the superabundance of this Anointing, may be saved."[101] Thus the glorified flesh of Christ became "the pledge of our own resurrection,"[102] that is, perfect possession of our own flesh by the Spirit: "And this is why this Spirit descended on the Son of God who became the Son of Man: in this way, with him, the Spirit became accustomed to dwell in the human race, to rest on men, to reside in the work modelled by God; it realised in them the will of the Father and renewed them by making them pass from their decay to the newness of Christ."[103] In the final books of the *Adversus Haereses*, Irenaeus offered almost unsurpassable—and today unfortunately forgotten—developments on the gift of the incorruptibility that all flesh will receive through the mediation of the glorified flesh of the Resurrected. As always in his work, the great theologian did not try to offer subjective innovations but a more penetrating understanding of Scripture, in this case of the passage from Saint Paul: "For this corruptible body must put on incorruptibility and this mortal body must put on immortality. When this corruptible body puts on incorruptibility, and this mortal body puts on immortality, then the Scripture will be fulfilled: 'Death has been swallowed up in victory'" (1 Cor 15:53–54). Whilst holding firmly onto the paradox

98. Irenaeus of Lyon, *Adversus Haereses* 5.3.2.

99. Irenaeus of Lyon, *Adversus Haereses* 4.20.2.

100. Tertullian, *De resurrectione mortuorum* 8.2.

101. Irenaeus of Lyon, *Adversus Haereses* 3.9.3.

102. Tertullian, *De Carne Christi* 1.

103. Irenaeus of Lyon, *Adversus Haereses* 3.17.1.

of the flesh and the Spirit that is only resolved in the Resurrection, Irenaeus interpreted the Pauline passage as follows:

> The weakness of the flesh will be absorbed by the power of the Spirit, and such a man will no longer be carnal, but spiritual, because of the communion of the Spirit. . . . For the weakness of the flesh, thus absorbed, brings forth the power of the Spirit; the Spirit, for its part absorbing weakness, receives in itself the flesh as an inheritance. And it is from these two things that living man is made: living thanks to the participation of the Spirit, man by the substance of the flesh.[104]

Commenting on the same Pauline quotation, he went on to describe how Christ, "the supreme conqueror of death," will introduce humanity possessed by the Spirit into the new creation:

> These words will be truly said when this mortal and corruptible flesh, facing death, crushed under the dominion of death, ascends to life and assumes incorruptibility and immortality: for it is then that death will truly be defeated, when this flesh, which was its prey, escapes its power. . . . But the transfiguration by which from being mortal and corruptible it becomes immortal and incorruptible, does not come from its own substance; this transfiguration comes from the action of the Lord, who has the power to bring immortality to what is mortal and incorruptibility to what is corruptible.[105]

Irenaeus did not specify when this would be accomplished and whether this gift of incorruptibility would only take place after death. For him, it was important, against all the Gnostics who were removing the carnal dimension from the salvation of mankind, to recall that "neither the substance nor the matter of creation will be annihilated"[106] but that everything will be subjected to the power of the Spirit. The holy bishop of Lyon resounded a promise for all—the spiritualization of the flesh and the gift of incorruptibility which are rooted in the Risen Christ, the one who is forever freed from the bonds of death and fully awakened in the light of the new creation. As he recalled again in the final amazing lines of *Adversus Haereses*:

> There is in fact only one Son, who has fulfilled the will of the Father, and only one human race, in whom the mysteries of God

104. Irenaeus of Lyon, *Adversus Haereses* 5.9.2.
105. Irenaeus of Lyon, *Adversus Haereses* 5.13.3.
106. Irenaeus of Lyon, *Adversus Haereses* 5.36.1.

> are fulfilled. These mysteries, the angels aspire to contemplate them, but they cannot fully examine the Wisdom of God, by whose action the work fashioned by him is made consistent and concorporeal with the Son: for God willed that his Offspring, the firstborn Word, descend to the creation, that is to say, to the work modelled and be seized by it, and that the creature in turn might grasp the Word and ascend to Him, thus surpassing the angels and becoming the image and likeness of God.[107]

THE PLEDGE OF THE RESURRECTION

So far, the *jīvan-mukta*, "Wanderer in the Sky" (*khecara*) in a sovereign freedom, and the Risen One, streaming with light on Easter morning and promising spiritualization to all flesh, seem not to have encountered each other in Hindu and Christian thought. The two traditions have been separated by too many abysses of ignorance to be able to live a fruitful emulation of sanctity of which we can perceive the whole potential enrichment at the end of this journey with each other. Some people whose lives have been conducted at the intersection of the two religious universes, have however anticipated the questions that were posed to their faith when confronted with the faith of the other. This is the case of Henri Le Saux (1910–1973) who in the content of his letters or his personal diary, offers some stimulating reflections on the Resurrection. On the 6th of April 1966, he wrote to Sister Thérèse de Jésus (1925–1976):

> And it is there where I come to Easter! You no longer feel it, you say. But Easter, like all that has to do with time and history, belongs to the world of signs.... Easter is the awakening to Being in each moment; it is the attainment in every moment to the further shore. It is the entire cosmic mystery, creator, incarnator and redeemer that is contained in each Yes.... Each awakening to God, is it not a Passover? And is there any awakening to God where Christ might not be present? Christ is without doubt the climax of this presence; of his own Easter, the summit; of this awakening, the point of pure light from which all splendour flows and converges.[108]

An attentive reader of the *Upaniṣad*, Le Saux had perceived with great acuity the new insights that the mystical writings of Hinduism brought to the

107. Irenaeus of Lyon, *Adversus Haereses* 5.36.3.

108. Le Saux and Thérèse de Jésus, *Le Swami et la Carmélite*, 1:180–81.

theological question of Christ consciousness. This theme became increasingly central to his thinking at the end of his life, when he distanced himself from the so-called theology of fulfilment in Christ. However, the way in which he interpreted the divine "ego eimi" (the very characteristic "I am" by which Christ referred to himself) brought him more towards the Shankarian non-duality (*advaita*) than the Trinitarian Revelation[109]—an almost inherent risk for those venture into unexplored lands. In a final letter to Sister Thérèse, dated the 14th of April 1973, he wrote:

> I will celebrate Easter, as so often, in total solitude. Beyond the symbolism of the Resurrection, there is the frightening discovery that there is no death, and indeed no birth. The "*I*" is there, from all time and forever. An awakening that nullifies all the threats of death because it is an awakening at a level that transcends all becoming—that of which one can only simply say *asti*, "it is."[110]

It would surely be of value to gather together all the notes that Le Saux made about Easter so that they help us to answer the stimulating question that the *jīvan-mukti* ideal poses for the Christian concerning the consciousness of the Risen Christ, as long as we are able to stammer something about a reality that will always remain largely hidden to us. Such an emulation would without doubt have the merit of revitalizing the theology of the Resurrection so that the great mystery of the Christian faith might regain its centrality not only in the thinking but above all in the life of the disciples of Jesus.

Another question is worthy of being briefly raised: that of the pledge of the Resurrection, or in other words, the presence of the "new creation" in the world in which we live today. During the first Easter vigil that he celebrated as Pope, Benedict XVI (1927–2022) declared that the Resurrection

> is—if we can for once use the language of the theory of evolution—the greatest "mutation," the absolutely most decisive leap into a totally new dimension that has ever happened in the long history of life and its developments: a leap of a completely new order, which concerns us and which concerns the whole of history. . . . The Resurrection was like an explosion of light, an explosion of love, which untied the hitherto indissoluble bond of "die and become." It inaugurated a new dimension of being, of life, in which matter has also been integrated, in a transformed way, and through which a new world arises. . . . It is a qualitative leap in the history of evolution and of life in general, towards a new future

109. Cf. Vagneux, *Co-esse*, 570–72.

110. Le Saux and Thérèse de Jésus, *Le Swami et la Carmélite*, 2:230.

> life, towards a new world which, starting from Christ, already continually penetrates our world, transforms it and attracts it to Him.[111]

To quote a parable from the Gospel (Matt 13:31–32), the Resurrection is like a tiny mustard seed embedded in the field of the world and sufficiently invisible to our own eyes that we may doubt its reality or its action. However the grain grows patiently until the day when it will have become a tree capable of sheltering all the birds of the world: the creation recapitulated in the Pleroma of Christ. The Eucharist celebrated "donec veniat," until the Parousia of Christ, is the anticipation here on earth of this final fulfilment. It is "a meal of the end of time, taken with the risen Christ in whom is the end of the world,"[112] it "is both a pasch already present, and a parasceve, a vigil of the feast. It is adapted to our interlude between two eras, a parousia which exists alongside our carnal state and at the same time a presence which looks forward with longing, a food which increases the hunger it satisfies."[113] However, the Eucharist is not only an anticipation but it is also a realization: that of the glorious body of the Risen Christ which in faith, manifests itself in this matter that is fully porous to the Spirit and fully assumed into the Trinitarian communion for which the Eucharist is already named. In the "transformed host" which "is the anticipation of the transformation of matter and its deification into the Christological 'fullness,'"[114] the Resurrection is given to be contemplated—not just that of Christ but also our own resurrection when our flesh will be fully spiritualized. Jules Monchanin (1895–1957) here likened "the Parousia" to "a cosmic transubstantiation, the universe being fully the Body of the Risen One—and our bodies as incorporated into his Body, participating in the universe transubstantiated in Him."[115] Thus the Eucharist is the promise of our incorruptibility, as Irenaeus of Lyon rightly saw it: "How can they still say that the flesh goes to corruption and has no part in life, while it is nourished by the body of the Lord and his blood? So let them change their way of thinking, or refrain from offering what we have just said! For us, our way of thinking is in tune with the Eucharist, and the Eucharist in return confirms our way of thinking. For we offer him what is his, proclaiming in a harmonious way the communion and the union of the flesh and the Spirit: for just as the

111. Benedict XVI, "Homily for the Holy Saturday Vigil."

112. Durrwell, *Resurrection*, 328.

113. Durrwell, *Resurrection*, 329.

114. Ratzinger, *L'esprit de la liturgie*, 25.

115. Monchanin, Unpublished letter to M. Prost.

bread that comes from the earth, after having received the invocation of God, is no longer ordinary bread, but the Eucharist that is made up of two things, one earthly and the other celestial, likewise our bodies that participate in the Eucharist are no longer corruptible, since they have hope of the resurrection."[116]

The Eucharist will always resist trivialization or being reduced to a pure rite because it leads to what the scholastics called the *res*: the Trinitarian communion and the eschatological communion of the creation in Christ. In order to celebrate it with an enhanced consciousness of what is being accomplished in it, it would be good to listen to the tantric traditions that have brought to an extreme interiority the ritual action which has structured Hinduism since the primordial times of the *Veda*. Rejecting any routine mechanism that threatens the rites, the *Tantra* were not afraid to claim that only a *jīvan-mukta* was actually able celebrate them: "devo bhūtvā devaṃ yajet,"[117] "without having become god one cannot worship god." Faithful to the great spiritualization that this new path preached with vigor, the *Vijñāna Bhairava* recalled here that "worship (*pūjā*) does not consist in offering flowers and other substances. The real worship consists rather in setting one's mind firmly on the supreme Void of thought-free consciousness. This worship is an absorption with great fervour and respect."[118] For sure, the Christian will not be able to renounce the humble reality of the matter being offered in the liturgy or the fact that the sacrament works on its own (*ex opere operato*) but is it not with an increased awareness of being immersed in the mystery of the Resurrection that he will be able to proclaim with a more intense truth: "Death has been swallowed up in victory. Where, O Death, is your victory? Where, O Death, is your sting?" (1 Cor 15:54–55).

116. Irenaeus of Lyon, *Adversus Haereses* 4.18.5.

117. Gandharva Tantra in *Words of Sri Anandamayi Ma*, 171.

118. *Vijñāna Bhairava*, 147; Cf. *Le Vijñāna Bhairava*, 165.

7

The Taste of the Absolute

When he composed his Sanskrit hymn "Vande Saccidānandaṃ," Brahmabāndhav Upādhyāya[1] (1861–1907) made one of the boldest hermeneutical acts in Indian Christianity. By contemplating the Father as the mystery of being (*sat*), the Son as the mystery of knowledge (*cit*) and the Spirit as the mystery of joy (*ānanda*), the Bengali Brahmin associated with the Trinity one of the most emblematic although recent terms[2] by which the Hindu tradition designates the Absolute. While the dimensions of being (*sat*) and knowledge (*cit*) were broadly highlighted by the *advaita vedānta* of Śaṅkara (788–820) and his successors, joy (*ānanda*) remained for a long time in the background of Hindu thought. The *Taittirīya Upaniṣad*, however, saw joy as the ultimate mystery of the Absolute,[3] its deepest layer (*kośa*): "He who knows this, having departed from this world, proceeds to that *Ātman* consisting of food, proceeds to that *Ātman* consisting of the vital principle, proceeds to that *Ātman* consisting of mind, proceeds to that *Ātman* consisting of bliss (*ānandamayātmānaṃ*)."[4] In a beautiful verse, the *Taittirīya Upaniṣad* further contemplated the Absolute as the perfect bliss

1. Born into a Hindu family, Brahmabāndhav Upādhyāya received baptism from Anglicans in February 1891 and entered the Catholic Church six months later. Largely misunderstood in his lifetime, he was one of the pioneers of a genuinely Indian form of Christianity. His hymn "Vande Saccidānandaṃ" is reproduced at the end of this book.

2. The *karmadhāraya* "Saccidānanda" is apparently first encountered in the minor *Upaniṣads*: *Nṛsimhottaratāpaniyopaniṣad* 1.7 and *Rāmapūrvatāpaniyopaniṣad* 9.2.

3. "Anyo'ntara ātmānandamayaḥ," "there is within another *ātman* which consists of joy" (*Taittirīya Upaniṣad* 2.5).

4. *Taittirīya Upaniṣad* 2.8.5.

enveloping the destiny of the living: "Joy (*ānando*) is Brahman. For from joy, beings are born; by joy, being born, they live; into joy they enter when they pass on."[5] More than mere pleasure (*sukha*), *ānanda*, joy, is ultimately the supreme bliss. It is a "felt experience,"[6] first of the Absolute which experiences itself as *ānanda*,[7] then of the awakened beings who plunge into the beatifying ocean of the Divine, discovering (*cit*) thus the reality (*sat*) that they have always been: "In the Upanishads, . . . the supreme beatitude is not something to be achieved, produced or arrived at, but like being, something to be 'realised.' The reality must shine in the pure and unobstructed light of its self-consciousness so that it may appear as supreme bliss and satisfaction: *sat-cid-ānanda*!"[8] Then "cidānandarūpaḥ śivo'haṃ śivo'haṃ"[9] resounds, the cry that Śaṅkara put on the lips of the awakened one—the *jīvan-mukta*—and which the *Vivekacūḍāmaṇi* explains as follows: "This is the result of that knowledge: one becomes free even in this body, externally and internally, always enjoying the ever-blissfulness of the Being (*sadānanandarasāsvāda*)."[10]

It is on the one hand with "the spread of the experimentation on induced states of pleasure and bliss promoted in the more Tantric cults and practices" and, on the other hand, "the *bhakti* [way of devotion] literature" proposing "the union in bliss with the Absolute as the religious ideal of the devotees" that "the importance of *ānanda* grew"[11] in later Hindu thought. Associated with the notion of *rasa* (taste), *ānanda*, the supreme bliss, was now understood, in the remarkable developments of the Tantric schools, as the gift promised to aesthetic experience, as well as to erotic experience. Here was found the thread developed by the ancient *Upaniṣad* which did not hesitate about resorting to the ardor of the conjugal bond to speak of awakening in its fullness of non-duality (*advaita*): "Having pleasure in the *Ātman* (*ātmamithuna*) experiencing bliss in the *Ātman* (*ātmānandaḥ*), he

5. *Taittirīya Upaniṣad* 3.6.1: "ānando brahmeti vyajānāt ānandādhyeva khalvimāni bhūtāni jāyante ānandena jātāni jīvanti ānandaṁ prayantyabhisaṁviśantīti."

6. Cf. Maritain, "L'expérience mystique," 154.

7. "Ānandaṃ brahmano vidvan," "that Brahman knowing the bliss" (*Taittirīya Upaniṣad* 2.9).

8. Gispert-Sauch, *Bliss in the Upanishads*, 20.

9. Śaṅkara, *Nirvāṇaṣaṭakaṃ*: "Having the form of knowledge and bliss, I am Śiva, I am Śiva."

10. Śaṅkara, *Vivekacūḍāmaṇi* 418.

11. Gispert-Sauch, *Bliss in the Upanishads*, 11.

becomes the lord of himself";[12] "As a man fully embraced by his beloved wife knows nothing that is outside, nothing that is within, thus this person embraced by the Supreme *Ātman* (*ātmanā saṃpariṣvakto*) knows nothing that is outside, nothing that is within."[13] By restoring the centrality of *ānanda*, the Tantric masters partly corrected "the danger of a dry gnosticism in the Indian tradition": certainly

> the search for the Absolute is indeed a way of knowledge (*jñāna*). . . . But the ultimate end of that search is not a mere intellectual vision not even a pure merging of the knower and the known or the pure light of self-consciousness: there is there also what we might call a meta-intellectual element, that is bliss, *ānanda*, which can never be reduced to philosophical categories.[14]

In this "bliss of Brahman and [this] supreme pleasure"[15] is the overflow of the experience of the Absolute beyond the limits of mere human knowledge, which is only able to grasp a small part of it: "This is his [awakened one] supreme goal, his supreme success, his supreme world, his supreme bliss (*ānanda*). On a unit of this bliss the other beings live."[16] By following the path of *ānanda* and harmoniously combining the aesthetic, the erotic and the mystical, Indian thought has guarded against the danger of desiccation, and this is sufficiently remarkable for us to now draw some lessons from it.

AESTHETIC BLISS

Although the *advaita vedānta* is often considered one of the most arid systems in Hinduism, its founder Śaṅkara did not hesitate to resort to aesthetic experience to describe the state of *jīvan-mukta*, the condition of the "one who is liberated in this life," as "savouring the taste of the blissfulness of Brahman" (*brahmānandarasāsvāda*).[17] Using the key term of *rasa* (taste), the great commentator on the sacred scriptures (*Śruti*) made an allusion to the *soma*, the mysterious drink mentioned in the *Ṛg Veda* whose property

12. *Chāndogya Upaniṣad* 7.25.2.

13. *Bṛhadāraṇyaka Upaniṣad* 4.3.21.

14. Gispert-Sauch, *Bliss in the Upanishads*, 230.

15. *Gurugītā*: "brahmānandaṃ paramasukhadaṃ."

16. *Bṛhadāraṇyaka Upaniṣad* 4.3.32.

17. Śaṅkara, *Vivekacūḍāmaṇi* 435. In the passage quoted above, a similar term was mentioned: 'sadānandarasāsvāda' (*Vivekacūḍāmaṇi* 418).

was to "produce joy"[18] in the union with the divine: "We have drunk the *soma*; we have become immortal; we have gone to the light; we have found the gods."[19] Thus from the very dawn of Vedic revelation, the Absolute was not only a mystery to be contemplated but also to be tasted.

Rasāsvādana, "the act of savouring (*āsvādana*) a specific taste (*rasa*)," is surely the best Sanskrit term to translate aesthetic experience as expounded in Bharata's *Nāṭya Śāstra*, a treatise dating from the beginning of the first millennium and magisterially codifying theatre, poetry, dance and music. Its famous sixth chapter expounds the theory of *rasa* as the aesthetic emotion that artistic performance provides. The term *rasa* has had a remarkable semantic fortune in India. If it was originally used to describe the juice of plants that is squeezed to obtain the *soma*, its meaning has gradually evolved towards "taste" and "flavour," before linking with the meaning of *ānanda*, the joy of the Absolute that artistic experience already gives one the opportunity to experience. In order to understand *rasa* properly, we have to therefore hold together its culinary meaning—as with Indian cuisine which marries different flavours together—and its mystical meaning:

> One may wonder why it is called *rasa*? To which one has to reply: because it is tasty. How is *rasa* tasty? In the same way that when gourmets eat a dish seasoned with different spices, they taste the flavours and experience intense pleasure, the spectator who is concentrated [on the event] savours the sensations of the different components of the *rasa* that are presented to the audience through the recitation of the text, the mimicry of the body and the involuntary reactions, to thus experience an intense pleasure. This is why *rasa* are called "the taste of theatre" (*nāṭyarasa*).[20]

For India, the aesthetic experience is fundamentally gustatory: it is about savouring a particular *rasa*. It is not in any way a judgement on "good taste" as Western aesthetics has developed it. So, how to better understand what a *rasa* is? According to, the *Nāṭya Śāstra*, the *rasa* is the result of one of the eight basic emotions (*sthāyibhāva*)[21] aroused by the spectacle. The eight

18. *Ṛg Veda* 9.113.6.

19. *Ṛg Veda* 8.48.3.

20. *Nāṭya Śāstra* 5.32.6–10, cited in Maillard, *Rasa*, 113–14.

21. The eight *sthāyibhāva* are: *rati*, love; *hāsa*, laughter; *śoka*, sorrow; *krodha*, anger; *utsāha*, energy; *bhaya*, terror; *jugupsā*, disgust; *vismaya*, astonishment. The other emotions (*bhāva*) are the thirty-three transient feelings (*vyabhicārabhāva*) as well as the bodily expressions of the actors (*anubhāva*) and circumstances depicted on stage (*vibhāva*). They are mentioned in a crucial verse: "*Rasa* is produced from a

rasa Bharata describes are: *sṛṅgāra*, the erotic; *hāsya*, the comic; *karuṇa*, the pathetic; *raudra*, the furious; *vīra*, the heroic; *bhayānaka*, the terrible; *bībhatsa*, the odious and *adbhuta*, the marvellous. If the artist has the essential role of communicating the different emotions, it is the spectator (*rasika*) who has been of the greatest interest to Indian aesthetics because it is in him that the different *rasa* are experienced.

The treatise of Bharata was constantly read by the later tradition, which considered it as a fifth *Veda*. Between the seventh and eleventh centuries, the land of Kashmir conferred the most decisive developments upon it. In his *Abhinavabhāratī*, a commentary on the sixth chapter of the *Nāṭya Śāstra*, Abhinavagupta (950–1020) brilliantly synthesised the ideas of his predecessors and gave full radiance to the *rasa* theory. He first distinguished *rasa* from mere worldly emotions, for its very nature is to lead the spectator even further into spiritual experience and open him to a reality full of light and bliss. Taking up the work of Bhaṭṭanāyaka (tenth century), Abhinavagupta first emphasized the universalising capacity (*sādhāraṇīkaraṇa*) that *rasa* operates on the fundamental emotions, allowing thus the spectator to plunge into an experience that goes beyond his or her subjectivity. The Kashmiri master explained that this universalization is due to the capacity of resonance (*dhvani*) of the poetic word. Here he was rediscovering the subtle descriptions that Ānandavardhana (820–890) had made in his *Dhvanyāloka* to show that the suggestion of an aesthetic feeling (*rasadhvani*) was the very essence of the poetry. Thus, three functions of the word were distinguished: the literal expressive meaning (*abhidhā*), the metaphorical indicative function (*lakṣaṇā*) and the power of suggestion (*vyañjanā*) which "calls to deeper connotations than those provided by . . . analogical metaphor" as it broadens "the mind by reaching subtler levels of consciousness."[22] It is through the *vyañjanā* of the poetic word that the resonance (*dhvani*) is made capable of leading the listener, through a particular *rasa*, out of his everyday world into a subtler realm of shared joy. However, for such an "echo" to occur, both the artist and his audience have to be in tune—that which Sanskrit calls *sahṛdaya*: "Only 'a-man-with-a-heart,' to translate *sahṛdaya* literally, the expert, the human attuned to the poetic experience, can capture the *vyañjanā*. For this one needs a faculty beyond that of the mind, a *pratibhā* which can be both the creative intuition of the poet as well as the intuitive

combination of determinants (*vibhāva*), consequents (*anubhāva*) and transitory states (*vyabhicārabhāva*)" (*Nāṭya Śāstra* 6.109).

22. Maillard, *Rasa*, 72.

receptivity of the responsive reader."[23] This requires the spectator to possess an established contemplative practice and the ability to forget himself. In such a purified heart, what Abhinavagupta calls *camatkāra*, "aesthetic wonder," can then arise, i.e., "a mental operation on the part of the spectator who feels enraptured by a vibration (*spanda*) of marvellous pleasure."[24] This is a sudden and extremely intense descent of the divine energy (*śaktipāta*) which is not obtained from any human effort, even if some preparation is required in order to be ready for such a grace, as Lilian Silburn (1908–1993) wrote:

> *Camatkāra*, the rapture proper to the *sahṛdaya* who appreciates the drama and to the mystic who, at a much higher degree, enjoy divine bliss. But in both cases the impression is spontaneous, it does not depend on any effort. The *guru* in the case of the second or the actor of the first do nothing but lifting the veil and removing the obstacle, so that the inner ecstasy wells up immediately.[25]

In this aesthetic ecstasy, the spectator experiences a veritable expansion of his personal consciousness until he immerses himself in the divine Consciousness (*saṃvid*), which gives him absolute enjoyment (*paramānanda*), as the *Vijñāna Bhairava* opens it out in one of its a hundred and twelve tantric meditations: "When the mind of a *yogin* is one with the unparalleled joy of music and other aesthetic delights, then he is identified with it due to the expansion of his mind which has merged in it."[26] This unparalleled joy is due to the recognition (*pratyabhijñā*) of the supreme Reality shining deep in the heart of the spectator who then becomes a mirror of the Absolute for the world. In his monumental *Tantrāloka*, Abhinavagupta shows how in a ceremony, this recognition is heightened by the presence of other participants with whom an aesthetic communion beyond words is established:

> In public celebrations, the consciousness returns to a state of expansion. . . . The radiance of one's own consciousness in ebullition (i.e., when it is tending to pour out of itself) is reflected in the consciousness of all the bystanders, as if in so many mirrors, and, inflamed by these, it abandons without effort its state of individual contraction. For this very reason, in meetings of many people (at a performance of dancers, singers . . .), fullness of joy occurs

23. Larson, "Sources for *Śakti*," 51.
24. Abhinavagupta, *Abhinavabhāratī* 162.
25. *Śiva-Sūtra et Vimarśinī de Kṣemarāja*, 172.
26. *Vijñāna Bhairava*, 73; Cf. *Le Vijñāna Bhairava*, 114.

> when every bystander, not only one of them, is identified with the spectacle. The consciousness . . . attains, in these circumstances a state of unity, and so enters into a state of beatitude which is full and perfect. In virtue of the absence of any cause for contraction, jealousy, envy, the consciousness finds itself, in these circumstances, in a state of expansion, free of obstacles, and pervaded by beatitude.[27]

The aesthetic and mystical experience of the *camatkāra* not only immerses the spectator in supreme bliss (*paramānanda*) but it provides his dilated consciousness with an unspeakable peace (*śānta*) that a Kashmiri tradition dating back to Udbhaṭa (eighth century) has called the ninth *rasa*: the *śāntarasa* which, according to Abhinavagupta, constitutes "the possibility of all *rasa* and their outcome."[28] Arising from the fundamental experience of calm (*śama*) which culminates in detachment (*vairāgya*), the *śāntarasa* is for the other *rasas*, which proceed from it and return to it whilst disappearing, "like a serene lake when the wind has calmed, and the waves have subsided."[29] It is the attestation of the final liberation (*mokṣa*)—that which will definitively bring the aesthetic experience into the mystical experience. However, as many later commentators have rightly pointed out, the *śāntarasa* is a limit state of *rasa* because such detachment brings to an end the aesthetic experience, the *rasāsvādana* which is the savouring of a particular *rasa* through a specific representation. Yet how can one represent absolute stillness? Between aesthetic experience and mystical experience, it would be better to speak of an analogy or "a twinning in the taste of the Absolute" (*brahmasvādasahodara*) as pointed out in the fourteenth century by Viśvanātha Kavirāja in his *Sāhityadarpaṇa*. If there is such an analogy, it is because the two experiences are both "felt experiences of the Absolute" but to varying degrees. Both dilate human consciousness and raise it to an extraordinary level (*alaukika*) of peace and joy—specifically the level of the Absolute as the *Vijñāna Bhairava* beautifully reveals: "If

27. Abhinavagupta, *Tantrāloka* 28.373–79. Following this, Abhinavagupta adds a very pertinent remark: "When, on the other hand, even only one of the bystanders does not concentrate on the spectacle he is looking at, and does not share, therefore, the form of consciousness in which the other spectators are immersed, this consciousness is disturbed as at the touch of an uneven surface. This is the reason why . . . no individual must be allowed to enter who does not identify himself with the ceremonies and thus does not share the state of consciousness of the celebrants; this would cause, in fact, a contraction of the consciousness."

28. Maillard, *Rasa*, 98.

29. Maillard, *Rasa*, 92.

one listens with undivided attention to the sounds of string instruments or others, which are played successively and are prolonged, then one becomes absorbed on the supreme ether of consciousness at the end."[30] However, unlike the experience of the mystic, "aesthetic rapture brings the receiver (*sahṛdaya*) closer to the Absolute Consciousness but for a limited time and only in a partial and roundabout way."[31] On the other hand, the mystical experience (*brahmāsvādana*) definitively burns up all duality in the blazing fire of the Divine Consciousness—which marks the end of aesthetic experience (*rasāsvādana*). Now, "whilst the mystical experience cancels oppositions and dissolves the self in the Absolute, aesthetic experience on the other hand requires the presence of the things of the world and without the knowledge and observation of these, pleasure cannot arise."[32] It is the glory of Abhinavagupta, as the heir to a distinguished tradition of thought, to have shown the profound relationship between these two experiences and through their mutual fertilization, to have made artistic creation worthy of its spiritual vocation—that of enabling everyone to experience the "star-spangled hours" like Maurice Zundel (1897–1975) before the tomb of Lorenzo de' Medici in Florence. For his part, the mystic needs the aesthetic dimension to translate his experience into terms that can resonate in the hearts of his listeners and readers. So, it is no surprise that many spirituals were distinguished poets, such as Saint John of the Cross (1542–1591) in Christianity or Utpaladeva (900–950) who so inspired the thinking and sensibility of his heir Abhinavagupta.[33] In the *Śivastotrāvalī*, the "hymns of praise to Śiva," Utpaladeva remarkably knew how to convey his experience of recognition (*pratyabhijñā*) of the Absolute in terms that still move us:

Show your grace, O Lord,
So that my mind continually
Absorbed in your imprint,
Having tasted so many things,
Shall be intoxicated, absorbed by it.[34]

Being self-luminous
You cause everything to shine:

30. *Vijñāna Bhairava*, 41; Cf. *Le Vijñāna Bhairava*, 91.

31. Maillard, *Rasa*, 88.

32. Maillard, *Rasa*, 88–89.

33. Abhinavagupta also used the poetic form of hymns to translate his mystical experience and expound his doctrine. Cf. *Hymnes de Abhinavagupta*.

34. *Śivastotrāvalī* 5.9. Cf. *Hymnes de louange à Shiva*, 44.

Delighting in your form
You fill the universe with delight;
Reeling with your own bliss
You make the whole world dance with joy.[35]

DIVINE EROTICISM

Traditionally, the *sṛṅgārarasa*, the erotic, is called the *ādirasa*, the "mother of all *rasa*." The *Nāṭya Śāstra* discerns two aspects in it: *saṃbhoga*, "the consummation of love" or "love in union" and *vipralaṃbha*, "the absence of the beloved" or "love in separation."[36] The reason why the *sṛṅgāra* holds such importance in Indian aesthetics is because human eroticism and its pleasure (*bhoga*) is a metaphor for divine eroticism and the perfect bliss (*ānanda*) that it promises. Such an analogy—admittedly fragile—"may explain the profusion of erotic art displayed on the exterior of so many ancient temples of India, to suggest perhaps that it is through the humble realities of his daily experiences that man can reach the inner sanctuary of the experiences of the Absolute."[37] In other words: in the mystery of divine enjoyment, "love and passion are the means of access *par excellence* to transcend the empirical self and reach the divine"[38] but it is a steep ridgeway!

To approach what Tantrism has explored in the arcana of erotic pleasure, one must remember first that "sex in India is not sinful. It is generally regarded as a normal activity, the practice of which however roots the human being within the world and to its joys and sorrows, wasting a force which it is better either to conserve in order to keep or increase one's power, or to use, transmute or transcend it in order to free oneself from the limitations of life on earth."[39] In the Hindu tradition, it was Abhinavagupta in chapter twenty-nine of his *Tantrāloka*—a collection of Tantric practices and theories—who set out the ritual of the Kula ascetics which is "suitable for the most advanced masters and disciples."[40] This remark is crucial to explain what Abhinavagupta testifies, namely a difficult path reserved

35. *Śivastotrāvalī* 13.15. Cf. *Hymnes de louange à Shiva*, 84.

36. *Nāṭya Śāstra* 6.46.8.

37. Gispert-Sauch, *Bliss in the Upanishads*, 145.

38. Padoux, *Comprendre le tantrisme*, 145.

39. Padoux, *Comprendre le tanstrisme*, 147–48.

40. Abhinavagupta, *Tantrāloka* 29.1. The Kulas were, in the first millennium, the followers of one of the tantric traditions of the "left-hand path" (*vāmamārga*).

for a few beings (*yogin*) sufficiently experienced in spiritual practice to understand, in total detachment, that sexual enjoyment (*bhukti*) is capable of giving access to definitive liberation (*mukti*): "Sex is . . . one of the forms of the effervescence of energy. . . . For the *yogin*, sexual union, where he experiences this effervescence, is therefore participation in the play of Divine Energy. It can therefore quite naturally—if one knows how to bring it into play and grasp its powers, whether or not within the framework of a rite—lead to mystical union. What the *yogin* and his partner then experience is no longer pleasure (*sukha*), but bliss (*ānanda*), which, as we know, is a characteristic of *Brahman*."[41] Sexual enjoyment is thus the lever that enables the unfolding of consciousness to the ultimate experience of *camatkāra*, the grace-giving wonder caused by immersion in Divine Consciousness, as we mentioned in the case of aesthetic experience. Herein precisely lies the danger of losing oneself by sinking like "animals"[42] into purely carnal pleasure that does not lead to the supreme joy. On the contrary, for the *yogin*—a true "ascetic of desire"[43]—pleasure (*kāma*) is not an end in itself but a means to the supreme liberation: "Sex . . . is used as a means of access to transcendence. . . . It is not an impulse to which one gives in, but a force that one dominates. It is a technical mastery and not hedonism: the tantric way is not a search for pleasure."[44]

Tantric view on sexuality has often been misunderstood both by the supporters of a certain puritanism and even more so, by those of unbridled licence, forgetting that if sexuality has a place in the spiritual path, it is in a circumscribed way. By reserving this path for a few rare "heroes" (*vīra*), Indian thought through Abhinavagupta was opening a door only to close it again to the common man. However, the path exists and the analogy between sexual pleasure and divine bliss (*ānanda*) has presided over the development of *bhaktimārga*, the "path of devotion and love" open to all, which is based on a transfigured *erōs* where human desire is certainly preserved but totally purified by the attraction of the divine desire. It is no wonder

41. Padoux, *Comprendre le tantrisme*, 162. One may recall here stanza 70 of the *Vijñāna Bhairava*: "O Goddess! even in the absence of a *śakti* (a woman), a flood of bliss appears by intensely calling to mind the pleasure experience with a woman when kissing, caressing, embracing" (*Vijñāna Bhairava*, 112).

42. The expression is taken from Jayaratha (twelfth century) in his commentary on the *Tantrāloka* 29.99–100a which John Dupuche has carefully studied. Cf. Dupuche, *Vers un tantra chrétien*, 80–109.

43. Cf. Kakar, *Ascetic of Desire*.

44. Padoux, *Comprendre le tantrisme*, 163.

then that some have seen *bhakti* as the tenth *rasa*, for this spiritual path, which transformed Hinduism at the deepest level, ultimately promises "the fullness of joy (*sukhaṃ ātyantikaṃ*)."[45] One of the cradles of *bhaktimārga* is surely the *Bhagavadgītā* which many date to the beginning of the first millennium. In this essential work, the Absolute is not only a mystery beyond everything but is also a mystery of love that draws the devotee (*bhakta*) into a *līlā*, a truly divine game filled with passion: "He who works for me, who loves me (*mad-bhaktaḥ*), whose supreme end I am, free from attachment to all things, and with love for all creation, he in truth comes unto me."[46] In *bhaktimārga*, the whole being must spiritually surrender (*prapatti*) and entrust itself to the Lord, as with the embrace of lovers. *Bhakti* is the truth of a love that responds to love, a love that makes every gift luminous, even the humblest, as Kṛṣṇa declares to Arjuna: "He who offers to me with devotion (*bhaktyā*) only a leaf, or a flower, or a fruit or even a little water, this I accept from that yearning soul, because with a pure heart it was offered with love (*bhaktyupahṛitaṃ*)."[47] One then grasps the vibrant beauty of one of the last verses of *Bhagavadgītā*: "Give your mind to me, and give me your heart (*madbhakto*), give me your offerings and your worship. This is my promise: you shall in truth come to me, for you are dear to me."[48]

For two thousand years, the *bhaktimārga* has sparked a veritable fire of love kept alive by a myriad of men and women, belonging to every social category, and enriching the local languages of India with sumptuous devotional poems in which one feels the quivering of a heart responding to the extravagant love of its Lord—be He Śiva or Viṣṇu—or of the Devī, the divine Mother. Tamil Nadu was one of the first hotbeds of this fire, especially with the twelve *Ālvār*: literally, those who "plunged into the love of Viṣṇu to drown in Him." Their hymns are preserved in the *Nālāyira Divya Prabandhaṃ* which the Vaishnavite tradition (*śṛīvaiṣṇava*) considers equal to the *Veda*. Among these twelve Tamil saints, there is only one woman, Āṇḍāl, but she deserves the title of *ālvār* more than anyone else, she who sang to her god: "If we, mouth overflowing with song, beseech rapture / He will flood us in beauty."[49] Āṇḍāl's brief work (eighth century)—in particular her *Nācciyār Tirumoḻi* or "The Songs of the Lady"—is part of the

45. *Bhagavadgītā* 6.21.

46. *Bhagavadgītā* 11.55.

47. *Bhagavadgītā* 9.26.

48. *Bhagavadgītā* 18.65.

49. Āṇḍāl, *Tiruppāvai* 8. Cf. Āṇḍāl, *Autobiography of a Goddess*, 9.

erotic trend in Indian literature, rich in magnificent poems that "reflect a culture that celebrates the pleasures of flesh without any inhibition in language that never gives offence, that never crosses the line but always observes the canons of good taste."[50] If the *bhaktimārga* has always resorted to erotic imagery and sentiments to express the passion that consumes souls enamoured of the Lord, no one other than the young Āṇḍāl has gone so far in the mystical alchemy transforming the *sṛṅgāra*, the erotic, into *ānanda*. It is from her breast, filled at the same time with both carnal desire and holy devotion, that she addresses her Lord. Her two breasts—essential elements of Indian erotic aesthetics—"swell for that Lord alone"[51] and wring out from her this confidence: "From childhood I longed for him alone, to him / I offer my growing breasts supple and full. / May Dvārkā's Lord cup my breasts."[52] In the same song, Āṇḍāl implores Kāmadeva, the messenger of love, with a boldness known only to those consumed by passion: "Make Lord Keśava accept me completely and make / Me the woman I yearn to be, I fear his embrace. / I will serve at his feet as an ecstatic slave who sole / Aim in life is this. Bestow on me Your favour."[53] If the young girl reveals her intimate emotions without modesty, it is because she is painfully awaiting the coming of her Lord to ravish her and overwhelm her with his presence. Eroticism (*sṛṅgāra*) for Āṇḍāl does not reside in the satisfaction of desire (*saṃbhoga*) but, on the contrary, in the pain of absence which the Indian tradition designates by the key term of *viraha*. Addressing the *kuyil*, the cuckoo that keeps her company and "knows the anguish of separation from a beloved,"[54] the girl confesses: "Because I yearn to unite with the Lord / who reclined upon the surging ocean of milk. / My breasts swell in excitement / they rise and fall, torture my very soul."[55] The more time passes, the more acute the suffering becomes: "The fire of desire has invaded my body / I suffer."[56] Always, it is her body that Āṇḍāl presents as a witness to her passion and extreme devotion—this body that bears the stigma of unfulfilled desire: "I weep for him. I worship him yet he does not show

50. Parthasarathy, *Erotic Poems from the Sanskrit*, xv.

51. Āṇḍāl, *Nācciyār Tirumoḻi* 1.5. Cf. Āṇḍāl, *Secret Garland*, 88.

52. Āṇḍāl, *Nācciyār Tirumoḻi* 1.4. Cf. Āṇḍāl, *Autobiography of a Goddess*, 39.

53. Āṇḍāl, *Nācciyār Tirumoḻi* 1.8. Cf. Āṇḍāl, *Autobiography of a Goddess*, 47.

54. Āṇḍāl, *Nācciyār Tirumoḻi* 5.4. Cf. Āṇḍāl, *Secret Garland*, 104.

55. Āṇḍāl, *Nācciyār Tirumoḻi* 5.7. Cf. Āṇḍāl, *Secret Garland*, 105. The image of Viṣṇu resting on the ocean of milk is classic.

56. Āṇḍāl, *Nācciyār Tirumoḻi* 8.2. Cf. Āṇḍāl, *Secret Garland*, 114.

himself. . . . He does not consume me with his caress. He does not envelop me in his embrace."[57] Traditionally, in Tamil poetry, the breasts exalt not only the most intense human pleasure but also the most intoxicating love of the Lord. This is why, at the climax of the *viraha*, the pain caused by the absence of the Beloved, Āṇḍāl, filled with fury, can cry out:

I melt. I fray. But he does not care
if I live or die.
If that stealthy thief, that duplicitous Govardhana
should even glance at me
I shall pluck these useless breasts of mine
from their roots
I will fling them at his chest
to stop fire scorching me.[58]

Paradoxically, the long pilgrimage in the land of exile that is the *Nācciyār Tirumoḻi* ends in peace. Completely consumed by the fire of the *viraha*, Āṇḍāl through every pore of her being has perfectly become an *ālvār*: she has united definitively with the Lord by drowning herself in the extreme love of the absent: "My looted self I hurl at you / accept what is yours. Cherish ruin / as residue of your glory."[59] Henceforth, the Beloved is no longer hidden from Āṇḍāl's eyes, for she has discovered that he fills the outer world, as he also resides deep in her heart, breath of her breath, life of her life—supreme joy: *ānanda*. And the legend goes on to relate that Āṇḍāl was taken to the great temple of Śṛīrangaṃ for her mystical marriage to Viṣṇu and in the shrine, where the divine effigy stands, she disappeared forever from view, totally immersed in the beauty of her Lord.

A THEOLOGY OF GLORY AND DESIRE

Like tears of joy that no one can contain, *bhakti* is a gift without a why that pours into the depths of the heart and "waters what is parched."[60] Here we reach a realm of emotions that goes beyond mere speculative knowledge. It is the glory of India to have always jealously guarded access to the experience of *ānanda* by combining, without confusion, the aesthetic, erotic and mystical dimensions. The brief diversions into the Hindu world of *Tantra*

57. Āṇḍāl, *Nācciyār Tirumoḻi* 13.5. Cf. Āṇḍāl, *Secret Garland*, 131.
58. Āṇḍāl, *Nācciyār Tirumoḻi* 13.8. Cf. Āṇḍāl, *Secret Garland*, 132.
59. Āṇḍāl, *Nācciyār Tirumoḻi* 13. Cf. Āṇḍāl, *Autobiography of a Goddess*, 157.
60. Cf. Stephen Langton's *Veni Sancte Spiritus*: "Riga quod est aridum."

and *bhakti* makes us measure with new acuity the poignant diagnostic that Hans Urs von Balthasar (1905–1988) once made of the desiccation of a certain Catholic theology:

> For in its greatest period, theology cannot be considered apart from the innumerable commentaries on the *Canticle*, as embodying the central mystery of all theology. The same impulse is given by the great mystical tradition. . . . Consider only the series of the great commentators on Dionysius the Areopagite, whose writings on the mystery of the divine eros are so liturgical in tone and breath a spirit of awe and reverence. How barren seems the modern, academic approach . . . in comparison with the *sensus catholicus* of the great visionaries and theologians . . . ! The loss of the erotic element of the *Canticle* and of the aesthetic element of the Dionysian writings has resulted in a desiccation of theology. What it needs is to be steeped anew in the very heart of the love mystery of scripture, and to be remoulded by the force it exerts.[61]

To understand what has been lost and perhaps to try to remedy it, it is good to listen to some of the great commentators on the *Canticle of Canticles* "in which they saw the celebration of the all-transforming mystery of God and of the world, of Christ and of the Church, from the perspective of love."[62]

In this long hermeneutical tradition, the "voice of the Alexandrian" is the first to resound, "like those burning, dry desert winds that sometimes pass over the Nile delta, driven by a passion that is not romantic, a pure impulse, an ardent breath."[63] Origen (185–253) made an interpretation of the *Canticle* based on an admittedly erroneous but extremely fruitful reading of a passage from the letter of Ignatius of Antioch (35–110) to the Romans which allows him to consider in God not only the mystery of *agapē* (cf. 1 John 4:8, 16) but also of *erōs*: "From then on, it does not matter whether we say that God is loved or that He is cherished, and I do not think we can be blamed if we give God the name of Love, as John does that of 'Charity' (*agapē*). Thus I remember that one of the saints, named Ignatius, said of Christ, 'My Love (*erōs*)[64] is crucified,' and for this I do not deem him worthy of blame."[65] Associating the *erōs* with Christ in this way makes it possible

61. Balthasar, "Revelation and the Beautiful," 124–25.

62. Balthasar, *Glory of the Lord*, 1:550.

63. Balthasar, *Parola e Mistero in Origene*, 11.

64. Rufinus of Aquileia (345–411), the Latin translator of Origen, uses the term *amor* here, equivalent to *erōs*, unlike *caritas* which refers to *agapē*.

65. Origen, *Commentary on the Canticle of Canticles* Prologue 2.36. The quotation

to contemplate the whole of the Redemption in its erotic dimension—that of God in search of man and that of man in search of God, following the example of the drama of the *Canticle of Canticles*, which "inspires in the soul the love of heavenly realities and the desire for divine goods, under the figure of the bride and the bridegroom, teaching it to arrive by the ways of charity and love at the communion with God."[66] A warning is in order here: since the eroticism of which we speak has God as its source, it is an eroticism that is infinitely purified and transfigured in relation to the crude conceptions that man may have of desire and love. Therefore, one must be spiritually prepared to read the *Canticle* "whose whole body is formed of words with mystical meanings."[67] As it is the case "among the Hebrews" where "unless one has reached a mature and perfect age, one is not even allowed to hold this little book in one's hands,"[68] "so the childish and puerile age of the inner man is not allowed to receive these words."[69] This is the "warning and advice" that Origen gives "to anyone who has not yet been delivered from the predicaments of flesh and blood and has not renounced the disposition of the material nature: let him absolutely abstain from reading this little book and from what will be said in its favour."[70] These precautions having been taken, Origen was able to develop an aesthetic symbolism that had an immense impact in the successive commentaries on the *Canticle*, in particular in the allegorical interpretations of the different members of the lovers' bodies.[71] Another image that was destined to a great fortune was that of the arrow, which Greco-Roman culture associated with Érōs, the God of love, and which for Origen is Christ himself, the Son sent by the Father:

> How beautiful, how noble, to receive wounds from charity! One receives the marks of carnal love, another is wounded by an earthly passion; as for you, bare your limbs and present yourself to the arrow of choice, the completely beautiful arrow, for it is God

from Ignatius is: "My earthly desire has been crucified, and there is no longer any fire in me to love the material, but in me a living water that whispers and says within me: 'Come to the Father'" (Ignatius of Antioch, *Letter to the Romans* 7.2).

66. Origen, *Commentary on the Canticle of Canticles* Prologue 3.7.
67. Origen, *Commentary on the Canticle of Canticles* Prologue 1.3.
68. Origen, *Commentary on the Canticle of Canticles* Prologue 1.7.
69. Origen, *Commentary on the Canticle of Canticles* Prologue 1.4.
70. Origen, *Commentary on the Canticle of Canticles* Prologue 1.6.
71. Cf. Chrétien, *Symbolique du corps*.

> who is the archer. Listen to the Scripture which speaks to you of this same arrow; moreover, marvel at it; listen to what the arrow itself says: "He set me down as an arrow of choice and kept me in his quiver. And he said to me: It is a great thing to be called my child." (Is 49:2) Understand what the arrow means, and how it was chosen by the Lord. What joy it is to be wounded by this arrow! It was by this arrow that those who were talking to each other were wounded, saying: "Were not our hearts burning within us on the way when he explained the Scriptures to us?" (Luke 24:32) If someone is wounded by our word, by the teaching of divine Scripture, and if he can say: "I am wounded with love" (Song 2:5), perhaps this applies to him? But why do I say "perhaps"? Is it not obvious?[72]

Commenting on this same verse of the *Canticle* by associating it with the same passage from the prophet Isaiah, Origen could see in the wound of the arrow not only the objective mystery of the Incarnation of the Word but also the spiritual itinerary of the one who has been wounded by divine love and is made capable of understanding the deep meaning of the Scriptures, not only with his mind but with his heart (*sahṛdaya*):

> If there is anyone somewhere who has been at times consumed by this faithful love of the Word of God, if there is anyone, as the prophet says, who has received the sweet wound of his "arrow of choice," if there is anyone who has been pierced by the kindly stroke of his knowledge to the point of sighing with desire towards Him day and night, to be able to speak of nothing else, to want to hear nothing else, to think of nothing else, to take pleasure in desiring, wishing, hoping for nothing else but Him, that soul rightly says: "I am wounded with love" (Song 2:5): it has received the wound of which Isaiah speaks: "He has made me like an arrow of choice, and hidden me in his quiver" (Is 49:2). It is fitting that God should strike souls with such a wound, pierce them with such beautiful arrows and darts, and bruise them with such salutary wounds, so that, "since God is love," they too may say: "I am wounded by love."[73]

Let us emphasize again that Origen associates what is said of the bride of the Canticle "either with the Church or with the ardent soul"[74]—a truly eccle-

72. Origen, *Homilies on the Canticle of Canticles* 2.8.
73. Origen, *Commentary on the Canticle of Canticles* 3.13–14.
74. Origen, *Commentary on the Canticle of Canticles* 3.11.

sial commentary because the Church is the communion of particular souls, precious and unique stones of the heavenly Jerusalem. Thus is launched the theme of the mystical marriage between the Word and the soul, a dramatic theme that Origen orchestrated in its whole erotic dimension, referring (*vyañjanā*) unceasingly to a higher mystery:

> And if the bridegroom also deigns to come to my soul, which has become his bride, how beautiful must it be to draw him to herself from heaven, to make him descend to earth, so that he may come to the beloved? How beautiful must it be, how ardent must its love be, for him to say to it what he said to the perfect bride: Your neck, your eyes, your cheeks, your hands, your belly, your shoulders, your feet.[75]

In the tradition of commentaries on the *Canticle*, Origen's most faithful heir is Gregory of Nyssa (335–395). Taking up the interpretation of the bride as the Church and as the singular soul, the Cappadocian Father centred his entire reading on the mystery of the *erōs*: first the burning, impassive and pure *erōs* of God but also the *erōs* of the flesh which is purified by the divinising attraction of the celestial beauty. As Charbel Maalouf[76] has masterfully explained, by deploying the themes of love and desire Gregory of Nyssa brought about a remarkable work of Christian inculturation, assuming, purifying and transfiguring the Greek concept of *erōs*, that is so significant in the *Symposium* of Plato (428–347) and the *Enneads* of Plotinus (205–270). In Gregory, *erōs* is no longer linked to deprivation and lack but to divine superabundance; it is no longer merely ascending but is also descending when God lowers himself to mankind—proof not of his decay but of his unfathomable glory; finally, *erōs* does not lead to the perfection of a final rest but on the contrary is infinitely dynamic until within the divine eternity. Moreover, as in Origen, the allegory of the arrow is central for Gregory and allows the doctrine of the two *erōs* to be developed with connotations that combine the most carnal with the most spiritual:

> The soul that rises through divine progress thus sees in itself the sweet arrow of love that has wounded it; it glories in such a wound, when it says: "I am wounded with love." What a beautiful wound! What a sweet wound that allows life to penetrate it, after having enlarged, like an entrance doorway, the opening caused by the

75. Origen, *Homilies on the Canticle of Canticles* 1.3.

76. Cf. Maalouf, *Une mystique érotique*. We are greatly indebted to this remarkable work for our reading of Gregory.

> arrow! Indeed, no sooner had she received the arrow of love than the shot was immediately transformed into nuptial joy.[77]

Once again, the arrow is first of all a metaphor for Christ, who in the "philanthropy" of his Incarnation "bends down to the earthly . . . in order to put himself within reach of those below" so as to wound them with love and thus enable them to rise "to the Most High."[78] Taking up a key term from Greek culture, Gregory makes Christ the *erastēs*, "the beautiful lover of our souls."[79] By lowering himself to us, the Lord inflames the human *erōs*, wounding the soul with the "incorporeal and burning arrow of [his] *erōs*."[80] The paroxysm of this divine eroticism is the Cross where Jesus "wanted to convince us that he loves us with a mad love. So he invents this abasement, puts himself in a state of suffering and torment, in order to convince of his love those for whom he suffers the Passion, so that he can draw men to himself."[81] There, at Golgotha, the soul "saw that the infinite and indescribable beauty of the beloved was always more powerfully discovered."[82] In the humbled glory of the bridegroom, a true apocalypse takes place, a revelation of divine love that awaits, as its only response, the purified love of the soul:

> Therefore, she who has removed the veil that covered her eyes sees with pure eyes the unfathomable beauty of the bridegroom, and for this reason she has been wounded by the incorporeal and burning arrow of the *erōs*; for when the *agapē* is stretched tight, it is called an *erōs* about which no one blushes, for the effect of the arrow hurled at her is not of the order of the flesh. On the contrary, one is glorified by this wound when one receives the sharp edge of immaterial desire deep in the heart.[83]

77. Gregory of Nyssa, *Homilies on the Canticle of Canticles* 4.

78. Gregory of Nyssa, *Homilies on the Canticle of Canticles* 10.

79. Gregory of Nyssa, *Homilies on the Canticle of Canticles* 13.

80. Gregory of Nyssa, *Homilies on the Canticle of Canticles* 13.

81. Cabasilas, *Life in Christ* 6.12–13. This passage on the "mad *erōs*" was quoted by Pope Benedict XVI in his "Message for Lent 2007": "On the Cross, God's *erōs* for us is made manifest. *Erōs* is indeed, as Pseudo-Dionysius expresses it, that force which 'does not allow the lover to remain in himself but moves him to become one with the beloved' (*De Divinis Nominibus*, IV, 13). Is there more 'mad *erōs*' (than that which led the Son of God to make himself one with us even to the point of suffering as his own the consequences of our offences?"

82. Gregory of Nyssa, *Homilies on the Canticle of Canticles* 12.

83. Gregory of Nyssa, *Homilies on the Canticle of Canticles* 13.

At the nadir of divine annihilation, the divine ascent of the souls can begin, which Gregory calls the "lovers (*erastas*) of the higher beauty"[84] and whose "clear gaze wounds the Spouse with love"[85] like arrows: "The text [of the *Canticle*] in fact shows that our bridegroom and our archer are the same, and that he sees in the purified soul a bride and an arrow: an arrow that he would direct towards a virtuous goal, a bride that he would make to enter and take part in his incorruptible eternity."[86] The soul that has "received God's chosen stroke" and "has been struck in the heart by the barb of faith, receiving in the mortal place the shot of love" can thanks to its unceasingly purified desire begin its erotic and divinising elevation towards "the one who cannot be reached, . . . the one who is ungraspable":[87]

> This is why the most violent of the effects of pleasure, I mean erotic passion (*to erōtikon pathos*), is placed here in an enigmatic way by Scripture, for the purpose of teaching: so that we might learn through this that the soul, fixing its eyes on the unattainable beauty of the divine nature, must be enamoured (*eran*) of that beauty as much as the body possesses the disposition towards that which is innate and connatural to it. This soul, transposing passion into impassibility such that with all carnal disposition extinguished, the thought moved by the Spirit alone burns lovingly within us, warmed by that fire which the Lord came to cast upon the earth (Luke 12:49).[88]

Since what attracts its desire is the unfathomable beauty of the divine love—the divine essence (*ousia*) which is incomprehensible—the soul's *epecstasis*[89] will never end. The soul will certainly unite with the beloved, but it will be with a desire that will never be satisfied, in a race that is constantly started over: "Then the bride, who has taken part in the beauty as much as she has been able, is again drawn towards participation in the transcendent beauty

84. Gregory of Nyssa, *Homilies on the Canticle of Canticles* 6.

85. Bruno of Cologne, "Letter to Raoul le Verd": "Here one acquires that clear gaze which wounds the Spouse with love, and by means of which, clean and pure, one sees God."

86. Gregory of Nyssa, *Homilies on the Canticle of Canticles* 4.

87. Gregory of Nyssa, *Homilies on the Canticle of Canticles* 12.

88. Gregory of Nyssa, *Homilies on the Canticle of Canticles* 1.

89. *Epecstasis* is a key concept coined by Jean Daniélou (1905–1974), the great commentator on Gregory of Nyssa, from the Pauline quotation: "Brothers, I do not think I have grasped this yet. Only one thing matters: forgetting what is behind, and running forward (*epekteinomenos*), I run towards the goal in view of the prize to which God calls us up there in Christ Jesus" (Phil 3:13–14). Cf. Daniélou, *Platonisme et théologie mystique.*

as if she had never yet taken part in it. Thus, as she progresses towards that which never ceases to appear before her, her desire is increased, and the superiority of that which is found in the transcendent makes the bride feel as if she is but starting her ascent."[90] Such is the paradoxical "perception of presence"[91] (*aisthēsis tēs parousias*) which gives of itself into "an eternal intensification of presence and union in a dynamism proper to a love, that is ever more intense and renewed, never stilled and exhausted for the God who reveals himself as love."[92] *Erōs*, desire, beauty, divinization: few are the Christian authors who like Gregory of Nyssa have so happily married in a unique theological style the aesthetic, erotic and mystical dimensions, not only describing with great power the mystery of salvation but also marking out the pathway of an experience of faith that the divine Bridegroom has opened up for his bride.

Before John of the Cross (1542–1591) brilliantly reinterpreted the *Canticle of Canticles* in his *Spiritual Canticle*, Bernard of Clairvaux (1090–1153) was one of the previous great commentators on the biblical book. Taking up the twofold reading of the bride as an allegory of the Church and of souls, from the opening verse of the *Canticle* he developed the image filled with a chaste eroticism of the spiritual kiss:

> I would like to know if any of you ever received the grace to say these words from the depths of his hearts: "Let him kiss me with the kisses of his mouth" (Song 1:1). For it is not for everyone to say this, but only those alone who have once received a spiritual kiss from the mouth of Jesus Christ, its unique experience constantly excites them, and leads them with even greater passion to repeat what they have already found to be so sweet.[93]

More than his predecessors, Bernard enjoined reading the *Canticle* as the "book of experience"[94] so that each one could recognise (*pratyabhijñā*) that touched his flesh and heart at the deepest:

> It is only the unction of grace that teaches it, and experience alone that learns it, may those who have experienced it recognise it; may those who do not yet have this experience burn with the desire,

90. Gregory of Nyssa, *Homilies on the Canticle of Canticles* 5.

91. Gregory of Nyssa, *Homilies on the Canticle of Canticles* 11.

92. Maalouf, *Une mystique érotique*, 336.

93. Bernard of Clairvaux, *Homilies on the Canticle of Canticles* 3.1.1.

94. Bernard of Clairvaux, *Homilies on the Canticle of Canticles* 3.1.1: "We read today in the book of experience."

> not to learn about it, but to experience it. For it is not a sound from the mouth, but a joy of the heart, nor a sound from the lips, but a movement of joy; it is a concert not of voices, but of wills. It is not heard outside, neither does it resound in public. Only the one who sings it and the one in whose honour it is sung—these are the bridegroom and the bride—can hear it. For it is a nuptial song which expresses chaste and sweet embraces of the spirit, a perfect union of wills, and a bond of affection and mutual inclinations.[95]

Like his cloistered companions, Bernard allowed himself to be read and stripped bare by the Scriptures, which go "to the point they divide soul from spirit, joints from marrow" (Heb 4:12) and abominate any half-heartedness: "In this wedding song, . . . love speaks everywhere. And if anyone wishes to gain any understanding of it, he must love. In vain, he who does not love will listen to or read this canticle of love, the passionate speeches cannot be understood by a cold soul."[96] The same experiential vein can be found in the theology of Hans Urs von Balthasar who more than any other in the twentieth century, like an industrious bee, knew how to extract the most precious sap from the ecclesial tradition. If in his monumental work the aesthetic and the erotic are so present, it is because these dimensions belong to the very style through which God-Trinity has revealed Himself to us. Commenting on the "per hunc in invisibilium amorem rapiamur"[97] of the preface to the Christmas Mass, he wrote in the very first volume of his trilogy that this was "a vision which occasions a 'rapture' and a 'transport' (*rapiamur*) to an '*erōs-love*' (*amor*) for those 'things unseen' (*invisibilia*) which had announced themselves by appearing in the visibleness and revelation of the Incarnation."[98] Doubtless recalling Origen and his reading of Ignatius of Antioch, Balthasar wrote that "the word used here is *amor* (*erōs*) and not *caritas* [*agapē*]" for "*erōs* captures the sense of the transport of man's being as such far better than does *agapē*, and this constitutes . . . an aesthetic as well as a soteriological statement."[99] The experience of rapture

95. Bernard of Clairvaux, *Homilies on the Canticle of Canticles* 1.6.11.

96. Bernard of Clairvaux, *Homilies on the Canticle of Canticles* 79.1.1.

97. "Quia per incarnati Verbi mysterium, nova mentis nostrae oculis lux tuae claritatis infulsit ut, dum visibiliter Deum cognoscimus, per hunc in invisibilium amorem rapiamur," "In the wonder of the incarnation Your eternal Word has brought to the eyes of faith a new and radiant vision of Your glory. In Him we see our God made visible and so are caught up in love of the God we cannot see."

98. Balthasar, *Glory of the Lord*, 1:120.

99. Balthasar, *Glory of the Lord*, 1:122.

of the soul referred to here is based on a "antecedent and con-descending divine *ekstasis* in which God is drawn out of himself by *erōs* into creation, revelation, and Incarnation."[100] Thus basing his aesthetics and theological eroticism on the originating ecstasy of the God-Trinity out from Himself as He engages with man and makes his glory shine at the heart of the sinful world, Balthasar was able to take up the reflections of Western philosophy on the beautiful, which "is above all a form (*Gestalt*)":[101] "In the luminous form of the beautiful the being of the existent becomes perceivable as nowhere else, and this is why an aesthetic element must be associated with all spiritual perception as with all spiritual striving."[102] From the primary consideration of the divine *erōs,* Balthasar then moved on to that of the human *erōs* which resonates fully before the beautiful and *a fortiori* before the glory of the Christic figure:

> All our senses are engaged when the interior space of a beautiful musical composition or painting opens itself to us and captivates us: the whole person then enters into a state of vibration and becomes responsive space, the "sounding box" of the event of beauty occurring within him. This all the more so where human *erōs* is concerned, and yet more in the encounter with the divine *erōs*![103]

Far from the desiccation of cold intellectualism within which a sterile Catholic theology was bogged down for centuries, Balthasar, by starting out mainly in the experiential school of the saints and mystics, knew how to recover the aesthetic and erotic force of a truly Catholic theology that had fully recovered the taste (*sapor, rasa*) of the Absolute:

> The convergence of the aesthetic and the mystical in the great mystical theologies—from Gregory of Nyssa and Dionysius the Areopagite to Bernard of Clairvaux, William of Saint-Thierry, the greater Mechtild, and all the way to John of the Cross and Teresa of Avila—is striking and can only be explained by affirming that what in God is formless and ineffable is offered as a super-form which fascinates and transports man, eliciting from man and claiming for itself the answer of man's shaping powers. The dangers involved are evident, but they need not make a successful outcome impossible. Besides, the personal existential dimension is

100. Balthasar, *Glory of the Lord*, 1:122.
101. Balthasar, *Glory of the Lord*, 1:151.
102. Balthasar, *Glory of the Lord*, 1:153.
103. Balthasar, *Glory of the Lord*, 1:220.

> never lacking in great classical theology; *sapientia* has always been related to *sapor*, and the personal appropriation of Christian truth in one's existence has always been regarded as an indispensable criterion for the manifestation of the truth.[104]

If the two thousand years of Christianity have generated remarkable commentaries on the *Canticle*, none of those that have passed into history are the work of women. This fact is sufficiently remarkable as not to be passed over in silence! There is, however, a Carmelite tradition which relates that Teresa of Avila (1515–1582) transverberated by the divine arrow, for fear of male censorship and at the suggestion of her confessor burned the original of her "Thoughts on the love of God, which is like an explanation of some of the words of the *Canticle of Canticles*." Yet we would so much have liked to put ourselves in the school of feminine sensibility and find within Christianity some distant sisters of Āṇḍāl. Fortunately, we are left with the voice of the two Hadewijchs, whose echo continues to reverberate in the hearts of those who are spiritually craving for strong spirits. While the Church Fathers have often been too quick to speak of transfigured *erōs*, at the risk of losing its carnal roots, it is with her whole body pulsing with emotive eroticism that Hadewijch of Antwerp (1200–1260) describes the vehement ardors of *Minne*, the divine love which took on for her the features of the courtly love of the medieval bards. Hadewijch is a woman and it is as a desiring woman that she wants to unite with the Absolute as naturally as possible:

> Love's sweetest thing is its violence; its unfathomable abyss is its most beautiful form; to lose oneself in it is to reach the goal; to be hungry for it is to feed and delight; love's anxiety is a safe state; its deepest wound is a sovereign balm; to yearn for it is our vigour; it is by eclipsing itself that it makes itself discovered; if it makes us suffer, it gives us pure health; if it hides itself, it reveals its secrets to us; it is by refusing itself that it gives itself up; it is without rhyme or reason and that is its poetry.[105]

Hadewijch speaks from experience and it is her whole feminine personality that attests to the truth of her words: "This is the testimony that I and many others can bear at any time, we to whom love has often shown wonders, for which we received derision, having thought we were holding

104. Balthasar, *Glory of the Lord*, 1:601–2.

105. Hadewijch of Antwerp, *Mengeldichten* 13.

what it kept only for itself,"[106] Hadewijch is a warrior, and if she gives herself without restraint to love, it is so that at the end of a succession of presences and absences, love finally gives itself up to her in its unfathomable newness: "May new light give you new zeal, new works, the fullness of new delights, new assaults of love, and a new hunger so vast that eternally new love devours its new gifts!"[107] There where she stops, her journey begins that of the beguine who succeeded her under the same name. "Drunk with a wine she has not drunk,"[108] the other Hadewijch "thinks, in the very agnosia, the absolute truth"; she "loves, at the extremity of aridity, the absolute love, . . . even going so far as to rejoice less in the gifts given by God to creatures than in what in Him is incommunicable, beyond participation, what in God is God."[109] Thus launched herself like Gregory of Nyssa into the unknowability of the divine essence and "led far and wide by the power of love,"[110] Hadewijch can silently approach the land of spacious joy: "How narrow everything is for me: I feel so vast! It is an uncreated Reality that I have wanted to grasp eternally: I have understood it, it has freed me from all limits; everything is too small for me, you know that too, you who live there."[111] The Carthusian Jean-Baptiste Porion (1899–1987), who helped rediscover Hadewijch, wrote that the beguines in wanting to "create a language to translate their passionate experiences," belonged to "one of those moments in history when woman, the mother of renewal and dawns, draws from the sacred depths of her being a fresh inspiration for the civilisations of the written word and iron."[112] May Catholic theology not have wait any longer for women to revive it in the light of a unique spiritual experience.

A TERRIFYING BEAUTY

Over time, the Indian aesthetic experience has come to be summarised in three regularly quoted terms: "satyaṃ śivaṃ sundaraṃ,"[113] "truth, goodness

106. Hadewijch of Antwerp, *Mengeldichten* 13.

107. Hadewijch of Antwerp, *Strophische Gedichten* 33.

108. Porete, *Mirror of Simple Souls*, 68.

109. Monchanin, "Au nom de l'Église," 23.

110. Hadewijch of Antwerp, *Mengeldichten* 18.

111. Hadewijch of Antwerp, *Mengeldichten* 21.

112. Hadewijch of Antwerp, *Écrits mystiques des béguines*, 14.

113. One tradition records that Tulsīdās (1532–1623), the author of the first vernacular translation of the *Rāmāyaṇa*, was challenged by the Brahmins of Benares, jealous

and beauty." These transcendentals, taken in reverse order, gave Hans Urs von Balthasar the outline of his trilogy. If he had known it, what would the Basel master have thought of the *via pulchritudinis* that India has traversed through the *Tantra* and *bhakti*? Beyond the radical Christian novelty that he vehemently affirmed, would he not have found an identical call to allow himself to be taught by the aesthetic experience and the erotic experience, each of which, in its own degree, is a harbinger of perfect joy, the fullness of mystical experience? Like the West, India has deeply loved and sought beauty in very original ways. Yet, is it only an Apollonian beauty that she has constantly craved? Is there not also a Dionysian element in India? In its eagerness to overcome all duality, *Tantra* enjoined the aspirant to final union not only to taste the beautiful but also to welcome the ugly and, similarly, to rejoice in pleasure as well as to go through suffering in full consciousness.[114] Those who have not yet confronted terrifying horror remain human, all too human, and are still prisoners of duality.

In "Christ at the centre of everything," a teaching given in 1936, Jules Monchanin (1895–1957) noted that "if all beauty is *de jure* Christian, all beauty must also be configured to the Passion."[115] Gregory of Nyssa already enjoined us to contemplate, *sub contrario specie*, the beauty of the "beautiful lover of our souls," but it is with Balthasar that the cross in all its terror becomes the ultimate measure of divine beauty:

> If the Cross radically puts an end to all worldly aesthetics, then precisely this end marks the decisive emergence of the divine aesthetic, but in saying this we must not forget that even worldly aesthetics cannot exclude the element of the ugly, of the tragically fragmented, of the demonic, but must come to terms with these. Every aesthetic which simply seeks to ignore these nocturnal sides of existence can itself from the outset be ignored as a sort of aestheticism. It is not only the limitation and precariousness of all beautiful form which intimately belongs to the phenomenon of beauty, but also fragmentation itself, because it is only through being fragmented that the beautiful really reveals the meaning of the eschatological promise it contains.[116]

---

guardians of the purity of Sanskrit. These only bowed down when the book, having been deposited in the great temple of Śiva, was found with the autograph of the god who had inscribed on each page "satyaṃ śivaṃ sundaraṃ."

114. Cf. Abhinavagupta, *Tantrāloka* 3.36.

115. Cf. Jacquin, *Jules Monchanin*, 143.

116. Balthasar, *Glory of the Lord*, 1:460.

It is at the Golgotha that we must complete this "course of recognition" by reading the fervent lines of a thinker who knew that theology is the memorial and the preparation for the encounter with the living and true God. And this he knew how to express superbly by summoning the aesthetic, the erotic and the mystical and through listening to the true lovers that are the saints, those who have kept the taste of the Absolute in their palate:

> This is why through the mysteries of humiliation and servitude, and even of the Cross, we catch a glimpse of the mysteries of Solomon's bridal *Canticle*, through the mysteries of the divine *agapē* a glimpse of the mysteries of the divine *erōs*. . . . And yet, the Bridegroom shows himself physically naked before the world only as the man of sorrows on the Cross, and the sinner must endure this nakedness resulting from the tearing off of his garments. What the sinner encounters here, along with the sight of the divine love, is the sight of his own shame. And only a gaze such as that of the virginal John could here contemplate the two unveilings as one: the unveiling of the *Canticle of Canticles*, whereby he shows himself bodily in the ardour of *erōs*, and the unveiling of the love of the triune God, who suffers in just as bodily a manner. Unheard-of balancing of corporal love: in the face of the Cross, love is sobered to its very marrow before God's agapē, which clothes itself in the language of the body; and, in the face of this intoxicating language of flesh and blood that gives itself by being poured out, love is lifted above itself and elevated into the eternal, in order there, as creaturely *erōs*, to be the tent and dwelling-place of the divine love![117]

117. Balthasar, *Glory of the Lord*, 1:672–73.

8

Love in Separation

One wonders what the foreign traveller might observe today, on arrival in Vṛindāvan, a small town on the banks of the river Yamunā in the heart of the Braj country? Looking beyond the revolting filth common to many Indian towns, might he be seized by the ardent faith of the pilgrims flocking in from the surrounding countryside and from much further afield? Might he be both irked and attracted by the rampant modernisation which year after year pushes up shimmering tower blocks for rich Delhi dwellers in search of peace and quiet? Or else, might he get caught up in the great spiritual business which is increasingly overlaying all the Hindu sacred sites? To a mere passer-by, Vṛindāvan remains disappointingly opaque . . . but anyone willing to linger longer will gradually begin to perceive the mystery of the place, as reflected in the faces of all the devotees of Kṛṣna lost in intense prayers, repeating the Name of the Beloved over and over. For Vṛindāvan is far more than a geographic reference on a map; it is truly a "landscape of the soul" into which one needs to enter wholeheartedly, having let go of everything that could hold one back.

Few mystics have sung the glory of this place with as much incandescent fervor as did the blind bard Sūrdās, who lived on the cusp of the fifteenth and sixteenth centuries. Sadly, this name is practically unknown outside India; and few indeed are those who have read the booklet written about him by the French Indologist Charlotte Vaudeville (1918–2006). It encloses a number of poems drawn from his huge volume called *Sūr-Sāgar*—literally "*Sūr's* Ocean." The title "Pastorales" of the French text might put off a reader not attracted to shepherdesses and herds of cows.

For sure, it is about the cowherds—that caste among whom Kṛṣna dwelt before his true royal identity was revealed. And yet, way above the naivety of its language, this poetic work is the unveiling of one of the highest Indian spiritual paths, the path of *viraha*—love in separation—for which, still today, thousands of Hindus are ready to forsake everything in order to remain forever in Vṛindāvan where this path has been taught and lived right up to its paroxysm.

Though he might be somewhat tuned into Hindu spirituality, a foreigner cannot have but a very partial acquaintance with it, since it is one-sidedly filtered by the kind of teachings on *vedānta* given through yoga ersatz forms studied mostly by people in search of "wellbeing" and "personal development." It is a fact that *vedānta*—and in particular the unequalled heights to which Śaṅkara took it in the eighth century—is one of the deepest traits of the Hindu quest. Who indeed could remain unmoved by this ascetic path which, with almost barbarous violence, bans all signs and images in order to lose itself in the Nameless, Formless Absolute beyond all? Yet India, carried by its insatiable desire to attain "the further shore," has displayed this same inner violence when treading other paths, particularly the path of *bhakti* so beautifully spelt out in the words of the ancient Tamil sage Tirumūlar: "The ignorant say that love and God are two; they do not know that love itself is God. Whoever knows that love itself is God shall rest in love, one with God."[1] Then, many centuries after this magnificent statement was formulated in South India, the *bhakti* path of devotion found a new lease of life in the North of the country, precisely in Vṛindāvan; this is attested in the sixteenth century *Bhāgavata Mahātmya*:

> I was born in Dravida, grew up in Karnātaka, was honoured here and there in Mahārāṣtra, but in Gujarāt I begun to grow old. There, due to the effects of the dreadful Kali Age, the hypocrites caused injury to my limbs. Since this condition lasted for a very long time, I became . . . weak and lifeless. Then I reached Vṛindāvan, I became again young and beautiful.[2]

Bhakti comes from the Sanskrit root [*bhaj*] meaning: "to share, partake in, belong to, be part of." In this way, once he wholly belongs to

1. Tirumūlar, *Tirumantiraṃ* 257.

2. *Bhāgavata Mahātmya* 1.47–49. The great names of *bhakti* in North India are those of the *sants*: Ravidās (1414–1526), Kabīr (1440–1518), Gurū Nānak (1469–1539) the founder of Sikhism, Sūrdās (1478–1573), Mīrabai (1498–1557), Tulsidās (1532–1623). Cf. Hawley, *Songs of the Saints of India*; Vaudeville, *Myths, Saints and Legends*.

Him, the devotee partakes in the mystery of his Lord. It is literally a divine sharing where man and the Absolute are but one—that consummation of unity which is the goal of all Indian spiritual paths. The *viraha* unremittingly sung by Sūrdās is not only the highpoint of the *bhaktimārga* but also its most paradoxical manifestation, for union is accomplished here only through the unbearable pain of separation.

THE WHIRLPOOL OF LOVE

At the time he composed his thousands of poems, Sūrdās was able to draw inspiration from the great storehouse called the *Bhāgavata Purāṇa*,[3] written between the seventh and tenth centuries, and especially from its tenth volume entirely dedicated to Kṛṣna. Nowadays the Divine Cowherd is one of the most popular figures in Hinduism, seen as an *avatāra* of Viṣṇu; he spends his childhood among the cow herds in Vṛindāvan before reclaiming his throne at Mathurā, which had been stolen by his uncle Kaṃsa. Another famous text, the *Bhagavadgītā*, written at the beginning of our era, presents Kṛṣna as the charioteer of Prince Arjuna in the heart of the battle narrated in the epic poem *Mahābhārata*. Yet elsewhere, in Gujarāt, one is reminded of the antique city of Dvārkā, now submerged, over which the *avatāra* reigned before leaving this earth to which he had come to re-establish the sacred order, *dharma*, that had been put in peril in sundry ways: "When righteousness (*dharma*) is weak and faints and unrighteousness exults in pride, then I manifest myself on earth. For the salvation of those who are good, for the destruction of evil in men, for the sake of firmly establishing righteousness, I am born from age to age."[4] Of this multifaceted life, Sūrdās picked only the Vṛindāvan episodes on the banks of the Yamunā. These begin briefly with his childhood spent with his adoptive parents and move on to his adolescent adventures with the shepherdesses known throughout India under the name *gopī*. The accounts of their thwarted love stories enabled him to expound the path of *viraha*.

The autumn full moon bathes the opening scene of these immortal love plays. Whilst their husbands and masters are in deep slumber, the

3. Sūrdās was surely taught the *Bhāgavata Purāṇa* by his Master, Vallabha, to whom we shall have occasion to return. This work lies at the heart of Krishnaite mysticism and furnished him with the main stages of the love drama so magnificently amplified in his *Sūr-Sāgar*.

4. *Bhagavadgītā* 4.7–8.

sixteen thousand *gopī*—who of course represent the *bhakta*, the devotees of Kṛṣna—set off for the woods in answer to the call of their desire: "Fired by their love for Śyām,[5] all the women left in a stir! Not a word of this secret did they breathe to their masters. In the middle of the night, these women escaped from their houses, crowds of them."[6] In the folly of their urge to find the love of their heart, they cry out: "We have forsaken our nearest and dearest. . . . Woe to this life far from You! . . . What we seek is the sweetness of Your smile, from which springs this longing."[7] And even more boldly: "We have no care for vice or virtue: henceforth, come what may!"[8] Then "contemplating this happy forest," Kṛṣna "put his lips to his flute and played a tender melody."[9] This divine music transports the sixteen thousand *gopī* in a whirl of love, the *rāsa-līlā*[10] in which the Lover multiplies himself so as to embrace each one of them at the same time: "It's an ocean of beauty wherein waves rise and swell."[11] Even some of the cowherds grazing their herds nearby cannot resist the intoxicating strains of that music: "a single note—and each one is lost in the exquisite melody of His flute."[12] Before going further we need to pause briefly on the Sanskrit word *rāsa-līlā*, composed of *līlā*, which is a divine play between the Lord and His devotee, in which there is no reference to non-duality leading to a dissolution of 'otherness,' as is the case in Śaṅkara's *advaita vedānta*. *Rasa* on the other hand confers a unique connotation to this spiritual experience as it designates the essence or savour. Here, beyond theoretical knowledge, it is a question of tasting and experiencing, and thus, as the *bhakti* path tells us, of acquiring the Real Knowledge. Our language does not possess the richness of Italian, which permits a play of words between *sapore* (to taste or savour) and *sapere* (to know). Yet, in all that follows, it is a question of taste, even if it may prove a very bitter taste.

5. Kṛṣna has a huge variety of names such as Śyām, Hari, Gopāl, Mādhav, Mohan, etc. The convention is that unless we indicate it otherwise in this text all these names refer to Him.

6. Soûr-Dâs, *Pastorales*, 89.

7. Soûr-Dâs, *Pastorales*, 93.

8. Soûr-Dâs, *Pastorales*, 94.

9. Soûr-Dâs, *Pastorales*, 100.

10. The *rāsa-līlā* is also described in the *Bhāgavata Purāṇa* 10.29.

11. Soûr-Dâs, *Pastorales*, 101.

12. Soûr-Dâs, *Pastorales*, 102.

Among the sixteen thousand *gopī*, one of them attracts very special favours from Kṛṣna, to such an extent that she is forever associated with Him in all the statues through which India worships this eternal couple. Her name is Rādhā and, in this night of love, the two lovers appear to be inseparable: "At will, they dance together in a mad embrace; they stamp their feet to mark the rhythm and sing out their heart's delight."[13] And yet, Kṛṣna has decided to lead His chosen one through the narrow footpath of tears and, this first time, he escapes from her sight; thus she, together with all her companions, is condemned to seeking Him in the depths of the forest. "Then the Lord disappeared: he deserted His beloved."[14] At this stage, Sūrdās immediately reveals to his listeners (his poems were sung) that this separation serves no purpose other than to purify her love—for true devotion, *bhakti*, alone can strip away from a human being the selfishness, self-centeredness and pride into which he has—so to speak—been plunged since the day of his birth. This is why Kṛṣna states: "I am the Non-Manifest, Unborn, Undivided Being—but Rādhā has not known this mystery! . . . When there remains only a single soul for two bodies, then all duality has been abolished. But if a human being harbours pride, in him I cannot abide."[15]

This first test of separation—*viraha*—leads Rādhā to experience deep depression and floods of tears. Here, Sūrdās has re-transcribed almost word for word the unforgettable verses of the twelfth century Sanskrit text *Gītagovinda*[16] written by Jayadeva (1170–1245). Yet he discards the work's movingly erotic descriptions of Kṛṣna's loves. "See, He the Charmer, Gopāl, has abandoned me: the pangs of separation have seized my whole body"[17]

13. Soûr-Dâs, *Pastorales*, 107.

14. Soûr-Dâs, *Pastorales*, 109. Cf. *Bhāgavata Purāṇa* 10.30–31.

15. Soûr-Dâs, *Pastorales*, 109. This statement might appear to contradict what we shall subsequently explain concerning the two paths of the "Non-Manifest" and the "Manifest," of the Unqualified Absolute (*nirguṇa Brahman*) and the Qualified Absolute (*saguṇa Brahman*) which convey the great divide between the *vedānta* spiritual path and that of *bhakti*. In India, however, things are never that simple, especially not with regard to Western logic's principle of non-contradiction. In reality, the path of *bhakti* ultimately recognizes the supreme "Non-Qualified" (*nirguṇa*) character of the Absolute; several *sants* (the great exponents of *bhakti* in North India between the fifteenth and eighteenth centuries) worshipped the *nirguṇa Brahman*; one such is Kabīr, the great Saint of Benares. No doubt—yet here again we should avoid hasty generalizations—the most notable difference between *bhakti* and *vedānta* lies in the question of non-duality between a human being and the Absolute.

16. Stoler Miller, *Gītagovinda of Jayadeva*.

17. Soûr-Dâs, *Pastorales*, 110.

moans Rādhā; then she falls silent and no longer replies to the questions that come: "Why did you fall down so distraught? Why don't you open your eyes?"[18] To make her think that her Lover had returned, all the *gopī* "start chanting 'here he is! here he is!' in order to console their friend."[19] Rādhā speaks once more: "I go hither and thither in search of my Beloved, consumed by the desire to see him again. . . . This time, if I find him just for an instant, I shall not let him part from me"[20] but once more: "She cries out and calls 'Kṛṣna Kṛṣna!' and then falls down, her body gone all stiff."[21] One of the final statements of this distraught woman—the person referred to as a *virahini*—is also one of the most deeply troubling—all the more so if, instead of perceiving in her the experience she had gathered over her sixteen thousand former lives, one dared to understand that this is Rādhā's endorsement of the pain borne by sixteen thousand *gopī*, due to a true mystical substitution: "In a single body, for your sake, I have endured sixteen thousand pains, and Rādhā's soul has traversed each body. . . . My body is prey to the fire of separation that destroys pride."[22]

Yet, during that clear autumn night, the separation was short-lived: Kṛṣna reappears and consummates his marriage to His Beloved beneath the benevolent gaze of all the *gopī* as well as the gods and goddesses in the sky. As a token of love and a bond He reveals to her the secret of his *līlā*, his divine play: "Thou art dearer to me than my own life. . . . Smiling, I dwelt deep in your heart: it is I who gave rise to this play."[23] Now, the chorus of all who attended this sylvan wedding can exclaim "A single soul inhabits their two bodies: what a marvel of love and tenderness!"[24]

A MESSENGER IS SENT

Anyone reading the *Sūr-Sāgar* for the first time might have thought that it ended here with a touching *epithalamium* but, as soon as the party

18. Soûr-Dâs, *Pastorales*, 110.

19. Soûr-Dâs, *Pastorales*, 110.

20. Soûr-Dâs, *Pastorales*, 111.

21. Soûr-Dâs, *Pastorales*, 112. Here, we recommend a comparative reading of the fourth and sixth chapters of Jayadeva's *Gītagovinda* in which the Sanskrit draws on all its skills to describe Rādhā's suffering.

22. Soûr-Dâs, *Pastorales*, 113.

23. Soûr-Dâs, *Pastorales*, 113. Cf. *Bhāgavata Purāṇa* 10.32.

24. Soûr-Dâs, *Pastorales*, 119.

was over a new chapter opens with the *gopī*'s cry: "We are enamoured of Mādhav, and now he has gone away without a word!"[25] This is typical of the spiritual path described by Sūrdās: the lovers' reunion and marriage are not the end of the journey but the mere beginning of it, the prologue to the most painful stages awaiting them. Up to now, the devotee has been guided through the stripping of his ego: henceforth it remains for him to live out the true *bhakti* in the incandescent light of *viraha*—the separation from the Beloved becoming the very condition of his life. And no sooner has the bridegroom disappeared on the wedding night, that the chorus of *gopī*, who yesterday were so joyful, now changes to a great desolate lament: "How strange, this pain of separation! Only one who has experienced can comprehend it: the torment of loneliness is unbearable!"[26] And, concerning those who exclaim that "the separation from Śyām is a devouring blaze,"[27] a single desire possesses them: to behold once more the face of the Beloved: "O Son of Nanda,[28] grant us the grace of Your Sight! Our hearts yearn for Your presence, and our eyes are parched for the want of Hari's beauty."[29] Also, from then on, all the landscapes of the Braj once shimmering with beauty and joy, become an empty desert of solitude wholly prey to the pain of *viraha*—the consuming fire which, in the absence of Kṛṣna's face, reduces everything to ashes.

These heartrending laments draw us into the core of the *Sūr-Sāgar* and to the heights of *bhakti* in the form bestowed by *viraha*. In composing these unforgettable verses still capable of moving us today if we are blessed to hear them sung on temple forecourts or on the wayside, Sūrdās was able to have recourse to the *viraha-gīt*, the "songs of absence" which in his day were very popular in North Indian villages. And above all, he found inspiration in the spiritual teachings of his contemporary, Vallabha (1479–1531) whom he met in Vṛindāvan and from whom he received the essence of Krishnaite devotion enclosed in the *Bhāgavata Purāṇa*.[30] Like the

25. Soûr-Dâs, *Pastorales*, 120.

26. Soûr-Dâs, *Pastorales*, 121.

27. Soûr-Dâs, *Pastorales*, 123.

28. Nanda and Yaśodā were two cowherds who became the adoptive parents of Kṛṣna, entrusted to them by his real father Vasudeva in order to protect him from the vindictiveness of his maternal uncle Kaṃsa, who reigned as a despot over Mathurā.

29. Soûr-Dâs, *Pastorales*, 124.

30. In his book 10, dedicated to the tale of Kṛṣna, the *Bhāgavata Purāṇa* refers four times to the *viraha* experienced by the *gopī* separated from their Beloved (cf. *Bhāgavata Purāṇa* 10.46.5; 10.47.27; 10.47.29; 10.47.53). Yet, by comparing these with

majority of the great Indian philosophers, Vallabha came from the South but grew up and remained in Benares up to his death, whilst spending years on visits to the great places of pilgrimage throughout India. From his earliest childhood, this Telugu Brahmin was initiated to his people's great spiritual tradition through study of the *Veda* and the *Upaniṣad* as well as of Śaṅkara's (788–820) commentaries on the Scriptures which constitute the basis of *vedānta*. Vallabha was also introduced to the vision of the other masters of *vedānta*: Rāmānuja (1017–1137), Madhva (1197–1276) and Nimbārka (thirteenth century) who softened Śaṅkara's harsh non-duality by the more emotional vein of *bhakti*. Vallabha, through his commentaries on the sacred texts, developed the *śuddhādvaita* (pure non-duality). His *puṣtimārga*, in which loving adoration is centred on the Child Kṛṣna, was not initially the privilege of monks, as in Śaṅkara's path, but was open to all men and women overflowing with *bhakti*. On the other hand, Vallabha's life crossed that of another great spiritual master of that time, one of the greatest exponents of the path of *bhakti*: the Bengali Caitanya Mahāprabhu (1486–1533) who set off in search of the places associated with Kṛṣna's *līlā*, and so sparked the spectacular development of Vṛindāvan. With special permission from the Muslim Emperor Akbar (1542–1605), impressive temples were built of the same pink granite employed exclusively for the construction of mosques and other royal edifices. Thus, it is in the highly Krishnaite context of the time that Sūrdās inscribed his work, with a very special focus on the pangs of separation undergone by the *gopī* after Kṛṣna had to leave the woods of Vṛindāvan in order to go to kill Kaṃsa and re-establish *dharma* (righteousness).

Let us here take up the thread of the story. Kṛṣna is now installed on the royal throne of Mathurā, and even if the *gopī* compare Him to the big black bees which buzz from flower to flower, He has nothing in common with a fickle lover and he, too, is seized by the pain of exile: "Only once I see the people of the Braj again, will joy return to my heart."[31] In order to allay somewhat the pangs of separation, he decides to send his servant Uddhav to the bereft women of Vṛindāvan with the mission of teaching them about their true nature: the Invisible, Ineffable, Omnipresent Being, which the great Indian tradition has designated as *Brahman*, who ultimately has

the preponderance given to this theme in the *Sūr-Sāgar*, which in a way "overstates" the pain, we may easily understand that the *viraha* constitutes the essence of Sūrdās' spiritual message.

31. Soûr-Dâs, *Pastorales*, 127.

no qualified form (*saguṇa*) but is essentially Unqualified (*nirguṇa*). Once again, just as before in his first separation from Rādhā before the episode of their wedding, Kṛṣna wants to lead them to love Him, not by worshipping His face, but by contemplating His Ineffable Mystery. Thus, Uddhav becomes the conveyor of the most traditional Shankarian *vedānta* and Yoga to the *gopī*.

> Hear me O *gopī*, hear Hari's message. Go into trance and become absorbed in meditation: such is the message He sends you. . . . He is Non-Manifest, Eternal, Infinite, filling each of the bodies; without comprehending the Supreme Reality there can be no salvation—this is what the Scriptures teach us! Detach yourselves from the 'Qualified' and meditate on the 'Unqualified' with unfailing concentration: you shall then overcome the pain of separation and attain the Supreme Being.[32]

However, Sūrdās writes that "hearing this awful message drove the *gopī* to despair"[33] and, far from being satisfied with Uddhav's misleading mystical consolations, the shepherdesses seized the idea of revealing to him the true spiritual path, the only one which recognizes the Absolute in the splendour of his face: "You come to talk of yoga to the women of the Braj! Aren't you ashamed of yourself? You think you are something—but you have no common sense if you act that dumb!";[34] "You can keep your knowledge of the 'Unqualified' for yourself, Uddhav! . . . It's for the face of Śyām, radiant as the moon, that our eyes are parched!";[35] "Why are you praising this dried up yoga devoid of tender love? . . . These our eyes which have contemplated the lotus eyes of Mohan with his entrancing face, would you have us shut them?"[36]

32. Soûr-Dâs, *Pastorales*, 129.

33. Soûr-Dâs, *Pastorales*, 129.

34. Soûr-Dâs, *Pastorales*, 130.

35. Soûr-Dâs, *Pastorales*, 132.

36. Soûr-Dâs, *Pastorales*, 133. Here it is interesting to note to what extent Sūrdās has distorted the teaching of the *Bhāgavata Purāṇa*. In this work, the passages that deal with Uddhav's visit to the inhabitants of the Braj (10.46) and to the *gopī* (10.47), the latter are portrayed as being wholly satisfied with the teachings transmitted by Kṛṣna through the words of His emissary, revealing that the fire of *viraha* is extinguished once the identification of Kṛṣna with the Supreme Being is grasped (10.47.53), since the *gopī* can never be separated from their Lover who is manifest in the entire universe (10.47.27). Sūrdās did not accept such a philosophical consolation of the pain felt by the sorrowful women.

THE MOST PRECIOUS PAIN

There are few pages in which one finds such a final condemnation of Vedantic wisdom and of Yoga as in the humorous poetic passages in the *Sūr-Sāgar* that make up the chapter entitled "the Messenger of the Bee." In this series of ever more scorching verses, each reply spat out by the *gopī*, in refusal of the teaching that Uddhav tries to push down their throats, spells out the superiority of the *viraha-prem*, 'love in separation' as a spiritual path:

> People in the Braj are beginning to snigger—quick, hide your "yoga" You strut about hither and thither to display your *ātma-Brahman*,[37] the one hidden in each of the bodies! You parade with your "Qualified-Unqualified" under your arm: but nobody wants it! But ah! the story of Love, one has to have suffered that to know it. . . . As for you, withered up as you are, what can you know of that? Go ask the people! See their suffering! You are a noble messenger come from a noble city, but your noble intelligence has sunk into the sea.[38]

By an astonishing reversal of roles, the teacher becomes the taught when he is grappling with the true "authority of suffering" which the *gopī* reveal to him: "Are you not aware of the distance between the pain of absence and meditating on the Absolute? . . . Why then do you call to drowning men to hang on to the foam?"[39]

The description of the path of *viraha* here gives rise to poems that are no doubt among the most beautiful ever composed in India and indeed in the world, for what experience can be more universal than that of pain and separation? "Nights, the torture of love is so intense that no heart can rest, in house or in forest; days, our eyes watch intently down the road, sending streams of tears down the breast. Even now we harbour the hope the pain will ease, but our stock of sighs is vanishing as we count the days of the awful separation that will cause us longing women to leave behind our bodies";[40] "What kind of love is this love of ours? For our bodies still

37. *Ātman* and *Brahman* are the two central concepts of the *vedānta*. *Ātman* is the innermost principle within man. *Brahman* is the Absolute beyond all, the ground from which springs everything. Following on from the *Upaniṣad*, Śaṅkara expounded the identical nature of *ātman* and *Brahman*: to realize this is to obtain *mokṣa*, the much sought-after mystical liberation.

38. Soûr-Dâs, *Pastorales*, 134.

39. Soûr-Dâs, *Pastorales*, 135.

40. Sūrdās, *Sūr's Ocean*, 457.

remain, though Hari has gone . . . They're pierced and pierced by the arrows of separation as they fill and fill, thinking of the time he said he'd come. Life and death have become two heavy burdens";[41] "Hari lives in our hearts, so you say, but day and night our eyes burn for him—our eyelids never rest: we scan the four directions, scorched by fire of separation."[42]

Such is *viraha*, the religion of Love in its highest form. It is a ceaseless meditation on the *guṇa*, the Beloved's features and qualities; this meditation becomes more and more painful at every stage because the Beloved has disappeared. Nonetheless, the more acute the suffering, the more intense becomes the love that unites us to Him, for it is precisely the crucible in which every trace of the ego that separates us from Him is finally burnt to cinders: "For Kṛṣna's dark body, for His radiant lotus face and for the sweet joyful laughter from His mouth—it is for a glimpse of That that our eyes are dying of thirst."[43] Thus we may easily understand how the *gopī*, with a sweep of the hand, refuse all the paths that would have them concentrate solely on an ineffable Absolute, *nirguṇa*—that is, literally, having no *guṇa*, no attribute nor quality. With a pinch of humour, all the adepts of *vedānta* are swept away in the direction of Benares on the banks of the Ganges: "All the supporters of the 'Unqualified,' they are in Kāśī, in the city of Śiva."[44] In Vṛindāvan on the banks of the Yamunā, the river of love, there is but a single spiritual path, the one in which pain is the most precious experience, for it is the hallmark of an unshakeable devotion (*bhakti*) towards the Lord, whatever the cost: "Uddhav, it is in separation that one truly loves! . . . Whoever has embarked on the path of love, takes no heed of pleasure or suffering!"[45]

The Western reader might stand open-mouthed when confronted with such a radical stance making *viraha* not only the final flowering of *bhakti*, but even, such as the *gopī* taught it to Uddhav, the only way open to the lovers of Kṛṣna. Indeed, such a radical spiritual path need in no way pale before the path in which Śaṅkara makes all material duality dissolve into the One-without-a-second (*ekam eva advitīyam*),[46] the Light of the eternal *Brahman*. It is no doubt a faculty peculiar to India, to at the same

41. Sūrdās, *Sūr's Ocean*, 461.
42. Sūrdās, *Sūr's Ocean*, 463.
43. Soûr-Dâs, *Pastorales*, 136.
44. Soûr-Dâs, *Pastorales*, 138.
45. Soûr-Dâs, *Pastorales*, 139.
46. *Chāndogya Upaniṣad* 6.2.1.

proclaim that Truth is One and that, in order to attain it, there are many paths. And so, it is a vertiginous path of "love in separation, in which the devotee, for whom nothing exists any longer but the Lord with Whom he is intimately united, yet feels the excruciating pains of separation from Him."[47] The luminous lines written by the Jesuit Pierre Fallon (1912–1985), whose ministry in the Bengali Hindu context of Calcutta was remarked for its intellectual excellence, state that "the *viraha* (pangs of separation) is itself the highest form of union possible for the *bhakta* who, as *jīvan-mukta* (liberated but still alive), is still tied to a material body, still deprived of the final and blissful *videha-mukti* (heaven)."[48] Charlotte Vaudeville used similar terms to describe the *viraha* path which, as opposed to Sankara's non-duality leads to *mokṣa* (freedom from web of *saṃsāra*) right in this life-time and this body (*jīvan-mukti*): "In this world there is no remedy for the pain of loneliness: the *gopī* have chosen to experience this torment and therein lies their *dharma*, their own religion, and the very essence of their devotion which, according to Sūrdās, constitutes the most perfect expression of Krishnaite *bhakti*."[49] If then "this beautiful triumph of *bhakti* over Yoga, of the feminine heart over the false wisdom of the savants"[50] carries with it no other destiny for Kṛṣṇa's lovers than to be wandering souls consumed by pain, one is brought to the understanding that the sole reason for the existence of Creation—an eruption into duality that Śaṅkara relinquished into the realm of illusion or *māyā*—is to enable the *līlā* to be enacted as a play of love and pain between the Lord and his true lover. Tears are what make it possible for a human being to survive, by quieting the inner fire, thus preventing it from totally destroying the one who is prey to its flames. This is how the *gopī* describe it to Uddhav the messenger:

> Make him show us some mercy, some love. Go tell Hari everything—tell him how things are moving along in the Braj these days. Go and tell him what your eyes have seen—the burning of this forest fire—for how can we ourselves describe the pain our hearts are bearing? It brings us too much shame. Once, long ago, we wanted to end it all, but then we'd get the wish to see him again,

47. Smet and Neuner, *Religious Hinduism*, 308.
48. Smet and Neuner, *Religious Hinduism*, 308.
49. Soûr-Dâs, *Pastorales*, 58.
50. Soûr-Dâs, *Pastorales*, 58.

> and now if our bodies are still not dead from burning, it's only thanks to tears we've shed for *Sūr's* Lord.[51]

Thereupon Uddhav went back to Kṛṣna, this time bearing the *gopī*'s message to their Beloved—telling the love and pain with which they are filled by the trial of separation from Him:

> How can one speak of what is happening in the Braj? Listen, Śyām, how they pass their days, the people who live there without you. Cowherd girls and cows, cowherds and calves with grimy faces and emaciated limbs—they're utterly bereft, like lotuses whose petals have been lost to the assault of winter snows. Wherever I would go, they'd all come out to see me, wanting to know how you are, and love has made them so sick at heart that they'd cling to my feet to keep me from leaving.[52]

"Hari, how can I tell you how terribly they suffer waiting to see you one day?"[53] The emissary himself is lost for words to describe the incandescence spilling over from the hearts of the inhabitants of Vṛindāvan: "O Hari, how to describe the pain of the Braj? . . . By their sighing, *gopa* and *gopī* revive the flame of the glowing embers of separation."[54] But the one who had set out to spread the teachings of *vedānta* does not return unscathed: now he himself is a convert to *viraha-prem*, the path of love in separation which knows no other joy and no other pain than to recall each one of the attributes (*guṇa*) of the Beloved: "I had come to teach them the 'Unqualified' and here I am, an adept of the 'Qualified.'"[55] This is why Uddhav could close his report to Kṛṣna with the words: "Blessed, blessed are those women of the Braj who have no other support than You! On beholding the overflowing love there, I was stunned; I stood stock still, like an owl."[56] "O Mādhav, hear how they love, there in the Braj! For a whole six months I watched and meditated on the love of the *gopī*: not for a single moment did they

51. Sūrdās, *Sūr's Ocean*, 513.

52. Sūrdās, *Sūr's Ocean*, 535.

53. Sūrdās, *Sūr's Ocean*, 539.

54. Soûr-Dâs, *Pastorales*, 141.

55. Soûr-Dâs, *Pastorales*, 140. The *Bhāgavata Purāṇa* did not intend Uddhav's conversion to the path of *viraha*; still, it attributes to him this confession made to the *gopī*: "By the wholehearted love that ruled you because of your separation (*viraha*) from the Transcendental Lord, oh glorious ones, you have done me a great favour" (10.47.27).

56. Soûr-Dâs, *Pastorales*, 142.

remove Śyām from their heart. . . . Once I'd I witnessed their love, I found all wisdom lacking in taste!"[57]

However, Uddhav's tale is not the final outcome of the *Sūr-Sāgar*: Sūrdās added one last chapter in which he relates the almost surreptitious return of Kṛṣna to the Braj, many years later. He was then reigning in far-off Dvārkā and was accompanied by his new spouse Rukminī. We need to remember that Kṛṣna himself suffered from being far from Vṛindāvan: "Only once I see the people of the Braj again, will joy return to my heart";[58] and in a way, the pain of *viraha* which filled the *gopī* is a partaking in Kṛṣna's pain at being separated from them. This, as we have said, is the real meaning of *bhakti:* partaking in the Divine Mystery—in the divine life and divine feelings, let us boldly state—so that in the final consummation, devotee and Lord become as One. This final Unity pervades the briefly exchanged glance in which Kṛṣna beholds Rādhā for a last time—a brief sunny interval in the gloom of daily exile: "When Mādhav finds Rādhā again, Rādhā and Mādhav, Mādhav and Rādhā are but one being! . . . Smiling, He said to her, 'You and I are a single being' and, so saying, He sent her back to the Braj."[59] Following these few instants of chaste intimacy with his chosen one, He went on to meet the *gopī* and delivered his final teachings: "Hari said to the women of the Braj: 'I hold the Braj dear above all else! Never was I far from you, I have always been close to you. . . . If anyone cherishes Me, I in turn cherish her with equal tenderness: My devotee is to Me as My own image in the mirror!' As He spoke, he embraced each one of them, His eyes brimming with tears."[60] Sūrdās, in concluding his immense tome of poems, now delivers the key of this *līlā* of love and of pain: "Yet, was there ever separation? No, it was merely so in appearance: forever, Kṛṣna's heart belongs to the Braj, and the heart of the Braj to Kṛṣna."[61] Here we have the other aspect of this unique truth of perfect devotion *Bhakti* which up to now had found expression only through the experience of *viraha*: that the separation and pain were but the proofs of the Lord's mysterious Presence in the heart of His devotee purified by ceaseless weeping. Only those can know it, who have suffered that burning love and who have drained its bitter cup to the dregs. Henceforth, because they have explored

57. Soûr-Dâs, *Pastorales*, 143.
58. Soûr-Dâs, *Pastorales*, 127.
59. Soûr-Dâs, *Pastorales*, 144–45.
60. Soûr-Dâs, *Pastorales*, 145.
61. Soûr-Dâs, *Pastorales*, 58.

one by one the pangs of separation, they truly know God—without the remotest danger of falling back into themselves. Pure *bhakti* is their nature now: a fiery tension, an ocean of love, a gaping emptiness silently permeated by a Presence.

THE BRIDEGROOM IS TAKEN AWAY

In the figure of Kṛṣna and all the forms of devotion he generated, there lies a powerfully erotic theme that is both poetic and mystical. Herein we find a specifically Indian trait which is "to choose everything"—as Thérèse of Lisieux (1873–1897) would have put it—to call everything into play and do all in one's power in service to the ceaseless spiritual quest. However India is not alone in employing erotic language to describe man's ultimate path; it would seem that on the contrary, among the many mystical traditions throughout the world, only a minority have not used this state as a kind of jumping-off board—not so as to remain wallowing in the flesh, but in order to spring up towards the highest peaks of the Spirit by concentrating, purifying, and transfiguring one of the noblest expressions of life swirling within the human being. Yet in comparison with the poems of Jayadeva in his *Gītagovinda*, the verses of Sūrdās display a sober containment of eroticism (*sṛṅgārarasa*), as if the blind bard of Vṛindāvan had sought to record a mere outline of it by simply reproducing its two major manifestations: the presence (*saṃbhoga*), and, especially, the absence (*viraha*).

As we are now opening out our enquiry into different mystical traditions, this is a good moment to take a closer look at Sufism. Going beyond the legendary encounter between Sūrdās and the young Muslim Emperor Akbar—renowned for his broad welcome to all religions—it is indeed quite natural to draw a parallel between Krishnaite Mysticism and Sufism, since each of these paths developed almost concurrently in North India, witness to the fact that religious and cultural intermingling are the most fertile soil for the destiny of humankind. We might be reminded of the unforgettable love stories of Leyla and Majnun which have traversed the various regions of Islam, inspiring marvellous *ghazals* and other Sufi poems. In Arabic, the word "majnun" designates someone who is madly in love until death, such as the noble Bedouin Qays, whose fiery gaze transfigured Leyla's almost ordinary appearance, leading him to worship her with ever more incandescent love whenever she was physically absent, for it was at that precise moment that he beheld the True Beauty of Leyla. . . . We might also speak of the *dhikr* (the act of remembering Allah) and of *samāʿ* (listening to praises of the Divine) which lead the Sufi on to *fanā*, the annihilation of his human personality and his absorption into God. It suffices to quote from Islam two wonderful passages—volcanic eruptions—the first of which is by al-Ḥallaj (858–922) who, in his *Dīwān*, had begged "the night of his abandonment to fall, now, be it slowly or suddenly, no matter, so long as it is He, my Friend:"

> Silence, deafness, thin speech
> Knowledge, discovery, emaciation
> Clay then fire then light
> Coal then shadow then the sun
> Rough then smooth then desert
> River then ocean then dryness
> Drunk then sober then love
> Nearness then abundance then kindness
> Gripping then loosing then erasing
> Parting then joining then effacing
> Taking then denying then pulling
> Describing then revealing then clothing
> Words for those for whom
> This world is not worth a farthing.[62]

The second is the unforgettable lament of the *ney*—the reed flute—with which Rūmī (1207–1273) opens his *Masnavī*:

> Listen to the reed, how it is complaining.
> It is telling about separations.
> "Ever since I was severed from the reed field,
> Men and women have lamented.
> I want a heart torn, torn from separation,
> So that I may explain the pain of yearning."
> . . .
> The reed's cry is fire . . . it is not wind!
> Whoever doesn't have this fire, may be nothing!
> It is the fire of Love that fell into the reed.
> It is the ferment of Love that fell into the wine.
> The reed is the companion of anyone who was severed from a friend.
> Its melodies tore our veils.
> Who has seen a poison and a remedy like the reed?

62. Al-Ḥallaj, *Dīwān*.

> Who has seen a harmonious companion and a yearning friend like the reed?
> The reed is telling the story of the path full of blood;
> It is telling the stories of Majnun's love.[63]

For those whose spiritual tradition asserts that: "stern as death is love" for "its flames are a blazing fire!" (Song 8:6), Sūrdās' poems and his path of *viraha* will not seem totally foreign, and thus it is in the Christian world that we wish to end our journey through the land of exile, guided by a remark of Benedict XVI (1927–2022): "I have dealt with the myth of the God Kṛṣna, which demonstrates astounding parallels to the history and character of Jesus, and is of great importance for interreligious dialogue."[64] We would have surely already remembered of the *Canticle of Canticles*: "I opened to my beloved, but my beloved has departed, gone. I sought him but I did not find him; I called to him but he did not answer me" (Song 5:6). Or even these even more dramatic verses at the opening of the splendid *Spiritual Canticle* of John of the Cross (1542–1591)—Sūrdās' faraway contemporary in the Golden Age of Spain:

> Where have you hidden, Beloved,
> and left me moaning?
> You fled like the stag
> after wounding me;
> I went out calling you,
> but you were gone.[65]

One would wish to quote the entire poem, especially in its original tongue, but we shall only add two other stanzas, still from the opening passage:

> Why, since you wounded
> this heart, don't you heal it?
> And why, since you stole it from me,
> do you leave it so,
> and fail to carry off what you have stolen?
>
> Extinguish these miseries,
> since no one else can stamp them out;
> and may my eyes behold you,

63. Rūmī, *Masnavī*, 1.1–6; 17–25.
64. Benedict XVI, *Last Testament*, 111.
65. John of the Cross, "Spiritual Canticle," stanza 1, in *Complete Works* (1979), 410.

because you are their light,
and I would open them to you alone.[66]

For most of his poems, John of the Cross wrote impressive commentaries in which he expounded his spiritual doctrine, at the cost of losing therein some of the intensely mystic quality which only poetry can express. In relation to our present enquiry it would be useful to re-read a few lines in which the Spanish Carmelite saint explains the first stanza—"Adónde te escondite, Amado, y me dejaste con gemido?"[67] and takes us back to the initial pain inflicted on the soul by the disappearance of the Bridegroom—on the soul who: "being wounded by her love . . . has still to suffer the absence of her Beloved and is not yet loosed from her mortal flesh that she may be able to have fruition of Him on the glory of eternity."[68] Here, John explains that "[the Spouse] hides and reveals Himself, as the Beloved is wont to do in the visits which He makes to the souls, and in the withdrawals and absences which He makes them experience after such visits."[69] In almost clinical fashion, he spells out the suffering born of the separation from the Beloved:

> There comes to pass in the soul this grief that is so great, inasmuch as when God inflicts upon the soul that wound of love its will rises with sudden celerity to the possession of the Beloved, Whom it has felt so near by reason of that His touch of love which it has experienced. And with equal celerity it feels His absence and is conscious of sighing thereat, since in one and the same moment He disappears from the soul and hides Himself, and it remains in emptiness and with the greater sorrow and sighing according to the greatness of its desire to possess Him.[70]

In these lines we can almost hear the poems of the *Sūr-Sāgar* and rejoice in such hidden harmonies that bring together spiritual beings beyond spaces and beyond times, signalling a secret unity of the human spirit in its

66. John of the Cross, "Spiritual Canticle," stanzas 9 and 10, in *Complete Works* (1979), 411.

67. "Where have you hidden, Beloved, and left me moaning?"

68. John of the Cross, "Spiritual Canticle A," stanza 1, exposition (1), in *Complete Works* (1934), 31.

69. John of the Cross, "Spiritual Canticle A," stanza 1, exposition (7), in *Complete Works* (1934), 34.

70. John of the Cross, "Spiritual Canticle A," stanza 1, exposition (10), in *Complete Works* (1934), 35.

insatiate quest for the Absolute. Nevertheless, we shall take care to avoid the trap of levelling down all the characteristics specific to each spiritual tradition to obtain a fallacious unity—a kind of "Mystics International"—whose anthem is always sung in opposition to—and with intent to discredit—the religious institutions to which these fiery beings belonged. Moreover, for a Christian, there lies a great temptation to cause the new wine which the Christ came to serve to the wedding guests to turn into vinegar.[71] . . . But let us get back to John of the Cross who, still in his commentary on the first stanza of his *Spiritual Canticle*, says: "this affliction and sorrow for the absence of God is wont to be so great in those that are approaching ever nearer to perfection, at the time of these Divine wounds, that, if the Lord provided not for them, they would die."[72] It is interesting to note here that the suffering caused by the separation is only temporary: it pertains to the spiritual state of the beginners, or rather, to the few chosen souls who "approach the state of perfection." For these, the day will come for the betrothal preceding the spiritual marriage: "And upon this happy day, not only is there an end of the soul's former vehement yearnings and plaints of love, but, being adorned with the good things . . . she enters into an estate of peace and delight and sweetness of love."[73]

Pain, then, is but a stage towards the fullness of the Presence of the Beloved in mystic marriage. It is quite astonishing to note at this point that the spiritual itinerary laid out by John of the Cross is on practically every count the exact opposite of that of Sūrdās. The Christian mystic goes from the absence to the presence, from suffering to infinite delights, whereas the path of *viraha* runs in the opposite direction:—from presence to absence, and from the whirlpool of *rāsa-līlā* to the bitterest tears which sear the devotee with pain. It would be wiser to cease all comparison here, for we are looking at very different spiritual worlds. Should a Christian however be tempted to sneer and proclaim that Hinduism holds no promise other than hellish torments, one would need remind him that more than one great saint of the Church experienced to the full Christ's words addressed to Silouan the Athonite (1866–1938): "keep your soul in hell and do not despair." One such is Thérèse of Lisieux whose very last months of her brief existence

71. I have dealt at length with the question of Christian mysticism in the light of mystics from the other religions, in another book. Cf. Vagneux, *Co-esse*, 461–542.

72. John of the Cross, "Spiritual Canticle A," stanza 1, exposition, in *Complete Works* (1934), 37.

73. John of the Cross, "Spiritual Canticle A," stanza 13, exposition, in *Complete Works* (1934), 75.

seemed to her like "travelling through a tunnel" leading to a "wall rising up to the heavens and covering the starry firmament."[74] Indeed, the young Carmelite confided this to her spiritual brother, a missionary in China: "the thought of eternal beatitude hardly thrills my heart" for "suffering has been my Heaven here upon earth."[75] Even closer to our time, we might recall the "Saint of Darkness,"[76] Mother Teresa (1910–1997) who for five decades was cast into an inner exile beyond all spiritual consolation—"terrible pain" about which she wrote that it "has never made me desire to have it different.—What's more, I want it to be like this for as long as He wants it."[77] There are no doubt other names one could quote, though God alone knows who are the souls He has immolated in order to enable them to in a way participate in the mystery of Redemption of the world. Moreover here, the pain of separation which inhabited both Thérèse of Lisieux and Teresa of Calcutta should not be considered only from a mere personal angle as a "night of the senses" and a "night of faith," such as John of the Cross described them. It is more appropriate to connect their inner suffering to the suffering of mankind, not only because the latter is separated from God, but also because painful exile has become a commonplace condition for modern man. Here we are dealing with a redeeming separation, leading Thérèse of Lisieux to say shortly before her death, that she was "from now, seated at the sinners' table," and Teresa to write that: "The physical situation of my poor left in the streets unwanted, unloved, unclaimed—are the true picture of my own spiritual life, of my love for Jesus."[78] So what, then, is this substitution by total identification with the other's pain, if not a true "participation"—a "com-passion." There is a good reason for having stressed that the etymology of the term "bhakti" lies in the Sanskrit root [*bhaj*]: 'to participate in.' Were we not surprised at Rādhā's cry: "In a single body, for your sake, I have endured sixteen thousand pains, and Rādhā's soul has traversed each body"?[79] Here, it is almost as if India unknowingly drew close to the mystery of Redemption—and the Buddhist world

74. Thérèse of Lisieux, Manuscript C.

75. Thérèse of Lisieux, letter to Father Adolphe Roulland, MEP, July 14, 1897.

76. Letter from Mother Teresa to Father Neuner, March 6, 1962, in Mother Teresa, *Come Be My Light*, 230. Cf. Vagneux, *Indian Portraits*, 35–44.

77. Letter from Mother Teresa to Father Neuner, May 12, 1962, in Mother Teresa, *Come Be My Light*, 232.

78. Letter from Mother Teresa to Father Neuner, May 12, 1962, in Mother Teresa, *Come Be My Light*, 232.

79. Soûr-Dâs, *Pastorales*, 113.

continues to state this mystery in the great prayer of the Bodhisattva: "For as long as space endures and for as long as the world lasts, may I live dispelling the miseries of the world."[80] All these testimonies from the Christian world and elsewhere ought to lead us to contemplate with deep reverence and extreme gratitude the Lord's elect souls, who, unbeknown to us, are called to love Him in the suffering of separation so that they, in an infinite merger, may be united with the painful destiny of all Mankind.

Furthermore, we might reverse our perspective to perceive this painful nocturnal love filling certain saints as a participation in God's very own suffering—He who was the first to feel the *viraha* on the evening of the first sin when He scoured all of Paradise calling to his first creature: "Adam, where are you?" (Gen 3:9). One who associated himself with the divine agony of the Eternal Father whose Son has left for the abysses of death was Francis of Assisi (1181–1226) who went so far as to welcome the scars of the most searing love—he, the *Poverello*, whom tradition is wont to depict roaming the countryside, blind from weeping, and crying out: "Love is not loved!" That is exactly what it is to "have the same attitude that is also in Christ Jesus" (Phil 2:5), according to Paul's exhortation to the Philippians. And it is the hallmark of great saints to completely enter into God's open heart and commune with the "great [painful] love he had for us" (Eph 2:4). Perceiving God in this way as being the first bereft, the first abandoned, had often led me to read the *Canticle of Canticles* back to front, no longer perceiving the beloved as the human soul, but as God himself, gone in search of whom his "heart loves" (Song 3:1). Lastly, although Christianity seems to be unsurpassable in this domain, it would still appear that India had glimpsed—as in a mirage—the mysterious way in which man can participate in the suffering and sense of abandon felt by God, as expressed by Kṛṣna to Uddhav; "Only once I see the people of the Braj again, will joy return to my heart."[81]

Thus, our reading of Sūrdās' poems and discovering of the path of *viraha* can bring new light to bear on certain Christian destinies and authentic spiritual paths, and other lives that remain hidden in the night. What one hopes for from a true "emulation of sanctity"[82] between religious traditions is a fresh look at the particular features of each one. In examining the theme of *viraha* as a spiritual accomplishment there lies however no

80. Śāntideva, *Bodhicaryāvatāra* 10.55.

81. Soûr-Dâs, *Pastorales*, 127.

82. Monchanin, Letter to M. Divien.

intent to question John of the Cross, insofar as he himself, as well as a number of authorized authors in his wake, added an inflection to the postulated succession of three stages—beginner, proficient, and perfect—which probably were originally outlined by Origen (185–253).[83] What is more, in a rare confidence concerning his mystical life, the great Alexandrian also had recourse to the term 'absence' to hint at his own spiritual experience:

> The bride then beholds the Bridegroom; and He, as soon as she has seen Him, goes away. He does this frequently throughout the *Canticle*; and that is something nobody can understand who has not suffered it himself. God is my witness that I have often perceived the Bridegroom drawing near me and being most intensely present with me; then suddenly He has withdrawn and I could not find Him, though I sought to do so. I long, therefore, for Him to come again, and sometimes He does so. Then, when He has appeared and I lay hold of Him, He slips away once more; and, when He has so slipped away, my search for Him begins anew. So does He act with me repeatedly, until in truth I hold Him and go up, leaning on my Beloved's arm.[84]

In addition to what has been said about pain as a participating in God's suffering, according to Saint Francis of Assisi, or in suffering mankind, as for Thérèse of Lisieux and Mother Teresa, we need to return once more to the incandescent fire in Origen's imperishable legacy to the Church. Whilst being aware that this requires further argumentation, we shall here make do with a passage of his seventh homily on *Leviticus* which, many years later, caused the monks of Clairvaux to tremble as Saint Bernard (1090–1153) read it to them. In this homily, whilst commenting on Jesus' promise at the Last Supper that "he would not drink the fruit of vine until the days when he will drink anew in the kingdom of his Father" (Matt 26:29), Origen gave a striking explanation of the painful passion to which the Christ submits himself today and continues so right up to the return of the last sinner: "At this very moment my Saviour is grieving over my sins. . . . How then could he, the advocate for my sins, drink the wine of joy while I grieve him by my sinning?"[85] Such is the "passion of love" endured by the Saviour, causing Him continuous suffering for our sake; the passion which, elsewhere, had brought Origen to ask himself whether "the Father . . . in some way suffers"

83. Cf. Origen, *Homilies on the Canticle of Canticles* Prologue 2.7.

84. Origen, *Homilies on the Canticle of Canticles* 1.7.

85. Origen, *Homilies on Leviticus* 7.2.

and come to the conclusion that "the Father himself is not without suffering. When he is prayed to, he has pity and compassion; he suffers the passion of love and comes into those in whom he cannot be, in view of the greatness of his nature, and on account of us he endures human sufferings."[86] In another passage of this same seventh homily on *Leviticus*, Origen opened up the field of vision to the entire extended Church (thus avoiding the trap of the selfish 'my soul and my God' into which self-styled spiritual seekers fall far too often) and he was bold to make the saints participate in God's suffering: "For not even the Apostles have entered as yet into their joy, but they must wait till I become a sharer in their joy. Nor do the saints when they leave this world receive the full reward of their merits, but they stand in waiting for us, tardy and sluggish though we may be. There can be no perfect joy for them while they still weep over our truancy and grieve for our sins."[87] Each of these luminous observations tell us that we are far from being done with our exploration of the fields of Christian mysticism, especially when it is firmly rooted in genuine solidarity with the entire body of the Church and the destiny of the world—a solidarity which, we may be bold to state, is one of the features of what is *properly* Christian. No doubt there are sainthoods, joys and pains still unknown and un-tasted by us. Also, let us not forget that the *Canticle of Canticles* does not end with the enjoyment of a couple in which the lovers take possession of one another, but on the contrary, its closing passage is the poignant call from the bride to her Beloved, as if no true love existed outside separation and the inextinguishable desire to be reunited: "Go away, my Beloved, like a gazelle or a young stag on the mountains of spices!" (Song 8:14).

Above all, it is my wish that this journey through the Hindu landscapes of the Braj, as well as the few incursions into Christian mysticism that in its own way bears witness to love in the pain of separation, might shed new light on an enigmatic phrase which Christ addressed to his disciples as an indication on how to behave during His Blessed Passion, revealing His infinite love for the Father though He is in the abyss of abandon:[88] "But the days

86. Origen, *Homilies on Ezekiel* 6.6.

87. Origen, *Homilies on Leviticus*, 7.2.

88. To further develop this idea that the Passion is the maximum extent of the Son's love for the Father whilst in the abyss of separation from Him—and also in a way, the maximum extent of the love Christ showed to men in the darkest depths of sin, which in essence is separation—we may refer to Hans Urs von Balthasar (1905–1988) and his theology of the Holy Spirit at the time of the Cross and the descent into Hell. On the subject of this Spirit of Love that unites Father and Son in separation (*Trennung*), we

will come when the bridegroom is taken away from them, and then they will fast on that day" (Mark 2:20). First He was taken away on the Cross, then through the Ascension into heaven, and thus, separation from the master became the daily condition of the disciple, who is called again and again to spiritual fasting from the Beloved Presence: "Men of Galilee, why are you standing there looking at the sky? This Jesus who has been taken up from you into heaven will return in the same way as you have seen him going into heaven" (Acts 1:11). The Eucharist is in some way the sacrament of separation from the physical presence of the Risen One since its celebration at an inn on the road from Emmaus to Jerusalem: "And it happened, as he was at the table with them, that he took the bread, said the blessing, then broke it and gave it to them. Their eyes opened and they recognised him . . . but he had vanished from before them" (Luke 24:30–31). Against all the theological deviations that have reified the presence of Christ in the Eucharist, it is worth remembering that this is a spiritual fast from the sensible immediacy—"Visus, tactus, gustus, in te fallitur"[89]—where we learn indeed to recognize Christ with the eyes of faith alone and "a burning heart within us" (Luke 24:32). *Viraha*, to love in separation, is it not precisely to fast and to adore in these dark and present times whilst we await the return in glory of the bridegroom when God will be "all in all" (1 Cor 15:28) and when "He will wipe every tear from our eyes" (Rev 21:4)?

---

shall only quote two texts: "It needs to be brought out that the divine abandonment (*Gottesverlassenheit*) of the Son during the Passion is one mode of His union with the Father in the Holy Spirit" (Balthasar, *Dramatique divine*, 4:234). "It is in the Cross and the abandonment (*Verlassenheit*) of Jesus that the distance (*Distanz*) between the Son and the Father is made clearly manifest for the first time, and even the Spirit, which joins both by forming their 'We,' in revealing their unity, takes the appearance of pure distance" (*Dramatique divine*, 3:296).

89. Thomas Aquinas, *Adoro te devote*: "The sight, the touch, the taste of you are lacking."

9

The Tree with Celestial Roots

Oṃ dyauḥ śāntirantarikṣaṃ śāntiḥ
pṛthivī śāntirāpaḥ śāntiroṣadhayaḥ |
śāntiḥ vanaspatayaḥ śāntirviśvedevāḥ śāntirbrahma śāntiḥ
sarvaṃ śāntiḥ śāntireva śāntiḥ sā mā śāntiredhi ||

To the heavens be peace, to the sky and to the earth,
to the waters be peace, to plants and all trees,
to the God be peace, to Brahma be peace,
to all men be peace, again and again
—peace also to me![1]

In this ancient prayer of the *Yajur Veda*, where the accumulation of the term *śānti*, "peace," has a performative role, it is striking that the cosmos is described in all its dimensions before gods and men appear. In the universe over which peace is still invoked today with the same ancient words, trees hold a special place. Five of them have been continually venerated by

1. *Yajur Veda* 36.17.

Indian people: the pipal (*aśvattha, ficus religiosus*), the banyan (*vaṭa, ficus indica*), the neem tree (*niṃba, azadirachta indica*), the bael (*bilva, aegle marmelos*) and the myrobolan (*amalā, phyllanthus emblica*). The trees with their majestic foliage lift the gaze and invite us to penetrate the mysteries of the cosmos. True mediators between earth and heaven, they recall also the *yūpa*, the sacrificial pole where at the dawn of time the Puruṣa, the primordial man, was tied. A hymn in the *Ṛg Veda* sings of the tree of sacrifice, the *kalpavṛkṣa*,[2] that tree "bringer of every spiritual and material treasure, [from which] flows grace from heaven."[3]

> At the time of sacrifice, O Lord of the wood, the worshipers smear you with sacred oil. When you stand upright or when you repose on earth's bosom, you still will grant us good fortune. . . . Lord of the wood, take now your stance on this, the loftiest spot of all earth. Well-fixed and measured one, give to the worshiper, who brings a sacrifice, honour and glory.[4]

One of the most emblematic images of Vedic revelation is the cosmic tree embracing the whole universe with its outstretched branches: "With your apex you touch the heavens, with your middle portion you fill the air, with your foot you establish the earth."[5] Similar to the sun which "sustains on high a heap of light, the rays of which are pointed downwards, while their base is above,"[6] it is the tree with celestial roots—*ūrdhvamūla*: "There is an eternal pipal tree with its roots above (*ūrdhvamūlo*), its branches below. It is the bright, it is *Brahman*; it is called the immortal. On it all the world depend: no one goes beyond it."[7] It was again in the shade of a pipal—*aśvattha* in Sanskrit—that Siddhārtha Gautama (563–483) sat and attained enlightenment. His followers left a lasting impression on Indian thought, causing it to lose its original optimism about the universe, which, in their eyes, was now seen as the snares of the *saṃsāra* from which liberation was

2. In fact, the legend, of the *kalpavṛkṣa*, the "wishing tree," is posterior to the *Veda*. It is found in the *Purāṇa*. The marvellous *kalpavṛkṣa* would be one of the gifts that surges from the primordial waters during the churning of the ocean of milk. The *Purāṇa* also speak of the *akṣayavaṭa*, the "eternal banyan" which alone will survive the flood at the final dissolution (*pralaya*).

3. Panikkar, *Vedic Experience*, 372.

4. *Ṛg Veda* 3.8.1–3.

5. *Śatapatha Brāhmaṇa* 3.7.1.14.

6. *Ṛg Veda* 1.24.7.

7. *Kaṭha Upaniṣad* 2.3.1.

needed at all costs. Even the *Bhagavadgītā*, in its reiteration of the previously quoted verse from the *Kaṭha Upaniṣad*, does not escape the pessimism that came to tarnish the sumptuous Vedic image:

> There is a tree, the tree of transmigration, the *aśvattha* tree everlasting. Its roots are above in heaven (*ūrdhvamūlaṃ*), and its branches are here below. Its leaves are sacred songs, and he who knows them knows the *Veda*. Its branches spread from earth to heaven, and the powers of nature give them life. It buds are the pleasures of the senses. Far down below, its roots stretch into the world of men, binding a mortal through selfish actions. Men do not see the changing form of that tree, not its beginning, not its end, nor where its roots are. But let the wise see, and with the strong sword of dispassion let him cut this strong-rooted tree and seek that path wherefrom those who go never return.[8]

It took a few more generations for the successors of Śaṅkara to affirm that "*Brahman* is real and the universe unreal," "Brahma satyaṃ, jagan mithyā."[9] At the same time, a later *Upaniṣad* concluded that the world is pure illusion, *māyā*: "On the very day one is disillusioned, on the same day one becomes a renouncer."[10] To gain the only thing necessary, one had to accept "to leave behind desires for sons, desires for wealth and desires for worlds" and "to live on alms."[11] Such radicalism had no other justification than "the mystery of glory and immortality, raised to the highest heavens, hidden in the secret of the heart, where only those who have renounced everything can penetrate."[12] An essential figure of Indian civilization, the *saṃnyāsin*, "the ascetic, swathed in wind, [who has] put dirty red rags on,"[13] was then the most faithful guardian of the quest for the Absolute which from the beginning had made the heart of his people beat, drawing them up towards the celestial roots of the eternal tree.

In its beginning and its end, the Bible also finds support in the powerful trunks of the divine trees. The book of *Genesis* mentions two of them: "The Lord God made all kinds of trees grow out of the ground, with a desirable appearance and tasty fruit; there was also the tree of life in the middle

8. *Bhagavadgītā* 15.1–4.
9. Śaṅkara, *Vivekacūḍāmaṇi* 20.
10. *Jābāla Upaniṣad* 4.
11. *Bṛhadāraṇyaka Upaniṣad* 4.4.22.
12. *Mahānārāyaṇa Upaniṣad* 12.14.
13. *Ṛg Veda* 10.136.

of the garden, and the tree of the knowledge of good and evil" (Gen 2:9). If the first disobedience took place under the shade of these trees and once Adam and Eve were expelled, God "set the Cherubim at the east of the Garden of Eden, armed with a sharp sword, to guard the entrance to the tree of life" (Gen 3:24), the vision of the heavenly Jerusalem in the book of *Revelation* indicates that "in the middle of the city square, between the two arms of the river, there is a tree of life that bears fruit twelve times: every month it brings forth its fruit; and the leaves of this tree are medicine for the nations" (Rev 22:2). A legend dear to medieval Christians relates that Seth implored the Cherubim to give him a branch from the tree of the knowledge of good and evil to plant on Golgotha, where only the eternal Son tasted its bitter fruit as he hung on the wood of the cross. In his hymn *Crux fidelis*, which once accompanied the Church's prayer on Good Friday, Venantius Fortunat (530–610) sang the austere glory of the new and definitive tree of life:

O faithful cross! The one noble tree, among all trees;
no forest yields your like, in foliage, flower and fruit;
sweet is the wood bearing, a sweet burden with a sweet nail.
Bend your limbs, O lofty tree, relax your tense fibres,
and let that hardness, which your nature gave you, soften;
that you may stretch on a tender trunk, the members of the heavenly king.
You alone were worthy, to bear the price of the ages,
and, as a seaman, to ready the port for the shipwrecked world,
whom the Precious Blood anointed, shed forth from the flesh of the Lamb.

A few centuries later, in the gold of the mosaics, the Roman artists of the basilica of Saint Clement immortalized the tree of the cross, bringing life from its dead beams, until its luxuriant branches embraced the whole of creation and fulfilled the ultimate prophecy of Jesus: "When I am lifted up from the earth, I will draw all men to myself" (John 12:32). This grand vision of the Saviour's cross was based on a Gospel parable: "The kingdom of heaven is like a mustard seed that a man took and sowed in his field. It is the smallest of all seeds, but when it has grown, it outstrips the other vegetable plants and becomes a tree, so that the birds of the air come and make their nests in its branches" (Matt 13:31–32). In this cosmic cross, the Church sees her fully Catholic identity reflected and contemplates the extension of her mission:

> This Tree, vast as heaven itself, rises from earth to the skies, a plant immortal, set firm in the midst of heaven and earth, base of all that

> is, foundation of the universe, support of this world of men, binding-force of all creation, holding within itself all the mysterious essence of man. Secured with the unseen clamps of the Spirit, so that, adjusted to the Divine, it may never bend or warp, with a foot resting firm on the earth it towers to the topmost skies, and spans with its all-embracing arms the boundless gulf of space between.[14]

Faced with the incomparable sacrifice of Christ, the Church can only have as her measure the disproportion of divine love—that inextinguishable love which leads her to cross over the porch again and leave the sanctuary in order to go forth into this world which, through the power of the cross, has become the "Galilee of the nations" (Matt 4:15) where the Risen One always precedes her. It is no longer a question of turning away from the world because, as Emmanuel Mounier (1905–1950) wrote, "there is no Christian renunciation except that which sets up its quarters in the midst of the world."[15] May this optimism, which is not an illusion but the mark of a true catholicism, always guide Christians in their conversations with their contemporaries, following the example of Hans Urs von Balthasar (1905–1988) who, in 1985, confided to Angelo Scola:

> I want to speak of my conviction, nourished by my spiritual journey and by the great men I have come to know, that the Catholic Church, in order to be able to communicate to the modern world the depth of its treasures, should not approach it as a stranger or as an enemy, but should rather infiltrate it in order to assimilate what is valid in the new systems, not externally, but in such a way that these new elements remind her of treasures contained within her, which she has forgotten or has not yet discovered.[16]

14. Pseudo-Chrysostom, "Sixth Homily on Easter," quoted in Lubac, *Catholicism: Christ*, 442–43.

15. Mounier, *L'affrontement chrétien*, 64.

16. Balthasar, *Entretiens sur l'Église*, 21.

10

An Emulation of Sanctity

When the first volume of *Glory of the Lord* was republished in 1967, Hans Urs von Balthasar (1905–1988) added a short note in which he confided: "The overall scope of the present work naturally remains all too Mediterranean. The inclusion of other cultures, especially that of Asia, would have been important and fruitful. But the author's education has not allowed for such an expansion, and a superficial presentation of such material would have been dilettantism. May those qualified come to complete the present fragment."[1] The man Henri de Lubac (1896–1991) called "the most cultured man of our time"[2] had the merit of recognising his shortcomings. However, alongside the sum of philosophical and theological knowledge deployed by Balthasar in his trilogy, we can be astonished that spiritual continents such as India or Buddhism in its twenty-five centuries of growth remained ignored. We would have so much liked Balthasar to have been able to converse with Śaṅkara or Abhinavagupta, and to have invited Āṇḍāl, Utpaladeva or Sūrdās to join the company of mystics who have so deeply inspired his remarkable studies. Like many thinkers who have marked Catholic theology in the twentieth century, Balthasar cannot escape the warning that Paul Tillich (1886–1965) made in 1963: "A Christian theology which is not able to enter into a creative dialogue with the theological thought of other religions misses a world-historical occasion and remains provincial!"[3]

1. Balthasar, *Glory of the Lord*, 1:11.
2. Lubac, *Paradoxe et Mystère de l'Église*, 184.
3. Tillich, *Systematic Theology*, 4:6.

Tillich's diagnosis should be received as the greatest encouragement for theology to be ever more catholic. Indeed, despite the emblematic gesture of the Fathers towards Greek philosophy and that of Thomas Aquinas (1225–1274) towards the Aristotelianism that was rediscovered thanks to Muslim thinkers, Western theology has always run the risk of shutting itself up in its sumptuous fortress, to the point of being autistic to the vast world that surrounds it. No one can doubt that German philosophy is a high-class interlocutor, but if we take a broader view, we will realize that it is only a *continental* philosophy that is fairly localized when seen at the level of the whole world. Of course, one could always retort that it is not the work of Europeans to deal with *vedānta*, but this would be forgetting that since the nineteenth century, the thought of Śaṅkara (788–820) has taken root in the United States, a veritable promised land for Hindu monks and mystics such as Swāmī Vivekānanda (1863–1902) or Paramahaṃsa Yogānanda (1893–1952). As for Buddhism, who could deny that it has become an essential component of Western culture? If one single theologian cannot embrace the whole of humanity, should we then imagine a truly catholic theology on the same model as the universal Church, which is a pluralistic communion of local Churches that is united by the same faith but with particular forms? In the early centuries, in addition to Latin theology, there was a Byzantine theology and a Syriac theology. Despite the sometimes-painful controversies, the twentieth century has seen the development of Latin American, African and Asian theologies which we hope will continue to grow and strengthen. Would it not be the role of the Church of Rome, which "presides in charity"[4] to encourage, in great freedom and "without any conditions other than those imposed upon any child of the Church,"[5] an ever more catholic deployment of theology? This seems to be the renewed ambition of Pope Francis: "The contrary of conversion is immobility, the secret belief that we have nothing else to learn from the Gospel. This is the error of trying to crystallize the message of Jesus in a single, perennially valid form. Instead, its form must be capable of constantly changing, so that its substance can remain constantly the same. True heresy consists not only in preaching another gospel (cf. Gal 1:9), as Saint Paul told us, but also in ceasing to translate its message into today's languages and ways of thinking, which is precisely what the Apostle of the Gentiles did. To preserve means to keep

4. Ignatius of Antioch, *Letter to the Romans*, prologue.

5. Letter from Henri de Lubac to Jules Monchanin, January 18, 1947, in Jacquin, "Henri de Lubac et Jules Monchanin," 11.

alive and not to imprison the message of Christ."[6] This was also the wish of the philosopher Jean-Louis Chrétien (1952–2019), in order that theology would not become exhausted by a lack of perspectives: "All Christian thought must in its own way be missionary and carry the proclamation of the Gospel. To do this it needs to translate and be translated, it must move forward and travel, from one language to another, from one horizon to another. The truth of the spirit cannot be that it wants to preserve the purity of what it thinks by protecting itself from all contact and all encounters, obsessed as it might be by the risk of contamination. Only a weakened life sees its salvation in a sterile claustration, and that which merely preserves itself is already condemned by its fatal and trembling allergy."[7]

A THEOLOGY IN CONVERSATION

In his memorable 1964 encyclical *Ecclesiam Suam*, Paul VI (1897–1978) wrote: "The Church must enter into dialogue with the world in which she lives. She has something to say, a message to give, a conversation to make."[8] It is in fidelity to this ever-present call that I have sought a conversation between the best of the Hindu traditions and Christian theology, guided by the call of Monchanin (1895–1957): "I would like to see reigning between Hindus and Christians, not ignorance and mutual contempt and certainly not the easy syncretism that smooths away the angles and reduces everything to a rather flat moralism, but a real philosophical emulation and above all an emulation of sanctity."[9] Surely, we can measure, at the completion of this journey, how much this is a ridgeline between several pitfalls. Firstly, the mutual ignorance that stultifies the intelligence and leads Christian disciple to deny his Catholicism. Secondly, syncretism which "is artificial, generally the work of rulers or literary men, and presupposes declining faith."[10] A sterile easy solution, this "concordism alters and perverts the two terms that it claims to join together by its arbitrariness and fallacious mediation."[11] "It is an insult to the living God,"[12] as well as to the religious

6. Francis, "Address to the Roman Curia."
7. J.-L. Chrétien, preface to Maalouf, *Une mystique érotique*, 16.
8. Paul VI, *Ecclesiam Suam*, 67.
9. Monchanin, Letter to M. Divien.
10. Lubac, *Catholicism: A Study*, 155.
11. Monchanin, "Guhāntara," 269.
12. Lubac, *Catholicism: A Study*, 155.

tradition with which it claims to enter into dialogue. It is because of this uncompromising rejection of syncretism that the studies in this book have sought to avoid hasty comparisons and reductive similarities between the two religions, because comparison "kills love," as a priest once told me, and does violence to the interlocutor by denying his distinctiveness. All the more so for religions whose system of thought is difficult to transpose. On the contrary, as in the noble debates that call for the best in us, I have always favoured "a real philosophical emulation and above all an emulation of sanctity"[13] between Hinduism and Christianity.

To be worthy of such emulation, it was necessary to deploy a genuine catholic listening to Hinduism in the hope that it would also elicit in the Hindu interlocutor a sympathetic listening to Christianity. At the beginning of our journey, we gave the different characteristics of this listening. At the end, we will recall the most salient elements. First of all, to consent to what the Desert Fathers called *xeniteia*, expatriation as a foundation for the spiritual life and, for us, to dialogue. It has been necessary to understand the other from within, like the stained-glass windows of cathedrals whose splendour will remain hidden if we remain outside the building. In order to facilitate the conversation, an abundance of quotations was required—something that has not been omitted throughout the different chapters. Moreover, like the Jains whose famous theory of *anekāntavāda* aims at the ultimate reality by multiplying points of view, we understood that, in a genuine dialogue, "our model is not the sphere . . . where every point is equidistant from the centre, and there are no differences between them. Instead, it is the polyhedron, which reflects the convergence of all its parts, each of which preserves its distinctiveness."[14] We also wanted to open up to the best of what each tradition has to offer, going beyond all the fundamentalist caricatures that are unfortunately present in every religion. "ā no bhadrāḥ kratavo yantu viśvato," "let noble thoughts come to us from all directions,"[15] as the *Ṛg Veda* sang three and a half thousand years ago, in a *śloka* still cherished by Hinduism. Undoubtedly, such a conversation will have led each tradition to rediscover the unique treasure it carries in a new light: "In contact with Hinduism and its components, the Christian will see, as if for the first time, certain aspects of the mystery of his faith that were hitherto latent. The Hindu will also look with new eyes at that which the

13. Monchanin, *Écrits spirituels*, 101–2.

14. Francis, *Evangelii Gaudium*, 236.

15. *Ṛg Veda* 1.89.1.

fact of being accustomed was still concealing from him."[16] No one will deny that such a conversation can also be a test. Each tradition must sometimes painfully leave its enclosure to expand what remains too narrow within it. As we well know, people sometimes prefer the sterility of inner desiccation to the renewal brought by the presence of the other. Such a danger threatens Hinduism as much as Christianity today, as well as so-called globalized societies that barricade themselves in bastions of identity where intelligence regresses. Here, the only remedy is the lands and the eras of cross-cultural fertilization, like the Kashmir valley which, although today plunged into an endless tragedy, was in former times the fertile crossroads for Buddhism, Shivaism and Sufi Islam, giving rise to a unique culture: the *kashmiriyat*.

Finally, our conversation was, I hope, *catholic*. Against all the narrowing of this adjective, forgetting that openness to the other is an integral part of Catholic identity, we want to passionately live the apparent paradox between an unfailing fidelity to the incomparable newness of Christ who is "the way, the truth, and the life" (John 14:6), "in whom men may find the fullness of religious life"[17] and a discerning welcome of the best of what mankind has produced under the breath of the Spirit. In this lifelong education, nothing is more profitable than to return to the great masters such as Yves de Montcheuil (1900–1944):

> Being worthy of the name of Catholic is to accept first of all the differences of others, to understand and love them as such. It is to repudiate the sectarian spirit which gives an absolute and universal value to particularities. . . . Moreover, the true Catholic on occasion seeks to be enriched by the differences of others; he does not believe that he possesses everything by himself. He does not close in on himself; he is not concerned to copy everything that is done and thought of well elsewhere, but he sees what he can assimilate from it. We must remain within this current of vital exchanges that flows through the whole Church, drawing from it as much as possible and wanting it to extend to the very limits of humanity.[18]

In a world that lacks nobility, we must learn the magnanimity of a Catholicism that goes so far as to "recognize, preserve and promote" the treasures of other religious traditions:

16. Monchanin, "Guhāntara," 269.
17. Paul VI, *Nostra Aetate* 2.
18. Montcheuil, *Aspects de l'Église*, 64.

> The Catholic Church rejects nothing that is true and holy in these religions. She regards with sincere reverence those ways of conduct and of life, those precepts and teachings which, though differing in many aspects from the ones she holds and sets forth, nonetheless often reflect a ray of that Truth which enlighten all men. . . . The Church, therefore, exhorts her sons, that through dialogue and collaboration with the followers of other religions, carried out with prudence and love and in witness to the Christian faith and life, they recognize, preserve and promote (*agnoscant, servent et promoveant*) the good things, spiritual and moral, as well as the socio-cultural values found among these men.[19]

FROM THE FULLNESS OF THE RISEN ONE

Today, some would like to go beyond the theology of fulfillment as conceived by Jules Monchanin, Henri de Lubac, Jean Daniélou or Hans Urs von Balthasar. Of course, some misleading versions could have presented the fulfilment in Christ as an insulting claim in respect of other religions. This non-Catholic attitude is a temptation that came from a radical reading of Karl Barth (1886–1968) and from Pentecostal groupings promoting a deculturated 'thought.' Nevertheless, no one can call himself a Catholic if he forgets the Father's "benevolent design": "to bring the times to their fullness, to recapitulate all things in Christ, those in heaven and those on earth" (Eph 1:9–10). For Monchanin, like Saint Irenaeus of old, recapitulation (*anakephalaiōsis*) was a central aspect of the Christian faith, even if it is difficult to perfectly explain the way in which the Risen One in his Pleroma fulfils the diverse paths that the Spirit has led humanity to take—the Kingdom of the eighth day is still a foreign shore for those walking in the uncertain dawn, as the disciples were on that Easter morning.

Anakephalaiōsis is the faith with which I conducted, in the Hindu temple and the Catholic cathedral, the various studies of this book. I must admit that this conversation often brought forth unexpected insights into the fullness of the risen Christ to burst forth, which in turn brought remarkable elements of Hinduism to light, to be discerned even more finely. Of course, it is not a question of comparing what is not comparable! It is undeniable however that listening to the great texts of Hinduism has been a call for the disciples of Christ to think more deeply, with "new eyes" freed

19. Paul VI, *Nostra Aetate* 2.

from "the fact of being accustomed,"[20] about the unfathomable newness of Christ and of the Christian life, expressed here in terms of sacrifice, childhood, Resurrection, desire and of beauty and loving abandonment. It often seemed to us that India had, as it were, an indistinct and distant intuition of what would later be fulfilled in the risen Christ "in whom are hidden all the treasures of wisdom and knowledge" (Col 2:3). We were reminded then of what Irenaeus of Lyon (140–202) wrote about the prophecies of Israel: "But then, you may think, what did the Lord bring that was new with his coming?—Well, know that he has brought everything new, by bringing his own person as announced in advance: for what was announced in advance was precisely that the newness would come to renew and revitalise man."[21] With regard to some Hindu myths and other metaphysical breakthroughs, we could be so bold as to say that Jesus gave flesh to them in an unprecedented way, without degrading the immemorial quest of those who conceived them:

> On the basis of its own particular form, the Christ-form relates to itself as the ultimate centre the relative uniqueness of all other forms and images of the world, whatever the realm they derive from. This relatedness of all myths and religious conceptions, indeed of everything in the world of man which can be and is an authentic revelation of God, to the centre of God's Incarnation necessarily has two sides: it is fulfilment through judgment. . . . Theologians necessarily had to treat this kind of "enlightenment" more carefully, since there can be no question of any straightforward progression in enlightenment but only of a veiled manner of relating myth to a centre which is itself veiled.[22]

The conversation carried out with the best of Hindu traditions poses some crucial questions for Christian theology, the answer to which goes beyond the scope of this book and calls for discernment firstly on the part of the Churches of India and of the universal Church thereafter. An essential point to note is that the light of Revelation in retrospect brings to light within Hinduism some intuitions the definitive meaning of which the Christian faith affirm that it was given in an incomparable way by the Saviour centuries later. In this connection, it should be recalled that when Brahmabāndhav Upādhyāya (1861–1907), the Brahmin convert to Christ,

20. Monchanin, "Guhāntara," 269.

21. Irenaeus of Lyon, *Adversus Haereses* 4.34.1.

22. Balthasar, *Glory of the Lord*, 1:507–8.

sang in his hymn to the Trinity of the eternal Son as the true *Puruṣa*, he was merely rediscovering the thread that ran through the whole of the Catholic Church's thought as she went out to meet cultures:

> It is not necessarily a contradiction of the Biblical tendency when theologians of history such as Justin, Clement and Eusebius, Alan de Lille and Nicholas of Cusa, Schelling and Hegel, and artists such as Calderon in his ecclesiastical mystery-plays, all want to illuminate the mythical world by relating it to Christ. Calderon succeeded in portraying convincingly the fact that Christ is not only the true Isaac and Boaz, but also the true Jason and Hercules, the true Amor with the human soul, Psyche, the true Theseus with the Minotaur, the true Orpheus with Eurydice, who represents humanity.[23]

What the fullness of the risen Christ illuminates with a bright light in the wisdoms of the world is not the sign of a mysterious work of the Holy Spirit within them? Here we must quote John Paul II (1920–2005):

> Whatever the Spirit brings about in human hearts and in the history of peoples, in cultures and religions serves as a preparation for the Gospel and can only be understood in reference to Christ, the Word who took flesh by the power of the Spirit "so that as perfectly human he would save all human beings and sum up all things."[24]

Nevertheless, we must remain cautious about these remarkable elements of Hinduism and perhaps not be too quick to use the patristic terms of "evangelical preparation" or "seeds of the Word," which were certainly taken up by the Second Vatican Council[25] but which refer to the theology of figures (*typos*) which is principally inscribed in the frame of the Revelation made

23. Balthasar, *Glory of the Lord*, 1:508.

24. John Paul II, *Redemptoris Missio* 29, citing Paul VI, *Gaudium et Spes*, 45.

25. Cf. Paul VI, *Lumen Gentium* 16: "Whatever good or truth is found amongst them [the non-Christians] is looked upon by the Church as a preparation for the Gospel. She knows that it is given by Him who enlightens all men so that they may finally have life"; Paul VI, *Ad Gentes* 11: "Let them [the Christians] be familiar with their national and religious traditions; let them gladly and reverently lay bare the seeds of the Word which lie hidden among their fellows"; John Paul II, "General Audience": "The 'seeds of truth' present and active in the various religious traditions are a reflection of the unique Word of God, who 'enlightens every man coming into world' (cf. John 1:9) and who became flesh in Christ Jesus (cf. John 1:14). They are together an 'effect of the Spirit of truth operating outside the visible confines of the Mystical Body' and which 'blows where He wills' (John 3:8; cf. John Paul II, *Redemptor Hominis* 6.12)."

to Israel. However, the question remains as to what status we should give to that which I am inclined to call the astonishing 'premonitions' of Indian thought. This raises the question of the need to formulate afresh an elaboration of a broader Catholic theology of history (not just a *Western* theology of history) in which the Indian insights could find their place. To do this, it would be necessary to distinguish our present time, in which the risen Christ pours out the Holy Spirit in fullness on the Church, from the time when the Holy Spirit worked at the heart of Israel's election (particularly in the inspiration of the Scriptures) and also from an Advent of the nations (still ongoing) in which the Spirit mysteriously sanctifies "not only the individuals but also society and history, peoples, cultures and religions."[26] Above all, as John Paul II put forward in 1990, there is a need to deepen a theology of the work of the Spirit "in the heart of every person, through the 'seeds of the Word,' to be found in human initiatives—including religious ones—and in mankind's efforts to attain truth, goodness and God himself,"[27] the Spirit which "is therefore not an alternative to Christ, nor does He fill a sort of void which is sometimes suggested as existing between Christ and the Logos."[28]

AN INDIAN-INSPIRED THEOLOGY

Accustomed as they are to seeing it as an *exclusively* Christian book, many believers forget that the Bible offers us astonishing examples of the integration of elements from non-Jewish and non-Christian cultures.[29] What would the book of *Genesis* be without the Babylonian myths and the wisdom of Israel without the wisdom of Egypt and the Hellenistic world? What would the letters of saint Paul be without the Stoic culture in which the apostle was steeped? Even the Greek poet Aratus found hospitality in the Acts of the Apostles: "For in him we have life, movement and being. As some of your poets have also said, 'We too are his offspring'" (Acts 17:28). What then can we say about the boldness of the Fathers of the Church with regard to Greek philosophy? In an eminently Catholic perspective that refused a solution of continuity between the order of creation and that of redemption, Justin of Rome (100–165) was able to put forward, not without

26. John Paul II, *Redemptoris Missio* 28.
27. John Paul II, *Redemptoris Missio* 28.
28. John Paul II, *Redemptoris Missio* 29.
29. Cf. Legrand, *Bible on Culture*.

some nuances, the term "suggeneia" (kinship) to evoke the links between the faith in Christ and certain eminent thinkers:

> It is not that Plato's teachings are strangers to those of Christ, but they are not similar to them in all respects, nor equally to those of the others, Stoics, or poets and writers of prose. Indeed, to the extent that each of them, by virtue of their participation in the divine Seminal Logos (*tou spermatikou theiou Logou*), contemplated what for them was related (*suggenes*), they spoke of it excellently, but the fact that some of them contradicted themselves on essential points clearly shows that they possessed neither an infallible science nor an irrebuttable knowledge. It is why what has been so well said by everyone belongs to us, to us Christians.[30]

A few years later, Clement of Alexandria (150–215) "reached the point of maintaining that God gave philosophy to the Greeks 'as their own Testament.'[31] For him, the Greek philosophical tradition, almost like the Law for the Jews, was a sphere of 'revelation'; they were two streams which flowed ultimately to the Logos himself."[32] Finally, Gregory of Nyssa (335–395) affirmed in *The Life of Moses* that "there is something in secular culture with which we must not disdain to unite ourselves in order to engender virtue."[33] These testimonies illustrate that Christian tradition is like a living river that "irrigates various lands, feeds various geographical places, germinating the best of that land, the best of that culture. In this way, the Gospel continues to be incarnated in every corner of the world, in an ever-new way."[34]

The long discernment that the Church has made with regard to Greek culture is the one that still awaits her in the face of the riches of Indian culture, even after two thousand years of Christian presence on the Subcontinent. In spite of eminent works, the Catholic Church is still waiting for an Indian-inspired theology, such as Henri de Lubac called for when Jules Monchanin left on mission:

> I have met again with Father de Lubac, alone and at length. He told me again all about his fellowship, my being what he was looking for, bringing about the intuition that he had had from

30. Justin of Rome, *Second Apology* 13.2–6.
31. Clement of Alexandria, *Stromata* 6.8.67.1.
32. Benedict XVI, "General Audience."
33. Gregory of Nyssa, *Life of Moses*, II.37, 126–27.
34. Francis, *Veritatis Gaudium*, 4.

> the seminary days: to rethink everything in the light of theology and this through mysticism, freeing it from all the incidentals and retrieving the essential by spirituality alone. He believes that confronted with India I will be able to rethink theology, far better than by digging over the philosophical problems for themselves.[35]

Throughout his eighteen years in India, Monchanin kept his friend's invitation to heart, but he also knew that before writing anything, a quiet incarnation in Indian culture and a deep knowledge of Hindu texts and traditions were necessary. In 1939, a few months after his arrival, he wrote:

> Increasingly, I believe that only the creation is worthwhile. But I am powerless to create myself. I am happy with this kenosis if it is for the enlightenment of India. It is necessary to generate a new school of Alexandria here: the obscure Pantaenus had thus paved the way for Origen. The Indianization in its outer, noetic and spiritual forms of the Christian Mystery seems to me a historical phenomenon of the same order of magnitude as its Hellenisation in related forms.[36]

In 1953, he recalled his hope that "India alone will one day give her own theology at the heart of theology"[37] but he also remarked "if the Christian West had been able to use pagan mythology in its symbolism, it was because paganism was dead; the situation is quite different in India where Hinduism is still very much alive."[38] Finally, in 1955, two years before his death, he confided to Henri Le Saux (1910–1973):

> I think that we can and must go beyond, but at our own risk, step by step. With the minimum of foolhardiness (with the maximum true reference to *theologia perennis*). We can be sure in advance that we will not end up with a canonisation of the *vedānta*. Revelation always means both at the same time: consummation (its truth included) and rejection (going beyond but by way of a death). Teamwork no doubt, which Indians will have to carry out (Europeans can initiate it and must show the necessity and urgency of it).[39]

Monchanin was a link in the development of an Indian-inspired Christian theology. Other names should be mentioned. Among them, the Jesuit

35. Monchanin, Letter to M. Prost.
36. Monchanin, Letter to É. Duperray, Dec. 14, 1939.
37. Monchanin, Letter to É. Duperray, Dec. 30, 1953.
38. Finance, Letter to F. Jacquin.
39. Monchanin, Letter to H. Le Saux.

Gispert-Sauch (1930–2020) who, like all great thinkers, had a deep knowledge of Hindu texts which he commented on with great intellectual honesty. He admired the spiritual heritage of Brahmabāndhav Upādhyāya, particularly as expressed in his two Sanskrit hymns, the "Vande Saccidānandaṃ" to the Trinity and the "Jaya Deva Narahare" to the Incarnate Word. About the former, Gispert-Sauch wrote: "Brahmabāndhav's hymn is a composition expressing the Christian faith. It is not in itself an attempt to find parallel doctrines between Hindu religious thought and the Christian faith. It is a Christian meditation on the mystery of the Blessed Trinity as revealed to us in Christ, and it would be impossible to find in the traditional literature of Hinduism any faith coming near to the faith expounded here. And yet, this faith, as we have said, is proclaimed in such a way that it does not appear completely extraneous to the religious history of India. With all its newness, the seed is received in a land that can give it a new body of expression. The terms that convey the Christian faith grow from the religious tradition of Hinduism and keep their full religious resonances and power of allusion for anyone educated in Hindu thought patterns. I believe that here is found the most successful example of a true adaptation or incarnation of the faith in India."[40] Brahmabāndhav Upādhyāya was a true precursor of what the Churches of India have yet to achieve. Yet, the political turmoil of recent history have surely caused many Indian Christians to lose the enthusiasm of the years that followed the Second Vatican Council, and especially the interest extended to other religious traditions. More than a systematic treatise, which it is not yet time to elaborate, the different studies in this book have had only one ambition: to revive a necessary conversation between Hinduism and Christianity in a true emulation of sanctity.

BEYOND THE BOOKS

I also hope that a breath of universality will have passed through this conversation. I believe that a religion cannot in differing degrees reject a genuine universalism, without risking a decline into a deadly barren state. Previously, on the Acropolis, Saint Paul was astonished that the Greeks, "especially religious men," had built "an altar with this inscription: 'To the unknown God'" (Acts 17:22–23). Hinduism, too, in its heights, has provided hospitality to the other believer. "Even those who in faith worship other gods (*anyadevatābhaktā*), because of their love they worship me, though not

40. Gispert-Sauch, "Sanskrit Hymns," 79.

in the right way,"[41] affirmed Kṛṣṇa in the *Bhagavadgītā*. As for Utpaladeva (900–950), he praised Śiva thus: "Glory to you, Great Lord, Lord of the universe who has put your imprint of glory on the whole world / And you have gone so far as to give your own self to the world"[42] and Abhinavagupta (950–1020) added: "I take refuge in you alone, Lord Śambhu, the Supreme, the beginningless one, beyond the abyss, the One who has entered many caves of the heart (*guhā*), the resting place of all, and dwelling in all animate and inanimate beings."[43] The Second Vatican Council is imbued with the same breadth: "For by his incarnation the Son of God has united Himself in some fashion with every man";[44] "For, since Christ died for all men, and since the ultimate vocation of man is in fact one, and divine, we ought to believe that the Holy Spirit in a manner known only to God offers to every man the possibility of being associated with this paschal mystery."[45]

Every thought has to confront an excess that it is not able to thematize and before which it must bow in silence. The tragedy of the later *vedānta*, as well of a certain Christian Neo-Scholasticism, is to have wanted to build closed and supposedly perfect systems which only finally end up as a sterile repetition. On the contrary, when two religious traditions meet in truth, they give mutual rise to stimulating incitements: incitement by the abundance of their intellectual and spiritual riches; incitement by the truth of the experience to which they bear witness; incitement finally by the silence to which each one is ultimately leading. Of these, the first two have become clear in the pages of this book while we were seeking to summon the best of what Hinduism and Christianity have produced, especially at the spiritual level which India grasps first and foremost. A few words will however be necessary to evoke the silence to which all true encounters invite, through a mental purification and inner stripping that can be experienced as a harsh spiritual test. For a Christian, this apophatic excess will always have the name of the love of the Father, the Son and the Holy Spirit which no words can circumscribe. That is why the hour of silence comes: "Beyond the books, there is prayer. There is silence before God. There is God who calls us."[46]

41. *Bhagavadgītā* 9.23.
42. Utpaladeva, *Śivastotrāvalī* 14.12.
43. Abhinavagupta, *Paramārthasāra* 1.
44. Paul VI, *Gaudium et Spes*, 22.
45. Paul VI, *Gaudium et Spes*, 22.
46. Monchanin, Letter to his mother, April 5, 1957.

Also for us who have been led through so many sacred Scriptures in this conversation between Hinduism and Christianity, it is time to allow the silence of experience to fill us. As a last word, let us quote an *Upaniṣad*: "Read, study and ceaselessly ponder the Scriptures; but once the light has shined within you, throw them away as you discard a brand which you have used to light your fire."[47] In a harmonic of the Spirit across time, saint Augustine (354–430) responded to these words when he exhorted the Christians of Hippo to "give heed" to the Scriptures "as to a lamp shining in a dark place, until the day dawns, and the day-star arises in [their] hearts" (2 Pet 1:19):

> When, therefore, our Lord Jesus Christ shall come, and, as the Apostle Paul also says, will bring to light the hidden things of darkness, and will make manifest the thoughts of the heart, that every man may have praise from God; then, in presence of such a day, lamps will not be needed: no prophet shall then be read to us, no book of an apostle shall be opened; we shall not require the witness of John, we shall not need the Gospel itself. Accordingly, all Scriptures shall be taken out of the way which, in the night of this world, were as lamps kindled for us that we might not remain in darkness.
>
> When all these are taken away, that they may not shine as if we needed them, and the men of God, by whom these were ministered to us, shall themselves, together with us, behold that true and clear light. Well, what shall we see after these aids have been removed? Wherewith shall our mind be fed? Wherewith shall our gaze be delighted? Whence shall arise that joy which neither eye has seen, nor ear heard, nor has gone up into the heart of man? What shall we see? I beseech you, love with me, by believing run with me: let us long for our home above, let us pant for our home above, let us feel that we are strangers here. What shall we see then? Let the Gospel now tell us: 'In the beginning was the Word, and the Word was with God, and the Word was God.' You shall come to the fountain from which a little dew has already besprinkled you: you shall see that very light, from which a ray was sent aslant and through many windings into your dark heart. . . .
>
> I feel that your affections are being lifted up with me to the things that are above. . . . I am about to lay aside this book, and you too are going to depart, every man to his own house. It has been good for us to have been in the common light, good to have been glad there, good to have rejoiced there; but when we part from one another, let us not depart from Him.[48]

47. *Amṛitanāda Upaniṣad* 1.

48. Augustine of Hippo, *Homilies on the Gospel of John* 35.9.

Postscript: A Marriage with Hinduism

"Therefore, the man will leave his father and his mother to join himself to his wife, and the two will become one flesh" (Gen 2:24). According to the description of our origin in Genesis which runs throughout Scripture before being found once again upon the lips of Christ (Matt 19:5) and in the Letter to the Ephesians (Eph 5:31), the man who marries must leave the paternal home to face up to the alterity of others whom he will come to know by stages. Firstly, his wife, then his children, whom he will discover with joy and the occasional bitterness to be inalienable freedoms upon which he will never be able to exert control. In this adventure of the 'other,' the destiny of Abraham is once again being lived out, the one whom the Lord enjoined to "leave his country, his kindred, his father's house for the land that he would show him" (Gen 12:1). In a very clear way Biblical man knows, even with a hint of sadness, that he must be separated from the place of his origin to undertake the pilgrimage into the unknown, with a naked faith towards the One who has called him to otherness.

Even if he does not create a family in the flesh, the Catholic priest is himself also called into such an adventure and even, we might say, in an exponential way because his priesthood is by default a response to all of the brothers and sisters that he meets daily. If he is faithful to his calling, the priest will not experience any of the complacency of the "shut-in homes" the "closed doors" and the "jealous possessions of happiness"[1] but on the contrary he will always be reaching beyond. I have had the chance to experience this myself for more than twenty-five years, by living at the centre of an unusual marriage with Hinduism which has been one of the most prominent realities of my consecration to India. In fact, at a young

1. Gide, *Nourritures terrestres*, 83.

age I left the 'house of my origin,' which risked acting as a sort of Christian self-segregation, in order to live a Catholicism in the wider world in the company of Hindu believers. A mysterious calling which brought together my Christian roots which had been firmly planted in the mystical soil of the Chartreuse—the land of my ancestors—my childhood in a Brittany of timeless faith and devotion and the Pontifical Rome where I completed my theological studies before departing for the multi-religious Benares, within which the tree of my attachment to the Saviour has stretched its canopy ever further afield.

In this exodus I am a bit like the younger son of the well-known parable who, having asked for his share of the inheritance, left the paternal home "for a distant country" (Luke 15:13). However, far from squandering my Christian inheritance, my missionary dispatch has in fact led me to make it bear fruit in Hindu lands, I have as my only model the eternal Son who "came from the Father" and "who came into the world" (John 16:28) to expose himself to the complete otherness of humanity through a total gift of his own person. Today after more than twenty-five years of marriage with the people of India, I would like to gather together some fruits of my pilgrimage into the heart of Hinduism—the religion with which I maintain an interior dialogue over the long term.

DEVOTION AND WISDOM

From my early days in India, I recall a Sunday in November 1997 where, sat on the steps of the pool of Mylapore in Madras, I was watching the faithful go down into the purifying waters before entering the sacred courtyard of the temple. Furthermore, I can see myself one month later on the night of the full moon of Karthikai, climbing the slopes of Aruṇāchala with thousands of pilgrims to receive the vision of the shining fire at the top the mountain. This inaugural encounter with the radiant religious devotion (*bhakti*) has kept me from attempting any intellectualist reduction of Hinduism—a temptation into which Westerners so often fall when, using Greek reason, they try to classify something that cannot be classified and to understand something that is unfathomable by virtue of being beyond a merely rational *logos*. On the contrary, with the interior openness of youth I allowed myself to be carried along by the faith of my new people in all their highly diverse and disconcerting manifestations—like the Tamil penitents whose tongues are pierced by a large needle. Thus, led in silence by the religious fervor that stirs our being to its roots, I have been able to reach the threshold of what lives in the Hindu soul without having to get there with the assistance of words and ideas. I have thus discovered something of the burning heart of Hinduism in the realm that is accessed through *prapatti*, surrender, the abandonment of oneself to the divine love—not a passive surrender, but by contrast one which is overlaid with an insatiable longing. I have also "understood" that in such a *bhakti*, it is precisely the giving over of oneself to the One that is beyond that gives the whole meaning to our lives at the centre of the universe. The proof of the totality of such a surrender is to be found in the humility of the offering that mankind makes to his God: "He who offers to me with devotion only a leaf, or a flower or a fruit or even a little water, this I accept from that yearning soul, because with a pure heart it was offered with love."[2]

Seized by the interior power of Hinduism as it is lived in the daily life, I mingled with the crowds of pilgrims and walked with them to the sanctuaries of the plains and in the mountains. With unalloyed joy, I experienced the religious festivals which provide a monthly rhythm to the lives of my friends. And thus, I entered into the powerful flow of the great river of devotion where the Beloved becomes present. One thing leading to another, starting out from the faith of the lowly, the peaks of the age-old wisdom (*jñāna*) appeared to me, not just in an intellectual way but with a sort of 'mystical premonition.' This let me see what it is that unites into one same adoration: the simplest soul, the sage who has himself "become like a child"[3] and the devotee who feels his way through the night of *viraha* where he must search in the dark night of separation for the one whom he loves in his heart. I understood then that there is a Himalaya of wisdom (*jñāna*) which will always rise up on the Hindu horizon to rekindle its unquenched quest for the heights. Moreover, it is there in the shadow of the peaks where the silent hermits hide themselves away and where the sacred streams spring up that we have to keep climbing up, struggling against the current of all that scatters us throughout the *regio dissimilitudinis*[4] that is covered over by the opaque and illusory veil of *māyā* which hides the true light.

It will always be difficult for me to say to what extent my daily journey with Hinduism will have transformed the Christianity that I inherited as my core identity. What I can say with clarity is that India continually

2. *Bhagavadgītā* 9.26.

3. *Bṛhadāraṇyaka Upaniṣad* 3.5.1.

4. "The realm of dissimilitude."

cleanses my faith of all that might be too intellectual within it, leading it towards the spiritual depth without which any religion is nothing but a shame which the world will quickly expose. The searing otherness of Hinduism has given me the appetite to rediscover the living springs of the two traditions which are blended together within myself in a unique way. To borrow an appropriate image from Christian de Chergé (1937–1996), the Prior of Tibhirine, I have to tirelessly "dig my well"[5] by living out with Hinduism a genuine "emulation of sanctity"[6] through the face to face experience of the emotive devotion (*bhakti*) of the lowly and the intensity of the search for wisdom (*jñāna*) of so many of those one meets on the road, whether they are still fully engaged in the world or those, such as the *saṃnyāsī*, who are already separated from it. This "ascent to the depth of the heart"[7] results in a deeper stripping away in order to reach the interior simplicity of those who in the words of the evangelist are called to be "like little children" (Matt 18:3)—those who belong to the *Krist bhakta:* the devotees of Jesus, the eternal Child of the Father.

Thus, over the years, I have come to better understand that it is not the words or the ideas that India wants to hear but rather the intensity of a silent presence where everything is rendered transparent to the Mystery. It is in this place of extreme simplicity that the *logos* can be awoken within ourselves. Indeed, the West has forgotten that this reason is not a fixed once and for all faculty, but a disposition called to grow, through the spiritual gift of wisdom, by deepening and simplifying itself so as to be capable of penetrating ever further into the weaving of reality that India designates by the term *tantra*.

SCRIPTURES AND RITUAL

It has to be recognized that nowadays Hinduism is studied more by foreigners than by Hindus themselves, who would have difficulty explaining their faith to an outsider. In this respect we must recognise the remarkable work carried out by numerous western universities in conserving so many of the spiritual traditions that appeared fated to disappear even though they give Hinduism its elusive multifaceted countenance. However, in this contrast between the intellectual work of foreigners and the simple faith of Hindus,

5. Salenson, *L'échelle mystique*, 68.
6. Monchanin, "Homage to Mahatma Gandhi," 200.
7. Cf. Abhishiktānanda, *Ascent to the Depth*.

there is an important point to emphasise. The young Brahmin in his Vedic school (*gurukula*) who spends years studying centuries-old texts from his tradition is not doing so in order to find new ideas but, on the contrary, he is uncovering the gateway to the original source so as to retrieve the intensity of the spiritual experience documented in the sacred Scriptures. Along with his predecessors, he knows that everything he will need for his way of union with the Absolute is contained within the *Veda*, the *Upaniṣad* and the *Bhagavadgītā*. In these world heritage spiritual monuments, the precious pearl has been embedded by means of the use of a perfect language—Sanskrit—where each word is charged with a depth of interior vision. It is the reason why the whole lengthy process of Vedic studies has to start with the learning of Sanskrit, a veritable vehicle of the divine that is perhaps without equal.

In Hinduism, all the Scriptures have their given place in the ritual which is the very framework of this religious universe. The Indian is a profoundly liturgical individual, who inhabits the splendor of the cosmos. In particular, the Brahmin is called to be the cult mediator between man and the gods. By stating that "the officiant recites the verses continually, without interruption" to "make the days and nights of the year continuous" and "so the days and nights of the years alternate continually without interruption,"[8] the *Śatapatha Brāhmaṇa* assigns to the Hindu priest the duty of saturating time with the rite so as to restore the original unity that was broken up by the sacrifice of the Puruṣa.[9] The life of the simple man of faith is also enshrined entirely within the ritual framework of the *saṃskāra*, the diverse ceremonies that follow on from his conception right up until his final funerary offering to the flames of Agni, the sacred fire that is the witness of his whole destiny. Contrary to what many would think, the rite has not been abandoned over the course of time in Hinduism. It has remained truly alive, all the while being overlaid with a new symbolic dimension in tantrism which has managed to unify the cult (*karmakhaṇḍa*), devotion (*bhakti*) and wisdom (*jñāna*) producing a new scriptural flowering that guides the spiritual path of man that is completely taken up and transformed in his bodiliness. It is in this way that the *tantras* have made each of the connections (*upaniṣad*) between the world (*cosmos*), the Absolute (*theos*) and man (*anthrōpos*) embracing everything in the flames of Agni, the ardor of ascesis (*tapas*) and the radiance of knowledge (*jñāna*).

8. *Śatapatha Brāhmaṇa* 1.3.5.16.

9. Cf. *Ṛg Veda* 10.90.

In the silence of my room at Benares, I spent years studying the Hindu sacred Scriptures, deciphering them word by word from Sanskrit, before opening the many commentaries of the *vedānta* masters. A severe and fruitful ascesis which by embracing the mindset of the other was a veritable spiritual healing for myself. In what can seem off-putting for a Westerner, I realized how much Christian theology at its beginnings in the patristic era, was in itself also a continuing commentary on the Bible, and not an attempt to formally conceptualise it into "summae" as was the case during the Middle Ages. Yesterday and today the Scriptures are offered to us as a text to decipher—and furthermore as a place to inhabit. Gregory the Great (540–604) said that they "accompany those who read them, being perfectly accessible to the simplest readers and disclosing themselves to be forever new to the wise."[10] Furthermore, by beginning to open up the Bible in the way that a Hindu enters into the *Veda*, it occurred to me very clearly how much the great Christian theology is a theology of the Eternal. This speaks to us of "the spring that flows and runs" that source "whose origin is unknown, because it does not have one" but of which one knows that "every origin has come from it" even if "it is at night."[11] Of course—and such is its particular character—Christianity is called to take in hand what is temporal and channel it towards the "blessed hope" but it can run the risk of spiritual exhaustion if it does not succeed in this contraflow pilgrimage to get back to the Trinitarian source from which all things come.

Equally in the Church the Scriptures have also powerfully reverberated in the liturgy, at least for many centuries. Whilst listening in awe to the Brahmins who chant the *Veda* from memory to music from ancient times, a sadness often overtakes me as I think of what has been lost with the disappearance of Gregorian chant. No other Christian song has been able to so greatly exalt the Christian Scriptures by immersing them within the language of music and in so doing, making the spiritual experience of the believer understood from the first notes, in the way that the call of the muezzin in Islam speaks so powerfully of the transcendence of Allah. Even if they did not usually know Latin, this loss has surely been most detrimental for the ordinary people, who have also lost their access to the great treasure of the Church. As a spiritual diary entry from the poet Marie Noël (1883–1967) makes clear:

10. Gregory the Great, *Commentary on Job* 20.90.

11. John of the Cross, *Song of the Soul*, stanzas 1 and 2.

> Although not learned . . . I am . . . so attached to the Latin of the Offices that I feel a great absence when the French version—secularized—tears it from us. How would I know the reason for this great nostalgia? Is it that in our liturgical chant transmitted to us across the ages by so many blessed voices there is an almost sacramental gift of the Spirit of Pentecost, that used to speak to simple souls in a hidden way through sacred vocables? Do they want to take this away from us because not being sufficiently educated, we would not know how to understand them? Well, of course we do not understand them all, despite our missals, but we used to let them flow over us like an outpouring of grace. The words of the *Veni Creator, Miserere, De profundis, Magnificat, Te Deum,* and all the others that were repeated time and time again, have become within us our family wealth, through the wide-open magnificence of the Catholic Church whose prayer in the world raises up and enhances the humble without their knowing it, far better than all the lessons and lectures in every age and place of the world.[12]

When one lives in India, one can see the evidence that the rite is an essential dimension of being human. It is the very foundation within which our spiritual growth is made possible because it ties us back to the immemorial and away from the endless web surfing into which the so-called developed world is locked. This fashionable malady, along with that of subjectivism never fails to descend upon the Church at regular intervals, somewhat like mildew on a potato field. Having the privilege of hours of contemplation during the Brahminical rituals, the best of which I have often found in remote shrines, I understood how much the Catholic priest when he celebrates the Mass, must disappear as an individual in the face of the mystery that he is celebrating so as not to make himself into a screen. It is thus only the sacrament that can truly beckon and the cosmos re-ignite itself in the tiny host of the God who was sacrificed and dismembered for the love of mankind.

KALIYUGA

My daily life with Hinduism has also allowed me to go ever deeper into the deep psychological wound that this religion carries, particularly in the North of India,[13] bearing the tragic history of the many foreign inva-

12. Noël, *Notes intimes*, 321–22.

13. Without doubt, it is necessary to nuance our analysis distinguishing between

sions. I have thus had to grow in compassion and share the anguish that passes through the broken memory of the past. How would one be able to abandon a spouse upon discovering her shadows and her fractures? Today Hinduism is the target of a problematic political revival led by the religious organisation *Rashtriya Swayamsevak Sangh* (R.S.S.) and the *Bharatiya Janata Party* (B.J.P), its political offshoot which is in power. Along with other branches of Hindu fundamentalism (*Hindutva*), these groups are trying to unify their polymorphic religion by any means possible in order to make it manipulable and receptive to their political interests. We have here the perfect incarnation of the well-known 1910 aphorism of Charles Péguy (1873–1914) concerning the Dreyfus affair: "Everything begins in mysticism and ends with politics."[14] In practice, this ideological stranglehold translates into the brainwashing of the masses that I also notice amongst the Brahmin students at Benares. We are witnessing the destruction of reason in a discourse reduced to slogans that are shot through with prejudice, which would be hilarious if they were not leading to the ongoing lynching and murder of Muslims. To that is added the triumph of bad taste such as the gigantic statues of gods which pop up like mushrooms in the Indian landscape, reducing Hinduism to a derisory folklore halfway between a religious Disneyland and the megalomania of the satraps. Ultimately the Hindu motto, "vasudhaiva kutumbakaṃ,"[15] "the world is all one family," seems now to be only a vague past memory, giving vent to a highly toxic communalism which polarises Indian society. From being the spiritual beacon of the world, Hinduism has become a caricature of itself. In this religion which has become corrupted by politics, there is no longer an ounce of the mystical. After all, is not this worrying spiritual emptiness just the trademark of all extremists, fundamentalists, hardliners and traditionalists?

Another fault line to be found in contemporary Hinduism is its fossilisation of a fragment of its distant past: a mythical golden age that never

Southern India where Hinduism is more serene and sovereign as it still is in Nepal. The south of India has a less complicated and wounded history than the north. In Tamil Nadu, Andhra Pradesh or Kerala, Hinduism remains alive and tranquil. Moreover, it is remarkable to observe how often across history Hinduism has been refreshed by great spirits who came from the South. At the same time, children of immigrant Indians settled in the United States are now starting to rediscover their religious tradition when they come into contact with western philosophy. Even if there are only a few of them, they are a source of hope for Hinduism.

14. Péguy, *Notre jeunesse*, 115–16.

15. *Mahā Upaniṣad* 6.72.

existed and which thus lends itself to all possible fabrications and manipulations. At the same time, an ominous crisis of priestly vocations can be observed amongst the Brahmins. One by one the gurukuls are emptying as the better-off families oppose their children committing themselves to a career that provides virtually nothing. None remain to learn the ritual other than the poorest Brahmins, who are incapable of making other studies to earn a living. So, from year to year the age-old traditions are disappearing and many learned pandits die without having been able to pass on the mantle to a disciple. At the same time, the Vedic cult and the *saṃnyāsa* (that is to say the coming together of the liturgical and the spiritual) is ridiculed within wider society: the Brahmins for their seeking financial gain and the renunciates for their licentious hypocrisy. In a religion which is losing its spiritual vitality, only the devotion of the faithful remains, but this has been taken hostage by the *Hindutva*.

When Hinduism adapts itself to the modern world, as it has done for example in the Unites States, then it becomes the harbinger of "wellbeing" which, as the name suggests, is the religion of the healthy. We need to mention here the astounding development of yoga in the West during the twentieth century, where it has been completely transformed—if not indeed distorted—returning to India by way of the affluent middle classes who find in it a practical and sanitized religion. In this Hinduism promoted by a few celebrity gurus, often with questionable objectives, it is no longer the ancient rites and the long, demanding ascesis but a cheap awakening for those who are only wanting a harmonious and peaceful supplement for their hectic lifestyles. It could be that this decaffeinated version of the religious quest is one of the greatest poisons which Hinduism has to face up to today.

However, all these pathologies take place within the understanding that the Indian makes of his destiny, and this is one of the most puzzling factors for a Westerner. In fact, Hinduism (along with Buddhism elsewhere) has contemplated its own disappearance in the present *kalpa*: the *kaliyuga* which started 5,000 years ago and stretches over a modest period of 432,000 years. In this age of darkness, everything must disappear, starting with the most venerable religious institutions being headed towards a massive collapse. Nietzsche's idea of the death of God appears as nothing in comparison with this Hindu teaching. However, there is no need for us to prepare for the shipwreck, because for a Hindu this cataclysm is inevitable! And all the disorders cited previously are nothing more than the symptoms of a disintegration that is already far advanced.

Personally, I have always considered that the other's wound is the mirror image of the wound within ourselves. I draw this from my experience as a confessor: in fact, very often, in the sin that the penitent confesses, the priest is able to recognise his own sin. In view of the problems of Hinduism, how would the Church not also be worried that the breath of the spirit has deserted many sections of its own institutions which are collapsing from day to day, as the unrelenting heat of modernity evaporates all the illusions of the traditionalists and their derisory folklore? How would the Christian faith also not be threatened with being drained of its theological lifeblood in so many places and reduced to be a simple 'lifestyle,' a placebo for all our existential anxieties, not on a quest for final salvation, but merely a bit of wellbeing?

In the face of this malady of Hinduism in the *kaliyuga* in which it is going to progressively disappear, an evangelical Protestant would be able to rejoice because for him all heathen religions are the work of the devil, but would this be so for a Catholic? He knows that he needs the spiritual emulation of other religions to give of the best of himself. Deeper still, he believes that religions—like all human manifestations—are mysteriously inhabited by the Spirit through which shines a "ray of that Truth which enlightens all men."[16] In order to keep all the spiritual treasures of Hinduism alive, it will not be enough to save its rich tradition with scholarly studies because all that will remain a dead letter as long as the sacred writings are not incarnated within the lives and progress of living beings. As with every religion in crisis, the only thing that can save it is the gift of saints who will re-live at the inner level the whole spiritual journey of earlier times.

My journey with Hinduism has not only been to receive, as far as practicable, the spiritual tradition of my Hindu brothers but also to do everything so that they might be proud of making a concrete manifestation of all of my hope within their religion. If, without being naïve, I have actually got the measure of the malady that is corroding present day Hinduism, I have never reduced it to the distortions that it is experiencing but on the contrary, I wanted to explore the highest peaks it has generated, its most intimate treasures, the very best of itself. It is for this reason that thanks to so many Hindu friends, I have been able to come to the heart of their faith—a heart that is very pure and cleansed of the slime with which the fundamentalists have covered it over. With my friends, I am highly delighted with the superabundance of greatness that they share with me, in this interior communion where we all become one within the depths of the heart.

16. Paul VI, *Nostra Aetate* 2.

It can certainly seem that when faced with such riches, this ancestral tradition has become too heavy to carry on the fragile shoulders of twenty-first-century men and women. However, over time nothing has been more moving than to receive the grace of the divine *darśana*[17] in the encounter with the most hidden beings who consecrate themselves totally to fulfilling their religious heritage with the utmost fidelity in order to transmit it to a new generation. Whether this is in the rite or in the renunciation, they want to fulfil this remarkable task not only by virtue of their intelligence but above all in the power of the Spirit that is the only true channel. All my Christian prayer goes out to them so that Hinduism never lacks some true spirituals who can stand up to all the political deformations and who will know how to preserve the riches of their religion, aware that this is related to an incalculable world heritage which will make humanity better through being more aware of the still small voice that murmurs within us all.

THEY WILL BECOME ONE FLESH

Nowadays we are a handful within the Holy Church who are existentially engaged with Hinduism. This inconsequential number may appear derisory in the face of a billion believers but who cares: we must go forward like a "voice in the desert." For me, this is how to be faithful to my consecration to India along with the very specific form that my priesthood has taken on over the course of time. In fact, I have tried to welcome as generously as possible the alterity of Hinduism into my being and my Christian faith. I have let myself be transformed by it in an ongoing spiritual dialogue, all the more real and burning when the Hindus themselves come to me calling me "Father Yann" with infinite tenderness, making me their friend, their brother, their father and also their priest. Looking at their faces, full of confidence towards me, I can say that the two traditions, Christian and Hindu, are inextricably linked in my being, as if they were of the one flesh whilst still remaining distinct. I also know that I will never finish knowing and learning from Hinduism. This will be a pilgrimage without end, made up of new discoveries that are not just intellectual but above all deeper, in the range of the mystical experience of which Abhinavagupta (950–1020),

17. *Darśana* is a key notion in Hinduism referring to the manifestation of the Divine in his different effigies, in the sacred Scriptures or just in the encounter of eminently spiritual beings.

the great spirit of Kashmir, said that aesthetic pleasure was the nearest equivalent. In one sense, in my Hindu wedding feast, there has not just been the seven inaugural steps (*saptapadī*) that the bride and groom take going around the sacred fire, according to the ancient ritual that is still in force. There will still be thousands of steps to make together in a covenant, within which we will be mutually transformed. But just as in union where the man and the woman remain what they are according to their sexual difference, it is very clear that for me there has never been a question of falling into a syncretism that for instance absorbs the forms of Hindu prayer or a number of its beliefs. On the contrary, it is about an actual expansion through Hinduism of my Catholicism, in order that it can reach its adult maturity.

It is in this precise way that I wanted to bring the heritage of my forefathers to fruition by learning how to be Christian at the heart of Hinduism, and how as a Christian to make myself understood by Hinduism, through speaking its language and in communion with its spiritual quest. Doing this, I have found myself to be more broadly Christian because going back to the language of Teilhard de Chardin (1881–1955), I have so powerfully felt the coming of the "ever-greater Christ"[18] who walks upon the sea of eternity as in the mosaics of the ancient Roman basilicas. But this Christ has so often come to me with the surprise of the Spirit—he who is "the wind that blows where it will" of which one knows "not where it comes from nor where it goes" (John 3:8). It has thus shown me some unimagined aspects of his person that I still did not know—the one who can assume all the human bye-ways whilst purifying them and transforming them in the newness of his mystery. This is also why my prayer to him has become simple till the point of being nothing but the yearning that brings the Bible to a close: "Maranatha, Come Lord Jesus" (Rev 22:20).

In this strange marriage that is my life, I am a bit like the Hindu husband who on the night of his wedding invites his bride to sit by his side under the heavenly firmament. There, he shows her the polar star that shines above them and says to her "You are firm and I see you. Be firm with me, o flourishing one! Bṛhaspati has given me to you, so live with me a hundred autumns, bearing children by me, your husband."[19] Inextricably united in the silence where there are no more words to speak, we stand

18. This is the title of a prayer that Teilhard de Chardin included in his essay *The Heart of the Matter*.

19. *Pāraskaragṛhyasūtra* 1.8.19.

side by side, with myself in Christian prayer and she in her Hindu prayer. And in our indissoluble love, I would like to designate for her the star that I am mysteriously gazing upon in the heavens: the Lord who comes, he whom the Apocalypse calls "the morning star" (Rev 22:16) the one "which never sets."[20]

Benares-Bangkok-Kathmandu,
September 2016—March 2023

20. "Exultet, the Proclamation of Easter," in *Daily Roman Missal*, 473.

Vande Saccidānandaṃ

Vande Saccidānandaṃ
Bhogilāncita yogivānchita caramapadaṃ

Parama purāṇa parātparaṃ
Pūrṇamakhaṇdaparāvaraṃ
Trisaṇgaṃ śuddham asaṅgaṃ buddham durvedaṃ

Pitṛ savitṛ parameśaṃ ajaṃ
Bhavavṛkṣa bījaṃ abījaṃ
Akhila kāranaṃ īkṣana sṛjanaṃ govindaṃ

Anāhata śabdaṃ anantaṃ
Prasūta puruṣa sumahāntaṃ
Pitṛ svarūpa cinmayarūpa sumukundaṃ

Saccidor melana saraṇaṃ
Śubha śvasitānanda ghanaṃ
Pāvana javana vāṇivadana jīvanadaṃ

I adore the Saccidānanda—
Being, Consciousness, Bliss—
scorned by worldlings, the desire of saints,
the supreme Goal.

The Most High, the Eternal, the One beyond all,
Fullness undivided, most Near and yet Inaccessible,
Threefold in Itself and Simple, pure Awareness, Holy
Pathless Mystery.

Father, Source of all, sovereign Lord, Unborn
Unsown Seed of the Tree of Life
Universal Cause, Creating by your Glance, All-Provider.

The Word, uttered in Silence, Infinite,
The Son of man, Begotten, Full of Glory,
The Father's Image, subsisting Thought, Deliverer.

Proceeding from the union of Being (*sat*) and Knowledge (*cit*),
Gracious Spirit, substantial Bliss,
Purifier, Swift and Free, Voice of the Voice, Life-giver.[1]

Brahmabāndhav Upādhyāya, 1898

1. Translation from Abhishiktānanda, *Saccidānanda*, 203–4.

Bibliography

Āṇḍāl. *The Autobiography of a Goddess*. Translated by P. Sarukkai Chabria and R. Shankar. Delhi: Zubaan, 2015.
———. *The Secret Garland: Āndāl's* Tiruppāvai *and* Nācciyār Tirumoli. Translated by A. Venkatesan. New Delhi: Harper Perennial, 2016.
Abhinavagupta. *La lumière sur les tantras*. Paris: de Boccard, 2000.
Abhishiktānanda, Swāmī. *Ascent to the Depth of the Heart: The Spiritual Diary (1948–1973) of Swami Abhishiktānanda (Dom Henri le Saux)*. Delhi: ISPCK, 1998.
———. *Saccidānanda: A Christian Approach to Advaitic Experience*. Delhi: ISPCK, 1974.
———. "The Upanishads." In *The Further Shore*. Delhi: ISPCK, 1975.
Aitareya Upaniṣad. In *Eight Upanishads*, translated by Swami Gambhirananda. Mayavati: Advaita Ashram, 2024.
Ajātānanda. *Années de grâce*. Unpublished.
Al-Ḥallaj. *Dīwān*. In *Le Diwan d'Al-Hallaj*. Translated by L. Massignon. Paris: Librairie Orientalists Paul Geuthner, 1955.
Amṛitanāda Upaniṣad. In *Upanishads du Yoga*, translated by Jean Varenne. Paris: Gallimard, 1971.
Andia, Ysabel de. "Le sacrifice parfait." In *Mystère du Christ, mystère de Dieu: Introduction à la mystique et la mystagogie*, 207–34. Namur: Lessius, 2019.
Augustin, Saint [Augustine of Hippo]. *Les Commentaires des Psaumes* [*Ennarationes in Psalmos*]. Paris: Bibliothèque Augustinienne, 2021.
———. *Homélies sur l'Évangile de Jean* [*Homilies on the Gospel of John*]. Paris: Bibliothèque Augustinienne, 1993.
Balthasar, Hans Urs von. *La dramatique divine*. Vol. 3: *L'action*. Louvain: Lessius, 1996.
———. *La dramatique divine*. Vol. 4: *Le dénouement*. Louvain: Lessius, 1996.
———. *Entretiens sur l'Église*. Paris: Le Cerf, 2022.
———. "The Eternal Child." In *Explorations in Theology*. Vol. 5: *Man Is Created*, 205–17. San Francisco: Ignatius, 2014.
———. *The Glory of the Lord: A Theological Aesthetics*. Vol. 1: *Seeing the Form*. San Francisco: Ignatius, 2009.
———. *My Work: In Retrospect*. San Francisco: Ignatius, 1993.
———. *Mysterium Paschale: The Mystery of Easter*. San Francisco: Ignatius, 2000.
———. *Parola e Mistero in Origene*. Milan: Jaca, 1991.
———. "Priestly Existence." *Explorations in Theology*. Vol. 2: *Spouse of the Word*, 373–420. San Francisco: Ignatius, 1991.

———. "Revelation and the Beautiful." In *Explorations in Theology*. Vol. 1: *The Word Made Flesh*, 95–126. San Francisco: Ignatius, 1989.

———. *Truth Is Symphonic: Aspects of Christian Pluralism*. San Francisco: Ignatius, 1987.

———. *Unless You Become Like This Child*. San Francisco: Ignatius, 1991.

———. "Young Until Death." In *Explorations in Theology*. Vol. 5: *Man Is Created*, 218–24. San Francisco: Ignatius, 2014.

Basile de Césarée [Basil of Caesarea]. *On the Holy Spirit*. Paris: Le Cerf, 2002.

Baudelaire, Charles. *Les fleurs du mal*. Paris: Gallimard, 1918.

Bäumer, Bettina Sharada. "From Puruṣa to Śakti." In *Witness to the Fullness of Light: The Vision and Relevance of the Benedictine Monk Swami Abhishiktānanda*, edited by W. Skudlarek and Bettina Sharada Bäumer, 31–46. New York: Lantern, 2011.

———. "Purusa." In *Kalatattvakosa* I. Indira Gandhi National Centre for the Arts. Delhi: Motilal Banarsidass, 1988.

———. *The Yoga of Netra Tantra: Third Eye and Overcoming Death*. Delhi: DK Printworld, 2019.

Benedict XVI. "Celebration of First Vespers with University Students of Rome." Dec. 17, 2009. https://www.vatican.va/content/benedict-xvi/en/homilies/2009/documents/hf_ben-xvi_hom_20091217_vespri-universitari.html.

———. "General Audience April 18, 2007." https://www.vatican.va/content/benedict-xvi/en/audiences/2007/documents/hf_ben-xvi_aud_20070418.html.

———. "Homily for the Holy Saturday Vigil." Apr. 15, 2006. https://www.vatican.va/content/benedict-xvi/en/homilies/2006/documents/hf_ben-xvi_hom_20060415_veglia-pasquale.html.

———. *Last Testament in His Own Words*. London: Bloomsbury, 2016.

———. "Message for Lent 2007." https://www.vatican.va/content/benedict-xvi/en/messages/lent/documents/hf_ben-xvi_mes_20061121_lent-2007.html.

Bergson, Henri. *La pensée et le mouvant*. Paris: Presses Universitaires de France, 1938.

Bernard of Clairvaux. *Homilies on the Canticle of Canticles*. Paris: Le Cerf, 1996.

Bhagavadgītā. Mayavati: Advaita Ashram, 2000.

Biardeau, Madeleine, and Charles Malamoud. *Le sacrifice dans l'Inde ancienne*. Paris: Presses universitaires de France, 1976.

Boyer, Frédéric. *Le dieu qui était mort si jeune*. Paris: POL, 1995.

Brahma Sutra Bhasya of Shankaracharya [*Brahmasūtra*]. Mayavati: Advaita Ashram, 2022.

Bṛhadāraṇyaka Upaniṣad. Mayavati: Advaita Ashram, 1997.

Bruno, Saint [Bruno of Cologne]. "Letter to Raoul Le Verd." In S. Bruno, Guigues and S. Anthelme, *Lettres des premiers chartreux*. Paris: Le Cerf, 1988.

Cabasilas, Nicholas. *La vie en Christ* [*The Life in Christ*]. Paris: Le Cerf, 2009.

Calasso, Roberto. *Ardor*. London: Penguin, 2015.

Chāndogya Upaniṣad. Mayavati: Advaita Ashram, 1983.

Chergé, Christian de. "Spiritual Testament." https://ocso.org/history/saints-blesseds-martyrs/testament-of-christian-de-cherge/.

Chrétien, Jean-Louis. *Symbolique du corps: La tradition chrétienne du Cantique des cantiques*. Paris: Presses Universitaires de France, 2005.

Clément d'Alexandrie [Clement of Alexandria]. *Les Stromates* [*Stromata*]. Paris: Le Cerf, 2023.

Clement of Rome. *First Letter to the Corinthians*. In *Patres Apostolici*, edited by F. X. Funk, 1:98–185. Tübingen: Henrici Laupp, 1901.

———. *Second Letter to the Corinthians*. In *Patres Apostolici*, edited by F. X. Funk, 1:185–211. Tübingen: Henrici Laupp, 1901.

Daily Roman Missal. Woodridge, IL: Midwest Theological Forum, 2012.

Daniélou, Jean. "D'une extrémité à l'autre." In *Histoire du cercle saint Jean-Baptiste: L'enseignement du père Daniélou*, edited by Françoise Jacquin, 246–47. Paris: Beauchesne, 1987.

———. *Platonisme et théologie mystique: Essai sur la doctrine spirituelle de saint Grégoire de Nysse*. Paris: Aubier, 1944.

Dhyānabindu Upaniṣad. In *Upanishads du Yoga*, translated by Jean Varenne. Paris: Gallimard, 1971.

Didachē: Doctrine du Seigneur enseignée aux nations par les douze Apôtres. Paris: Nouvelles Lectures d'Antan, 2019.

Dupuche, John. *Vers un tantra chrétien*. Paris: Les deux océans, 2021.

Durrwell, F.-X. *The Resurrection: A Biblical Study*. New York: Sheed and Ward, 1960.

Finance, J. de. Letter to F. Jacquin. Apr. 20, 1987. In *Lettres à sa mère*, by Jules Monchanin, 475. Paris: Le Cerf, 1989.

Forsyth, P. T. *The Person and Place of Christ*. London: Hodder & Stoughton, 1909.

Francis. "Address to the Roman Curia for the Exchange of Christmas Greetings." https://www.vatican.va/content/francesco/en/speeches/2022/december/documents/20221222-curia-romana.html.

———. *Evangelii Gaudium*. https://www.vatican.va/content/francesco/en/apost_exhortations/documents/papa-francesco_esortazione-ap_20131124_evangelii-gaudium.html.

———. "Interview aux revues culturelles jésuites." *Études*, Oct. 2013.

———. "Theology After *Veritatis Gaudium* in the Context of the Mediterranean." https://www.vatican.va/content/francesco/en/speeches/2019/june/documents/papa-francesco_20190621_teologia-napoli.html.

———. *Veritatis Gaudium*. https://www.vatican.va/content/francesco/en/apost_constitutions/documents/papa-francesco_costituzione-ap_20171208_veritatis-gaudium.html.

Gide, André. *Les nourritures terrestres*. Paris: Mercure de France, 1897.

Gispert-Sauch, George. *Bliss in the Upanishads: An Analytical Study of the Origin and Growth of the Vedic Concept of Ānanda*. New Delhi: Oriental Publishers & Distributors, 1977.

———. "The Sanskrit Hymns of Brahmabandhav Upadhyay." In *The Gospel and the Newspaper: Theological Queries Digging the Indian Quarry*. Delhi: ISPCK, 2013.

González de Cardedal, Olegario. *Cristologia*. Milan: San Paolo, 2004.

Grégoire de Nysse [Gregory of Nyssa]. *Le Cantique des cantiques* [*Homilies on the Canticle of Canticles*]. Paris: Brépols, 1992.

———. *La vie de Moïse* [*The Life of Moses*]. Paris: Le Cerf, 2000.

Grégoire Le Thaumaturge [Gregory Thaumaturgus].*Remerciement à Origène*. Paris: Le Cerf, 1976.

Gregory the Great. *Homélies sur Ézéchiel* [*Homilies on Ezekiel*] Paris: Le Cerf, 1986.

———. *Morales sur Job* [*Commentary on Job*]. Paris: Le Cerf, 1989.

Grosjean, Jean. *Le Messie*. Paris: Gallimard, 1974.

Guardini, Romano. *The Lord*. Allahabad: St. Paul, 1962.

Hadewijch d'Anvers [Hadewijch of Antwerp]. *Écrits mystiques des béguines*. Paris: Le Seuil, 2019.

———. *Mengeldichten*. In *Écrits mystiques des béguines*. Paris: Le Seuil, 2019.

———. *Strophische Gedichten*. In *Écrits mystiques des béguines*. Paris: Le Seuil, 2019.

Hadewijch of Antwerp. *The Complete Works*. Translated by Mother Columba Hart. New York: Paulist, 1980.

Hawley, John Stratton. *Songs of the Saints of India*. New York: Oxford University Press, 1998.

Heraclitus. *Fragments*. Paris: Presses universitaires de France, 2011.

Hilaire de Poitiers [Hilary of Poitiers]. *La Trinité* [*De Trinitate*]. Paris: Le Cerf, 1999.

Hymnes de Abhinavagupta. Translated by L. Silburn. Paris: Éditions de Boccard, 1970.

Les hymnes de louange à Shiva. Translated by R. Bonnet. Paris: Adrien Maisonneuve, 1989.

Ignace d'Antioche [Ignatius of Antioch]. *Letter to the Magnesians*. In *Lettres*. Paris: Le Cerf, 2007.

———. *Letter to the Romans*. In *Lettres*. Paris: Le Cerf, 2007.

Ignace de Loyola, Saint [Ignatius of Loyola]. *Exercices spirituels* [*Spiritual Exercises*]. Paris: Le Seuil, 2004.

Irenaeus of Lyon. *Adversus Haereses*. In *Contre les hérésies: Dénonciation et réfutation de la gnose au nom menteur*. Paris: Le Cerf, 2001.

Īśa Upaniṣad. In *Eight Upanishads*, translated by Swami Gambhirananda. Mayavati: Advaita Ashram, 2024.

Jacquin, Françoise. "Henri de Lubac et Jules Monchanin, lettres commentées." *Bulletin de l'Association internationale cardinal Henri de Lubac* 5 (2002) 4–24.

———. *Jules Monchanin, prêtre*. Paris: Le Cerf, 1996.

John of the Cross. *The Complete Works of Saint John of the Cross*. London: Burns Oates & Washbourne, 1934.

———. *The Complete Works of Saint John of the Cross*. Translated by Kieran Kavanaugh and Otilio Rodriguez. Washington: ICS, 1979.

———. *Song of the Soul That Rejoices in Knowing God Through Faith*. In *The Complete Works of Saint John of the Cross*. Translated by Kieran Kavanaugh and Otilio Rodriguez. Washington: ICS, 1979.

John Paul II. "General Audience." Sept. 9, 1998. https://www.vatican.va/content/john-paul-ii/en/audiences/1998/documents/hf_jp-ii_aud_09091998.html.

———. *Redemptor Hominis*. https://www.vatican.va/content/john-paul-ii/en/encyclicals/documents/hf_jp-ii_enc_04031979_redemptor-hominis.html.

———. *Redemptoris Missio*. https://www.vatican.va/content/john-paul-ii/en/encyclicals/documents/hf_jp-ii_enc_07121990_redemptoris-missio.html.

Justin of Rome. *Second Apology*. In *Les Pères Apostoliques*. Paris: Le Cerf, 2001.

Kakar, Sudhir. *The Ascetic of Desire*. New Delhi: Penguin, 1999.

Kaṭha Upaniṣad. In *Eight Upanishads*, translated by Swami Gambhirananda. Mayavati: Advaita Ashram, 2024.

Kena Upaniṣad. In *Eight Upanishads*, translated by Swami Gambhirananda. Mayavati: Advaita Ashram, 2024.

Larson, Gerald. "The Sources for *Śakti* in Abhinavagupta's Kashmir Shaivism: A Linguistic and Aesthetic Category." *Philosophy East and West* 24 (1974) 41–56.

Legrand, Lucien. *Bible on Culture: Belonging or Dissenting*. Maryknoll, NY: Orbis, 2000.

Le Saux, Henri. "Dans le pays tamoul, Dieu, c'est l'enfant: Enfance spirituelle et *Upaniṣad*." In *Les yeux de lumière: Écrits spirituels*. Paris: ŒIL, 1989.

Le Saux, Henri, and Thérèse de Jésus. *Le Swami et la Carmélite*. Vol. 1: *L'appel de l'Inde*. Orbey: Arfuyen, 2022.

———. *Le Swami et la Carmélite*. Vol. 2: *La beauté du Gange*. Orbey: Arfuyen, 2022.

Lévi, Sylvain. *La doctrine du sacrifice dans les Brâhmanas*. Paris: Ernest Leroux, 1898.

Lubac, Henri de. *Catholicism: A Study of Dogma in Relation to the Corporate Destiny of Mankind*. New York: Sheed and Ward, 1958.

———. *Catholicism: Christ and the Common Destiny of Man*. San Francisco: Ignatius, 1988.

———. *Images de l'Abbé Monchanin*. Paris: Aubier, 1967.

———. *Paradoxe et Mystère de l'Église*. Paris: Aubier, 1967.

Maalouf, Charbel. *Une mystique érotique chez Grégoire de Nysse*. Paris: Le Cerf, 2017.

Maillard, Chantal. *Rasa: El placer estético en la tradición india*. Varanasi: Indica, 1999.

Maritain, Jacques. "L'expérience mystique naturelle et le vide." In *Quatre essais sur l'esprit dans sa condition charnelle*, 131–77. Paris: Desclée de Brouwer, 1939.

Massignon, Luc. *Badaliya, au nom de l'autre (1947–1962)*. Paris: Le Cerf, 2011.

———. "L'involution sémantique du symbole dans les cultures sémitiques." In *Écrits mémorables*, 2:262–73. Paris: Robert Laffont, 2009

———. "Un nouveau sacral." In *Écrits mémorables* 1:343–49. Paris, Robert Laffont, 2009.

Monchanin, Jules. "Au nom de l'Église." In *Ermites du Saccidānanda*. Tournai-Paris: Casterman, 1956.

———. "*Bhagavadgītā*." In *Swami Parama Arubi Anandam (Fr. J. Monchanin) 1895–1957: A Memorial*, by Saccidānanda Ashram, 162–63. Shantivanam: Trichinopoly United, 1959.

———. *Écrits spirituels*. Paris: Le Centurion, 1965.

———. "Essai de spiritualité missionnaire." In *Théologie et spiritualité missionnaires*, 163–66. Paris: Beauchesne, 1985.

———. "Guhāntara." In *Mystique de l'Inde, mystère chrétien*. Paris: Fayard, 1974.

———. "L'hindouisme." In *Mystique de l'Inde, mystère chrétien*. Paris: Fayard, 1974.

———. "Homage to Mahatma Gandhi." In *Swami Parama Arubi Anandam (Fr. J. Monchanin) 1895–1957: A Memorial*, by Saccidānanda Ashram, 200. Shantivanam: Trichinopoly United, 1959.

———. Letter to É. Duperray. Dec. 14, 1939. In *Une amitié sacerdotale*, edited by Françoise Jacquin, 110. Bruxelles: Lessius, 2003.

———. Letter to É. Duperray. Dec. 30, 1953. In *Une amitié sacerdotale*, edited by Françoise Jacquin, 221. Bruxelles: Lessius, 2003.

———. Letter to H. Le Saux. Jan. 28, 1955. In *Lettres au Père Le Saux*, 180–81. Paris: Le Cerf, 1995.

———. Letter to his mother. Apr. 5, 1957. In *Lettres à sa mère*, 568. Paris: Le Cerf, 1989.

———. Letter to M. Divien around 1950. In *Écrits spirituels*, 101–2. Paris: Le Centurion, 1965.

———. Letter to M. Prost. Apr. 20, 1939. In *Mystique de l'Inde, mystère chrétien*, 146–47. Paris: Fayard, 1974.

———. *Mystique de l'Inde, mystère chrétien*. Paris: Fayard, 1974.

———. "Problèmes du yoga chrétien." In *Mystique de l'Inde, mystère chrétien*, 256–63. Paris: Fayard, 1974.

———. "Religions et civilisations indiennes." In *Mystique de l'Inde, mystère chrétien*. Paris: Fayard, 1974.

———. "Spiritualité de l'Inde." In *Mystique de l'Inde, mystère chrétien*, 237–40. Paris: Fayard, 1974.

———. Unpublished letter to Édouard Duperray, June 29, 1951.

———. Unpublished letter to M. Prost. Jan. 25, 1940.
———. Unpublished note: “Contemplation.”
Montcheuil, Yves de. *Aspects de l’Église*. Paris: Le Cerf, 1949.
Mother Teresa. *Come Be My Light: The Private Writings of the “Saint of Calcutta.”* New York: Doubleday, 2007.
Mounier, Émmanuel. *L’affrontement chrétien*. Paris: Parole et silence, 2017.
Muṇḍaka Upaniṣad. In *Eight Upanishads*, translated by Swami Gambhirananda. Mayavati: Advaita Ashram, 2024.
Mus, Paul. “Où finit Puruṣa?” In *Mélanges d’indianisme à la mémoire de Louis Renou*, 539–63. Paris: De Broccard, 1968.
Netra Tantra. In *The Yoga of Netra Tantra: Third Eye and Overcoming Death*, by Bettina Sharada Baümer. New Delhi: D. K. Printworld, 2019.
Nikhilānanda, Swāmī. “Introduction.” In Śaṅkara, *Ātmabodha, Self-Knowledge*, 115–17. Madras: Sri Ramakrishna Math, 1947.
Noël, Marie. *Notes intimes*. Paris: Stock, 1984.
Origène [Origen]. *Commentaire sur le Cantique des cantiques I* [*Commentary on the Canticle of Canticles*]. Paris: Le Cerf, 1991.
———. *Homélies sur le Cantique des Cantiques* [*Homilies on the Canticle of Canticles*]. Paris: Le Cerf, 2007.
———. *Homélies sur l’Exode* [*Homilies on Exodus*]. Paris: Le Cerf, 1985.
———. *Homélies sur Ezéchiel* [*Homilies on Ezekiel*]. Paris: Le Cerf, 1989.
———. *Homélies sur le Lévitique* [*Homilies on Leviticus*]. Paris: Le Cerf, 1981.
Padoux, André. *Comprendre le tantrisme: Les sources hindoues*. Paris: Albin Michel, 2010.
———. *The Hindu Tantric World: An Overview*. Chicago: University of Chicago Press, 2017.
———. *Vāc: The Concept of the Word in Selected Hindu Tantras*. Delhi: Sri Satguru, 1992.
Panikkar, Raimon. *Blessed Simplicity: The Monk as Universal Archetype*. New York: Seabury, 1982.
———. *The Vedic Experience, Mantramañjarī: An Anthology of the Vedas for Modern Man and Contemporary Celebration*. Delhi: Motilal Banarsidass, 1977.
Parthasarathy, R. *Erotic Poems from the Sanskrit: An Anthology*. New York: Columbia University Press, 2017.
Paul VI. *Ad Gentes*. https://www.vatican.va/archive/hist_councils/ii_vatican_council/documents/vat-ii_decree_19651207_ad-gentes_en.html.
———. *Ecclesiam Suam*. https://www.vatican.va/content/paul-vi/en/encyclicals/documents/hf_p-vi_enc_06081964_ecclesiam.html.
———. *Gaudium et Spes*. https://www.vatican.va/archive/hist_councils/ii_vatican_council/documents/vat-ii_const_19651207_gaudium-et-spes_en.html.
———. *Lumen Gentium*. https://www.vatican.va/archive/hist_councils/ii_vatican_council/documents/vat-ii_const_19641121_lumen-gentium_en.html.
———. *Nostra Aetate*. https://www.vatican.va/archive/hist_councils/ii_vatican_council/documents/vat-ii_decl_19651028_nostra-aetate_en.html.
Péguy, Charles. *Mystique et politique*. Paris: Robert Laffont, 2015.
———. *Notre jeunesse*. Paris: Gallimard, 1993.
Porete, Marguerite. *The Mirror of Simple Souls*. London: Burns, Oates & Co., 1927.
Praseed, George. *Sacrifice and Cosmos: Yajña and the Eucharist in Dialogue*. New Delhi: Decent Books, 2009.
Praśna Upaniṣad. In *Eight Upanishads*, translated by Swami Gambhirananda. Mayavati: Advaita Ashram, 2024.

Ramanujan, A. K. *Speaking of Śiva*. Baltimore: Penguin, 1973.
Ratzinger, Joseph. *L'esprit de la liturgie*. Geneva: Ad solem, 2001.
———. *Many Religions, One Covenant: Israel, the Church and the World*. San Francisco: Ignatius, 1999.
Renou, Louis. *Hymnes spéculatifs du Véda*. Paris: Gallimard, 1956.
The Rig Veda [*Ṛg Veda*]. New Delhi: Penguin Classics, 2000.
Rimbaud, Arthur. *Poésies completes*. Paris: Léon Vanier, 1895.
Rūmī. *Masnavī*. In *La religion de l'amour*. Paris: Points, 2011.
Saccidānanda Ashram. *Swami Parama Arubi Anandam (Fr. J. Monchanin) 1895–1957: A Memorial*. Shantivanam: Trichinopoly United, 1959.
Salenson, Christian. *L'échelle mystique du dialogue de Christian de Chergé*. Montrouge: Bayard, 2016.
Śaṅkara. *Brahmasūtra Bhāṣya*. Kolkata: Advaita Ashrama 1965.
———. *Vivekacūḍāmaṇi*. In *Sri Sankaracarya's Vivekacūḍāmaṇi*. Mayavati: Advaita Ashram, 2010.
Scheuer, Jacques. *Parole et silence: Un patrimoine de l'Inde hindoue*. Paris: Almora, 2022.
Scholtus, Robert. *Petit christianisme d'insolence*. Louvain: Lessius, 2015.
Shantideva [Śāntideva]. *Bodhicaryâvatâra: La Marche vers l'Éveil* [*Bodhicaryāvatāra*]. Chanteloube: Padmakara, 2008.
Śivasūtra et Vimarśinī de Kṣemarāja. Translated by L. Silburn. Paris: É. de Boccard, 1980.
Smet, R. de, and J. Neuner. *Religious Hinduism*. Mumbai: Saint Paul's, 1997.
Soûr-Dâs. *Pastorales*. Translated by C. Vaudeville. Paris: Gallimard, 1971.
Stoler Miller, Barbara. *The Gītagovinda of Jayadeva: Love Song of the Dark Lord*. Delhi: Motilal Banarsidass, 2007.
Sūrdās. *Sūr's Ocean*. Translated by John Stratton Hawley. Cambridge: Murty Classical Library of India, 2015.
Śvetāśvatara Upaniṣad. In *Eight Upanishads*, translated by Swami Gambhirananda. Mayavati: Advaita Ashram, 2024.
Taittirīya Upaniṣad. In *Eight Upanishads*, translated by Swami Gambhirananda. Mayavati: Advaita Ashram, 2024.
Teilhard de Chardin, Pierre. *The Heart of the Matter*. Translated by René Hague. New York: Harcourt Brace Jovanovich, 1978.
———. "Panthéisme et christianisme." In *Comment je crois?* Paris: Le Seuil, 1969.
Tertullien [Tertullian]. *La chair du Christ* [*De Carne Christi*]. Paris: Le Cerf, 1976.
———. *La résurrection de la chair* [*De resurrectione mortuorum*]. Paris: Le Cerf, 2023.
Thérèse de Lisieux [Thérèse of Lisieux]. Letter to Father Adolphe Roulland. MEP of July 14, 1897. In *Œuvres completes*. Paris: Le Cerf, 2023.
———. Manuscript C. In *Œuvres completes*. Paris: Le Cerf, 2023.
Tillich, Paul. *Systematic Theology*. Vol. 4: *Life and the Spirit*. Chicago: University of Chicago Press, 1963.
Utpaladeva. *Śivastotrāvalī of Utpaladeva*. New Delhi: D. K. Printworld, 2008.
Vagneux, Yann. *Co-esse: Le mystère trinitaire dans la pensée de Jules Monchanin—Swâmi Paramârûbyânanda (1895–1957)*. Paris: Desclée de Brouwer, 2015.
———. *Indian Portraits: Eight Christian Encounters with Hinduism*. New Delhi: Nirala, 2021.
Varenne, Jean, trans. *Upanishads du Yoga*. Paris: Gallimard, 1971.
Vaudeville, Charlotte. *Myths, Saints and Legends in Medieval India*. New York: Oxford University Press, 2005.

Vesci, Uma Marina. *Heat and Sacrifice in the Vedas.* Delhi: Motilal Banarsidass, 1992.
Vidyāraṇya, Swāmī. *Jīvan-mukti-viveka.* Kolkata: Advaita Ashram, 1996.
Le Vijñāna Bhairava. Translated by L. Silburn. Paris: É. de Boccard, 1999.
Words of Sri Anandamayi Ma. Translated and compiled by Atmananda. Kankhal: Shree Shree Anandamayee Sangha, 1995.
Yogatattva Upaniṣad. In *Upanishads du Yoga*, translated by Jean Varenne. Paris: Gallimard, 1971.

Name Index

Abhinavagupta, 12, 14, 16, 68–69, 87–92, 107, 138, 150, 163, 169, 172
Abhishiktānanda (see Le Saux)
Ajātānanda, 71, 169
Akbar, 116, 123
Alan of Lille, 145
Ānandavardhana, 87
Āṇḍāl, 14, 93–95, 105, 138, 169
Andia, Ysabel de, 34,169
Aratus of Soli, 146
Asaṅga, 3–4
Augustine of Hippo, 7, 14, 46, 151, 169

Bādarāyaṇa, 14, 51, 66
Balthasar, Hans Urs von, 4, 6–8, 10, 15, 33–35, 45–46, 48–49, 54–55, 96, 103–105, 107–8, 131–32, 137–38, 143–45, 169
Barth, Karl, 143
Basil of Caesarea, 188, 170
Baudelaire, Charles, 1, 10, 170
Bäumer, Bettina Sharada, 15, 24, 31, 33, 69, 70, 170, 174
Benedict XVI (see Ratzinger)
Bergson, Henri, 2, 170
Bernard of Clairvaux, 14, 102, 104, 130, 170
Bharata, 86–87
Bhaṭṭanāyaka, 87
Biardeau, Madeleine, 33, 170
Boyer, Frédéric, 50, 170
Bruno of Cologne, 101, 170
Bulgakov, Sergei, 33

Cabasilas, Nicholas, 100, 170
Caitanya, 116
Calasso, Roberto, 25, 170
Calderón de la Barca, Pedro, 145
Chergé, Christian de, 18, 156, 170, 175
Chrétien, Jean-Louis, 97, 140, 170
Chrysostom (Pseudo-), 137
Clement of Alexandria, 54, 145, 147, 170
Clement of Rome, 10, 54, 170

Daniélou, Jean, 2, 101, 143, 171,
Dupuche, John, 92, 171
Durrwell, François-Xavier, 15, 72–73, 75–76, 81, 171

Eusebius of Caesarea, 145

Fallon, Pierre, 120
Forsyth, Peter Taylor, 33–34, 171
Francis (Pope), 8–9, 18, 139–41, 147, 171
Francis of Assisi, 129–30

Gauḍapāda, 66
Gispert-Sauch, George, 84–85, 91, 149, 171
González de Cardenal, Olegario, 73, 171
Gorakhnāth, 43
Gregory of Nyssa, 14, 99–102, 104, 106–7, 147, 171
Gregory Thaumaturgus, 5, 171
Gregory the Great, 38, 158, 171
Grosjean, Jean, 73, 171
Guardini, Romano, 15, 47–49, 171

Hadewijch of Antwerp, 15, 55, 105–6, 171–72

Ḥallaj, Mansour al-, 124, 169
Hegel, Georg Wilhem Friedrich, 145
Heraclitus of Ephesus, 50, 172,
Hilary of Poitiers, 74–75, 172

Ignatius of Antioch, 54, 96–97, 103, 139, 172
Ignatius of Loyola, 5, 172
Irenaeus of Lyon, 6, 14, 35, 73, 77–79, 81–82, 143–44, 172

Jacquin, Françoise, 107, 139, 148, 171–73
Jayadeva, 113–14, 123, 175
Jayaratha, 92
John of the Cross, 6, 15, 90, 102, 104, 125–28, 130, 158, 172
John Paul II, 145–46, 172
Justin of Rome, 145–47, 172

Kabīr, 110, 113
Kakar, Sudhir, 92, 172
Kauṭilya, 61
Kṣemarāja, 69–71, 88, 175

Langton, Stephen, 95
Larson, Gerald, 88, 172
Legrand, Lucien, 146, 172
Le Saux, Henri, 15, 33–34, 38, 50–54, 58, 79–80, 148, 156, 168–70, 172–73
Lévi, Sylvain, 25, 173
Lubac, Henri de, 3–4, 15, 18, 137–40, 143, 147, 172–73

Maalouf, Charbel, 99, 102, 140, 173
Madhva, 61, 116
Maillard, Chantal, 86–87, 89–90, 173
Malamoud, Charles, 33, 170
Marie Noël, 158, 174
Maritain, Jacques, 84, 173
Massignon, Louis, 2–4, 169, 173
Mechtild of Magdeburg, 104
Mīrabai, 110
Monchanin, Jules, 3–6, 9–11, 15, 36–37, 39, 43, 55, 81, 106–7, 129, 139–44, 147–48, 150, 156, 171–73, 175
Montcheuil, Yves de, 142, 174
Mounier, Emmanuel, 11, 137, 174
Mus, Paul, 27, 174

Nānak, 110
Neuner, Josef, 120, 128, 175
Nicholas of Cusa, 145
Nietzsche, Friedrich, 161
Nikhilānanda, 65–66, 174
Nimbārka, 116

Origen of Alexandria, 4–5, 14, 18, 75, 96–99, 103, 130–31, 148, 169–71, 174

Padoux, André, 16, 67–68, 91–92, 174
Panikkar, Raimon, 15, 21, 25–26, 28, 30, 33, 41, 45, 53, 134, 174
Pantaenus of Alexandria, 148
Parthasarathy, 94, 174
Patañjali, 43
Paul VI, 13, 73, 140, 142–43, 145, 150, 162, 174
Péguy, Charles, 8, 160, 174
Peter Lombard, 14
Plato, 99, 147,
Plotinus, 99
Porete, Marguerite, 106, 174
Porion, Jean-Baptiste, 106
Praseed, George, 33, 174

Rāmānuja, 14, 61, 116,
Ramanujan, Attipate Krishnaswami, 24, 175
Ratzinger, 4, 8, 15, 80, 81, 100, 125, 147, 170, 175
Ravidās, 110
Renou, Louis, 21, 22, 174–75
Rimbaud, Arthur, 10, 175
Rufinus of Aquileia, 96
Rūmī, 124–125, 175

Salenson, Christian, 156, 175
Śaṅkara, 14, 51–52, 61–66, 70, 83–85, 110, 112, 116, 118–20, 135, 128–39, 174–75
Śāntideva, 129, 175

Schelling, Friedrich Wilhem Joseph von, 145
Scheuer, Jacques, 12, 175
Scola, Angelo, 137,
Siddhārtha Gautama, the Buddha, 13, 60, 134
Silburn, Lilian, 68–70, 88, 172, 175–76
Silouan the Athonite, 127
Skudlarek, William, 170
Smet, Richard de, 120, 175
Sūrdās / Soûr-Dâs, 14, 109–23, 125, 127–29, 138, 175

Teilhard de Chardin, Pierre, 37, 73, 164, 175
Teresa of Avila, 104–5
Teresa of Calcutta, 15, 128, 130, 174,
Tertullian of Carthage, 77, 175,
Thérèse de Jésus, 34, 79–80, 172
Thérèse of Lisieux, 15, 123, 127–28, 130, 175
Thomas Aquinas, 34, 73, 132, 139
Tillich, Paul, 138–39, 175
Tirumūlar, 110
Tulsīdās, 106, 110

Udbhaṭa, 89
Upādhyāya, Brahmabāndhav, 15, 83, 144, 149, 168–69
Utpaladeva, 14, 90, 138, 150, 175

Vallabha, 111, 115–16
Vasugupta, 70
Vātsyāyana, 61
Vaudeville, Charlotte, 109–10, 120, 175
Venantius Fortunat, 136
Vesci, Uma Marina, 29, 31, 33, 176
Vidyāraṇya, 65, 176
Viśvanātha Kavirāja, 89
Vivekānanda, 139
Vyāsa, 43, 61

William of Saint-Thierry, 104

Yogānanda, 139

Zundel, Maurice, 90

www.ingramcontent.com/pod-product-compliance
Lightning Source LLC
Chambersburg PA
CBHW062046220426
43662CB00010B/1670